Data Replication

Data Replication

Tools and Techniques for Managing Distributed Information

Marie Buretta

WILEY COMPUTER PUBLISHING

John Wiley & Sons, Inc.
- New York • Chichester • Weinheim
Brisbane • Singapore • Toronto

Executive Publisher: Katherine Schowalter
Editor: Robert Elliott
Managing Editor: Carl Germann
Text Design & Composition: Publishers' Design and Production Services, Inc.

Designations used by companies to distinguish their products are often
claimed as trademarks. In all instances where John Wiley & Sons, Inc. is
aware of a claim, the product names appear in initial capital or all capital
letters. Readers, however, should contact the appropriate companies for more
complete information regarding trademarks and registration.

This text is printed on acid-free paper.

Library of Congress Cataloging-in-Publication Data:

Buretta, Marie, 1946–
    Data replication : tools and techniques for managing distributed
information / Marie Buretta.
        p.   cm.
    Includes index.
    ISBN 0-471-15754-6 (pbk. : alk. paper)
    1. Distributed databases.   2. Database management.
    Qa76.9.D3B867   1997
    005.75'8—dc21
                                                                96-44019
                                                                CIP

Printed in the United States of America
10 9 8 7 6 5 4 3 2 1

Contents

Foreword

Data, alas, is everywhere. This is good news for businesses today if their data is of good quality. This is also good news for those of you who are reading this book. Most likely, you play an important role in delivering good quality data to the enterprise you serve. This job will never end, but it is forever changing.

First, the enterprise itself is changing. It is rapidly becoming organizationally flatter. Second, the job responsibilities of its workers are becoming customer-centric. Third, business activity is beginning to occur through a collection of highly distributed, collaborative, and knowledgeable centers. At each center eventually is a human, supported by one or more information systems.

This means that business workers will require instantaneous access to accurate, reliable data. Only in this environment can cooperative workers in workflow situations perform their jobs with confidence and consistency. As data professionals, we will need to be able to deliver this data environment to the enterprise. *Data Replication Tools and Techniques for Managing Distributed Information* is a monumental contribution to our ability to do so. There is no one I know more qualified than

Marie Buretta to write this book. I have always admired her abilities to be articulate, knowledgeable, and technically accurate.

This book covers concepts. Chapter 1 is an overview of replication concepts, while Chapter 3 presents variations in vendor approaches. Marie also covers technical topics; in Chapter 2 as a baseline and in Chapter 7 as an advanced treatment. She presents elements of application design in Chapter 4 and of database design in Chapter 6. For the practitioner designing and delivering a replication service, she provides an in-depth practical methodology in Chapter 5, real world replication infrastructure concerns in Chapter 8, and an application-oriented methodology in Chapter 9.

Of utmost value are Chapters 10–13. In these chapters, Marie pulls together her methodologies and examines four realistic and challenging case studies. For those of you wanting a quick insight into the wealth of information in this book, these chapters will be essential reading.

I am honored to have reviewed Marie's book as it progressed. I am even more honored to write the foreword for it. The book will serve its readers well, since it is based on Marie's technical expertise and her magical ability to communicate complex topics with practical insights. This book is a gift to those of us struggling to make sense of the complexities of today's data-obsessive world.

—Barbara von Halle
Co-founder
Knowledge Partners, Inc.

Acknowledgments

I would like to thank my daughter Heidi, who produced all the technical drawings for the book. She is a bright, competent young lady who is both my daughter and my friend. Through this adventure we truly experienced mother/daughter computer bonding. I would also like to thank my friends for their patience and support, as running a consulting practice and producing a book at the same time can be challenging. My friends always offered the right mix of encouragement and sympathy. A special thanks to Jon Raymond, who diligently proofed every page and corrected all those errors that got past the spell checker.

I also want to thank Barbara von Halle, my technical reviewer and friend. She initially recommended me to Bob Elliott of John Wiley & Sons, Inc., as a good prospective author on the topic of data replication. I had a lot of technical experience with various replication products and had implemented several global replication solutions. When Bob approached me I was both flattered and a little apprehensive. I was delighted with the opportunity to share my experiences and confident that I could articulate the issues clearly, drawing on my background as a former chemistry instructor. The challenging part was that, even though I had produced numerous technical papers and best-practice guides as part of my consulting practice, I had never written a complete book. Bob was diligent in keeping me to our aggressive schedule; through his expert advise and direction I believe we produced a work of high quality. My objective was to clarify the murky terms and architectures associated with the topic of replication and provide a simple road map for firms wishing to integrate replication into their infrastructure.

I would also like to thank Rob Goldring of IBM and Mark Deppe and Richard Drechsler of Sybase. They were generous with their time and knowledge. A final thanks to my consulting clients. They have offered me exciting assignments and challenging opportunities to implement this technology. I would especially like to thank John Ritter and Fred Spencer who afforded me the initial opportunity to technically lead an internal consortium to establish replication best practices and implement a global replication initiative.

Introduction

Today, most businesses must be able to create and maintain multiple copies of redundant data—that is, replicated data. These redundant copies are typically used to improve data availability and application performance at remote sites, for decision-support systems that remove analytical query processing from online production systems, and for warm-standby recovery alternatives. Maintaining and administering these copies is both complex and resource-intensive. Firms have been looking to vendors for off-the-shelf solutions. As a result, vendors have marketed replication software that will provide this system-managed copying facility. The key to using these products successfully is two-fold. The first is to strategically distribute data across the organization, thereby optimizing network and hardware resources and administrative skills. The second is to standardize the firm's use of replication software, thereby creating a service that will ensure maximum flexibility and scalability *across heterogeneous systems*. It is in these areas of judicious distribution of data and establishment of firmwide procedures for software use that organizations meet their greatest challenges. While vendor-supplied documentation adequately explains product use, it does not address these two key topics. This book presents tactics for effective data distribution and strategies for building a firmwide replication service.

At first glance, implementing replication might appear to be simply a matter of copying data from point A to point B. But if the necessary support infrastructure has not been established and the databases have not been appropriately designed, a firm might successfully implement replication for a small number of isolated applications but is sure to fail when it attempts to implement replication on an enterprisewide scale.

This book presents a well-defined road map for successfully implementing a replication service within an organization. It should be used as a guide by application designers and implementers, and by *infrastructure architects* who define and build the technical environment for a firm. The concepts apply to all vendor-supplied solutions as well as home-grown solutions. The author has successfully implemented global replication services using this technology; tips and warnings highlight the knowledge gained from those experiences.

WHO USES REPLICATION SOFTWARE

Firms requiring a replication software solution include those that meet *any* of the following criteria:

- They have distributed data and/or processes in a multiple site environment and wish to improve application availability and performance.
- They have requirements for warm-standby recovery solutions.
- They have distributed data environments currently being made consistent via data extract/refresh solutions and would like to reduce existing network WAN cost and improve data timeliness.
- They have decision support systems that require near-real-time data consistency with their online transaction environment.
- They have requirements to consolidate data from multiple processing locations.

Clearly, most midsized and larger firms are candidates for replication services.

Today most firms are migrating from a two-tier architecture, where the application code communicates directly with the database management systems, to a three-tier architecture, where the application is partitioned into business services that use a data access layer to communicate with the database management systems. This new multitier approach creates a service-based architecture. The advantages to this architecture are that it promotes code reuse, thereby potentially shortening the time to market for applications, and protects the investment in coding by isolating application code from the underlying technology. Replication software fits perfectly into this new paradigm by providing a distributed technical service for maintaining data consistency.

Early replication products provided data consistency using complete refreshes to copy sites. This entailed unloading and loading huge amounts of data, consumed large amounts of computer and network resources and due to its batch nature was only able to maintain data consistency with a 24-hour lag. The new breed of replication software is based on forwarding only the data changes to copy sites. This permits near-real-time data consistency across all replicas and greatly reduces the quantity of computer and network resources used.

A READER PROFILE

This book is written for application designers and developers who are responsible for implementing the replication solution, for enterprise architects who are responsible for the firm's global infrastructure, and for managers responsible for both organizational groups.

Implementing a successful firmwide solution requires expertise from various organizations within a firm. The application designers and developers, who are ultimately responsible for the replication design as it relates to a specific business problem, have a good grasp of issues related to their specific hardware platform, operating system, and database management system (DBMS). However, they often do not understand all the underlying infrastructure issues that should be considered in that implementation. For this group of users, this book presents a tactical "cookbook" approach for data distribution and replication implementation so that no design task is inadvertently omitted and all decisions are made with a full understanding of the technical trade-offs.

The enterprise architects, who are responsible for defining the technical environment and standards as they relate to replication, need a more strategic approach than is addressed in vendor documentation. For this group of users, this book addresses approaches for building a replication service. It advocates a top-down approach and identifies the areas where enterprise architects and data administrators should be paving the way for seamless replication both within and across applications. The goal is to have the flexibility to replicate anything, anywhere in a consistent, efficient, and easily maintained manner. This requires an established infrastructure.

HOW THIS BOOK IS ORGANIZED

I begin by presenting the critical issues involved in data and process replication at a conceptual level. Once the underlying concepts have been explained, I present a step-by-step approach for data distribution and for building a replication service. The possible pitfalls from a design, administration, and implementation perspective are identified so that the reader is prepared to tackle these hurdles. After reading this book, the reader should be able to make intelligent decisions regarding the use of replication as a solution to specific business problems.

The book is organized as follows:

Section I presents an overview of replication technology:
- Chapter 1, "Why Business Firms Need a Replication Service," sets the foundation for the book by describing what is meant by replication, data replication in particular, and the concepts behind a replication service. It is essential reading for everyone who wants to understand this technology.
- Chapter 2, "Establishing a Technical Baseline," presents the basic concepts necessary to build a robust replication infrastructure. For technical readers, some sections within this

chapter can be skimmed quickly because they essentially are review materials. The sections that address data distribution alternatives and application models that use asynchronous replication should be read by all. The templates presented here are used in other sections of the book.

- Chapter 3, "Vendor Approaches to Replication," presents a sampling of the architectures vendors use to implement their replication alternative. It is presented as background material but is especially beneficial to any reader wishing to implement a home-grown replication solution. It includes a checklist for evaluating replication software.

Section II presents guidelines for architecting a distributed environment that uses replication services:

- Chapter 4, "Application Partitioning and Placement Alternatives," presents guidelines for the partitioning of application functionality. It is tightly aligned with Chapter 5. Together, these two chapters address key factors for implementing distributed computing systems.
- Chapter 5, "Data Distribution Methodology," presents an approach for optimal data placement. The step-by-step workplan is valuable reading for all.
- Chapter 6, "Designing and Configuring Databases for Replication," presents techniques for designing databases that make efficient use of replication. The goal is to ensure a high degree of performance, flexibility, and scalability. This is a critical chapter for all technicians.
- Chapter 7, "Advanced Replication Topics," addresses the integration of replication across OLTP and OLAP environments, and across new development efforts and legacy systems. In addition, it addresses the integration of synchronous and multiple asynchronous replication alternatives.
- Chapter 8, "Implementing a Replication Service—An Infrastructure Perspective," presents all the best practices (policies, templates, and procedures) needed to support an efficient and effective replication environment. It is essential reading for anyone wanting to implement replication as a service within his or her firm.
- Chapter 9, "Implementing a Replication Service—An Application Perspective," presents a tactical approach for using

the replication service defined in Chapter 8. It makes suggestions regarding the selection of the initial applications that will use the replication service and presents a workplan that outlines the tasks required by these application teams.

Section III presents four case studies that illustrate the methodologies and techniques presented in earlier sections. The case studies are designed to present a good cross-section of business requirements.

- Chapter 10, "Case Study 1—Using Replication Within the OLTP Environment," illustrates the judicious use of data distribution and replication in an OLTP environment. The requirement is for the distribution of processes and data to multiple investment trading locations.

- Chapter 11, "Case Study 2—Using Replication with an Operational Data Store," illustrates the use of asynchronous replication in an OLAP (i.e., decision-support) environment. Replication is used to support an operational data store that needs near-real-time consistency with the OLTP operational data. It builds on the replication environment established as part of Case Study 1.

- Chapter 12, "Case Study 3—Using Replication Within a Mobile Computing Environment," illustrates the use of asynchronous replication in an OLTP environment that supports mobile users. The requirement is for the distribution of processes and data to many mobile workers that are part of a domestic insurance claims system. This case study presents many challenges because the tenets associated with client/server computing break down when using a model where the client is only intermittently connected to the network.

- Chapter 13, "Case Study 4—Using Replication for a Fault-tolerant Warm Standby," illustrates the use of replication to provide application failover. When a hardware or software error occurs to the primary data server or location, the application is switched over to use a standby data server.

Overview of Replication Technology

Section

Why Businesses Need a Replication Service

Most firms today use a diverse set of multivendor hardware and software platforms. Within this environment, they run a myriad of business applications. Much of the data that supports these applications is redundantly stored. The challenge for these firms is to ensure that all applications and business users make decisions with consistent copies of this redundantly stored data. If these data copies are not consistent, users may make different and possibly diametrically opposed business decisions, thereby putting the firm at risk. To reduce risk, all redundantly stored data either must be totally consistent with all other copies at all times or must have an acceptable level of inconsistency for short periods of time. An inconsistent copy can be made consistent by synchronizing the data with what has been designated as its primary source, that is, the master copy, or by resolving any data conflicts that exist across copies. Maintaining data consistency across all redundantly stored copies is not an easy task, but it can be achieved efficiently and effectively using a replication service. This chapter sets the foundation for the book by describing replication and data replication in particular, and the concepts behind a replication service.

WHAT IS REPLICATION?

According to its dictionary definition, replication is the act or result of reproducing—in short, a copy. As such, any type of data processing object can be replicated. This includes data, processes, and true objects as defined by object-oriented technologists (data and processes stored and used as a single unit). Note that the definition describes replication as the act of reproducing. Therefore replication is much more than simply the copying of any object; it must also address the implementation and management of the complete copying process. In essence, replication is a copy management service.

The replication of different types of objects poses both similar and unique problems. This book focuses on the replication of data; however, most of the recommendations and suggested design alternatives for data replication also apply to the replication of processes and objects. Where appropriate, I will point out the similarities; I will provide a thorough discussion of process and object replication in future publications.

Currently there are no standards in the area of replication. Therefore, each vendor uses its own terms for representing replication features and functions. In addition, vendor replication solutions differ widely in their architectures. This book provides concise explanations of what data replication is, when it benefits the information user as well as the firm, what application architectures are available, and how to evaluate competitive products.

> ### Changing Definitions of Replication in Technical Literature
>
> Technical literature used the term *replication* to identify the automatic maintenance of replicates of relational tables in a distributed environment. This definition implies the use of a participatory commit process to keep all tables consistent synchronously. In recent years, however, the term has been used more loosely to represent the asynchronous propagation of data from one system to another.

WHAT IS DATA REPLICATION?

A firm's data represents a recorded history of the information evidence that documents the firm's activities. As such, it must be given respect and appropriate care. Any application, tool, or service updating this asset must in no way compromise the integrity of these recorded events. Similarly, wherever data is persistently stored, it must be secure, free from any possible integrity compromises, and accessed only through designated applications, tools, and services.

Data replication is much more than simply copying data between data stores. It encompasses the analysis, design, implementation, administration, and monitoring of a service that guarantees data consistency across multiple resource managers in a distributed environment. As such, a data replication service should provide the following functionality:

- *It should be scalable.* With respect to replication, scalability means the ability to replicate both small and large volumes of data across heterogeneous resource managers.
- *It should provide data transformation and mapping services.* These services allow source and target data schemata to be different without losing essential semantics. For example, copies can be identical or semantically equivalent. Identical copies would have the same platform, same informational content, and same data types, whereas semantically equivalent copies would have the same informational content but different platforms and possibly different data types.
- *It should support the replication of not only data but possibly other types of objects.* An example of an object other than data that can be replicated is a database stored procedure.
- *It should support replication in both synchronous (real time) and asynchronous (non-real time) modes.*
- *It should provide a mechanism to describe the data and objects to be replicated.*
- *It should provide a mechanism to subscribe to the data and objects available for replication.*
- *It should provide a mechanism for initialization of a target, that is, a receiving replica.*

- *It should support end-to-end management of security and quality of service agreements.* For example, the service must guarantee that no corruption of the data or object can occur during the replication process. In other words, the data can change in format but not in content.
- *It should provide a log mechanism that records any failed replication effort.*
- *It should support an automatic recovery mechanism.* This mechanism provides recovery after specific types of failures.
- *It should support a GUI (graphical user interface) or user friendly monitoring tool.* This monitoring tool should provide information regarding the state of the entire replication environment. In addition, it should be able to interface with other industry-standard administrative tools.

In addition to the above functionality, appropriate meta-data—information about the data—must be stored and made available to designated users. With respect to replication, this meta-data includes specific information about primary sources and target replicas. For primary sources, it should identify such items as data owner (the person or group that defines the business and administrative rules governing that data element), complete description of data content, and security requirements for replication. For each target replica, it should identify such items as the name of each data element's primary source and a statement identifying the measure of data latency with the designated primary source. The *measure of data latency* is the amount of time a target can be in an inconsistent state with its designated primary source before data consistency is achieved. Some technical literature refers to this as the *degree of data currency.* I have found this term confusing when consulting in financial institutions because currency in this field has a totally different meaning. Throughout this book the terms *measure of data latency* and *degree of data currency* are synonymous.

WHY IS DATA REPLICATION A REQUIREMENT?

The principle driver for data replication is the requirement for data consistency when data is stored redundantly. Once multiple copies of any data exist, some means of keeping these copies consistent must follow. Vendors developed replication software to meet this demand. However, this begs the question of why do firms store data redundantly. Four major reasons account for this phenomena: (1) firms use a wide range of hardware and software platforms; (2) firms are becoming more distributed; (3) firms need a disaster recovery solution; and (4) the basic fact that humans do not like to share.

Most mid-sized or larger firms, I have found, have on average six distinct hardware and software platforms across which they try to maintain data consistency. This diverse lot usually includes the following:

- *Robust mainframe or mainframe-like environment.* Most of the legacy systems still reside within this environment.
- *Client/server, usually UNIX, database environment.* Newer applications, both critical and non-critical, reside within this environment.
- *Groupware environment.* Applications using small, LAN-based databases and spreadsheets reside within this environment.
- *Decision support environment.* The management information systems that reside within this environment are usually the start of a firmwide data warehousing effort. The data for these systems can reside on any of the aforementioned technologies or within a specialty resource manager, such as a multidimensional database.
- *Specialty or firm non-standard environment.* Within this environment resides the one or two industry-standard but not firmwide standard databases that were brought in specifically to satisfy the requirement of a vendor package. For example, the firm might have decided on Sybase SQL Server as its database vendor of choice; however, because a financial package that runs only in an Oracle database environment was the users' adamant choice, the Oracle environment must also be supported.
- *Leading-edge solutions.* Within this environment reside the small sampling of leading-edge technologies such as object-oriented applications with complex data types or data mining. Each of these technologies has its own associated data store.

A replication service is required to maintain data consistency across these diverse environments.

The current trend within firms is to migrate to a more distributed data and process model. Not only does distribution bring applications and information closer to the business user, it also has a significant impact on the communication issues associated with remote user access. Distribution reduces the network costs for query access, and it improves application availability and performance. However, as with any other decision, there are trade-offs. What the user gains in availability and performance, the firm pays for with additional administration and maintenance. Consequently, some individuals have become strong advocates for a very centralized—that is, non-distributed—data solution. These individuals predict that once communication limitations are no longer an issue (due to lower cost, better reliability, and unlimited bandwidths), a monolithic, centralized corporate data store will again become a strong alternative. I believe that this statement may be true strictly from a "is this technically feasible?" perspective, but it does not reflect the current direction in organizational structure. Firms are becoming flatter and putting more control in the hands of the business user. This can be seen in the decentralization of business functions to a widening set of locations. These new information users truly are the creators, owners, and maintainers of the data. As such, they are demanding all the benefits of a distributed environment—not only remote access to centralized data stores but also all the freedoms associated with mobile computing. They want to do their business anywhere, anytime and experience no technology impedance. To meet this requirement, data will have to be stored redundantly, and some sort of replication service will be needed to maintain its consistency.

With respect to disaster recovery, data is stored redundantly to provide application failover. In case of a hardware or software error to the primary data server, the application can be switched to a standby data server. The business user experiences only a small delay before the application can continue. This fault tolerance can be provided in either a "hot standby" or a "warm standby" mode. To implement a hot-standby solution, redundant data is kept consistent in real time using either a hardware alternative or what is called *synchronous data replication*. To implement a warm standby solution, redundant data is kept consistent in *near* real time using what is called *asynchronous data replication*. When a warm-standby disaster-recovery solution is used the standby data server's state lags that of the primary data server. Consequently, when the primary data server fails, some transactions will probably be lost. Definite trade-offs exist between a hot- or warm-standby solution, but in either case a replication service is required. The case study in Chapter 13 illustrates the use of asynchronous replication to provide a fault tolerant system. It also addresses the issue of transactions that are perceived as lost.

Think of the very human trait that we believe we have more control when we do not share. Therefore, the firm must establish an environment in which sharing does not have either a perceived or an actual negative impact on developers and users. Once this environment is established, users will find it easier to give up control, and the amount of redundancy of all resources will be reduced. This can result in tremendous cost savings for the firm.

 TIP

Data should be redundantly stored only if the performance and availability gains outweigh the cost associated with maintaining its consistency.

HOW IS REPLICATION IMPLEMENTED?

We can classify various approaches to data replication in several ways. The most succinct approach is to classify replication by the amount of latency that exists before data consistency is achieved across the replicas. The two types within this classification are *synchronous replication* and *asynchronous replication*.

Synchronous data replication

Synchronous data replication provides what is called "tight consistency" between data stores. This means that the latency before data consistency is achieved is zero. Data at all replicas is always the same, no matter from which replica the update originated. This can be accomplished only through a two-phase commit protocol. See Appendix A for a complete discussion of a two-phase commit protocol.

Synchronous replication can be provided by database management system software (DBMS) or by distributed TP monitor/transaction manager. In either case, all updating within the synchronous replication process occurs as one logical unit of work. In other words, it is an all-or-nothing transaction. Transactions exhibit what is commonly called ACID properties—when the operation is Atomic, data is Consistent, activity is Isolated, and results are Durable. See Appendix B for a complete discussion of the ACID properties of transactions.

TP monitors/transaction managers, such as IBM's CICS, have been used for a long time in mainframe environments. They are now becoming part of robust client/server environments. Distributed TP monitors/transaction managers provide a much wider range of services than does a replication service. Distributed TP monitors provide process-level recovery, which includes the ability to load-balance transaction execution and restart transactions after failure. Transaction managers administer and control transactional resources on a single server or across multiple servers. This includes the ability to cooperate with other transaction managers in federated arrangements, thereby permitting global transaction management across heterogeneous resource managers. When global transaction management is used to implement synchronous replication, data consistency is maintained in real time across all participating replicas. Any user with appropriate access authority can issue a synchronous updating transaction, and all participating replicas will be updated.

When to use synchronous replication - distributed transaction managers

Whenever the business requirement demands the data consistency that only a global commit protocol can supply, synchronous replication must be used. Distributed transaction management is the only means of ensuring real-time data consistency across n homogeneous and/or heterogeneous resource managers. If this tight data consistency is not a business requirement, then an asynchronous replication technique that preserves the required level of transactional integrity and sequential consistency should be considered. (See "Asynchronous Data Replication" below for a complete discussion of transactional integrity and sequential consistency.) Asynchronous replication lowers the cost, improves concurrency within resource managers (shortens the time any data is locked), and generally shortens the length of the originating database transaction.

Important issues to consider when using synchronous replication

Due to the synchronous nature of this type of replication, a number of critical design and infrastructure issues should be addressed. These infrastructure issues relate to the actual physical support structure required to bolster this type of replication. With a full understanding of the underlying concepts associated with each issue, designing and implementing an efficient synchronous replication environment should be relatively straightforward. These issues include the following:

- *Ensuring that transaction design reflects the fundamental unit of recovery.* The translation of a business event (that is, a business transaction) into its corresponding software transaction(s) is probably the most critical application design task. It is the software transaction that binds the client to one or more servers and services. It is transaction demarcation that provides the fundamental unit of recovery and consistency within the client/server system. This demarcation must reflect a recoverable unit from a business perspective.

- *Ensuring a sufficiently robust support infrastructure.* Robust multisite updating from within a logical unit of work assumes the appropriate dependability—availability, reliability, and serviceability—of all resource components. This includes a network infrastructure that provides the appropriate bandwidth with possible alternate routing capabilities. Appropriate network resources will ensure that the amount of time that database locks are held is kept to a minimum, thereby optimizing data concurrency within each resource manager. In a distributed transaction—a transaction that updates more than one resource manager—each resource manager maintains locks for its own data items. Each local lock manager can decide whether to grant a lock or make the requesting transaction wait. In addition, it cannot release any locks until it knows that the transaction has been committed or aborted at all the servers involved in the transaction. When locking is used for concurrency control, the data items remain locked and unavailable for other transactions during the commit processing.

- *Keeping the number of resource managers to a reasonable limit.* When using synchronous replication, the number and location of resource managers involved in the commit scope must not exceed the technical limits of the infrastructure components. If the number of locations is large or the underlying support infrastructure is not sufficiently robust, there is a strong possibility that one or more of the commit locations will be unavailable due to either a resource-locking condition or a component failure. In these situations, services and procedures must be available to provide some sort of transaction retry logic, notify the sending application that a failure has occurred, or provide a queuing service for the unavailable resource manager.

- *Understanding the transaction nesting capabilities of the resource manager(s) under the control of the distributed transaction manager.* XA is a component of X/Open Distributed Transaction Processing (DTP) standards as they relate to the interfaces between a resource manager and a transaction manager. Currently the XA standard does not address the implementation of nested transactions, parent transactions that spawn subtransactions. Therefore, resource managers vary in how they implement this functionality. When a transaction manager is used to coordinate across multiple resource managers, it is important to know what type of nesting models can be used. For example, can individual branches of the whole transaction (that is, subtransactions) be aborted without forcing a total transaction rollback, or can resource manager locks be inherited from a parent within the nesting? Because a number of models exist, a firm should develop its own Best Practice recommendations that identify the models supported by its in-house resource managers and provide templates for use within applications. See sidebar in Chapter 6 for a complete discussion of transaction nesting.

- *Defining limitations and appropriate procedures for updating files not controlled by resource managers.* For files not associated with a resource manager (any sort of flat file, for example an ISAM file) to be involved in a software transaction's recoverable unit of work, either a TP monitor/transaction manager or a transactional workflow system must be used. Currently it is the only means available to support the rollback functionality should a failure occur. When a failure does occur within a transactional workflow system, a compensating transaction is used to return the flat file to its pre-transaction state. This transactional workflow software can be of the vendor or home-grown variety.

Asynchronous data replication

Asynchronous data replication provides what is called "loose consistency" between data stores. This means that the latency before data consistency is achieved is always greater than zero; the replication process occurs asynchronously to the originating transaction. In other words, there is always some degree of lag between when the originating software transaction is committed and when the effects of the transaction are available at any replica(s). If the appropriate infrastructure resources are sufficient, the latency is usually measured in seconds.

Asynchronous data replication can occur in a variety of ways. A hierarchy of the approaches and a subsequent detailed discussion of each approach follows. Asynchronous data replication can be implemented using the following:

- *Complete or incremental refresh.* Refresh technology implies batch processing.
- *Delta propagation of events.* Event propagation implies near-real-time processing. The delta propagation of events can be accomplished through two distinct approaches: *database-to-database communication* or *process-to-process communication.*

Complete or incremental refresh

For a complete refresh, extracts from what is considered the primary data source(s) are scheduled and executed. Any data merging or transformation that may be required occurs. Finally the target replicas are loaded. For an incremental refresh, the same processing occurs except only the changes that have occurred from the last extraction are collected. The assumption for any type of refresh is that this processing is of a batch nature. In batch replication, the real-time transactional nature of the originating event is lost when the extracted data is written to persistent storage (the queuing or staging mechanism) in preparation for merging, transformation, and distribution. At this time the transactional BEGIN and transactional COMMIT are discarded. A further assumption of refresh replication is that the target replica is available in a single writer mode during the loading process. This means that the load utility is the only user of the target resource manager. All other users are denied access until the load utility has completed.

Delta propagation of events

When delta propagation of events is used for asynchronous replication, targets must first be initialized to bring them to a consistent state with the primary sources. After the initialization, only the changing events that occur at primary sources are forwarded to the target replicas. Generally with this type of replication each event preserves its discrete identity during the replication process. The event can be a software transaction or a message that represents the software transaction itself or some subset or superset of the software transactions. This event propagation can occur either through database-to-database communication or through process-to-process communication. Each of these approaches has its own characteristics and is applicable for specific situations.

Database-to-database asynchronous replication

Many of the existing vendor-supplied solutions for asynchronous replication are of the database-to-database communication type, largely because these packages are supplied by database vendor companies. This type of asynchronous data replication can be thought of as having three separate and distinct components. The first component is the collection process from the primary data source; the second is the distribution process; the third is the apply process at the designated targets. An optional fourth component, a monitoring process for all the other processes, also is usually present. There is no one standard way that these distinct processes should be implemented. Because the technology is still new, each vendor has implemented its own strategy. Chapter 3 thoroughly discusses a number of these approaches. What is important for the current discussion is that all of the database-to-database approaches have the following characteristics:

- *They are implemented as middleware with a complete or at least extremely high degree of application transparency.* Application transparency is important because it allows the data used by existing applications to become part of the asynchronous replication process without changing any lines of the existing application code. Depending on the vendor implementation, database objects to a greater or lesser extent may have to be altered, but the actual existing user application code need not be changed. For example, some vendors require that triggers be installed at primary source databases to propagate the originating event. Application transparency preserves the investment in existing applications and shortens the entry time into the asynchronous replication arena.
- *They provide both table-to-table event-based replication and the replication of stored procedures.*
- *They guarantee delivery within the distribution process.* This ensures that every database event will be delivered only once.
- *They maintain some level of sequential integrity throughout the delivery process.* (See Asynchronous Replication Issues below.)
- *They preserve the transactional nature of the originating event during the collection, distribution, and apply processes.* For most online transaction processing (OLTP) environments, the preservation of transactional semantics is critical. For online analytical processing (OLAP) environments where most updating occurs as part of a batch process—refresh technology—it is not as critical. OLAP, the analysis required to create, manipulate, animate, and synthesize enterprise information, now represents what was formerly called decision-support systems. If transactional semantics are preserved across the replication process, then the logical unit of work that was exe-

cuted as the originating transaction is also executed at the replica(s). The more near-real-time the asynchronous replication, the more important this concept becomes. Transactions provide a simple model for success or failure. They exhibit the ACID properties—atomic, consistent, isolated, and durable. (See Appendix B for a complete discussion of the ACID properties of transactions.) Figure 1.1 illustrates the effect of preserving transaction semantics across the asynchronous replication process.

As can be seen in Figure 1.1, the target replica where transactional semantics is preserved is always consistent transactionally with the source. No matter what cross-section of tables is queried at the target, the data is always transactionally consistent. For example, if this were a banking application and a debit and a credit were part of the originating software transac-

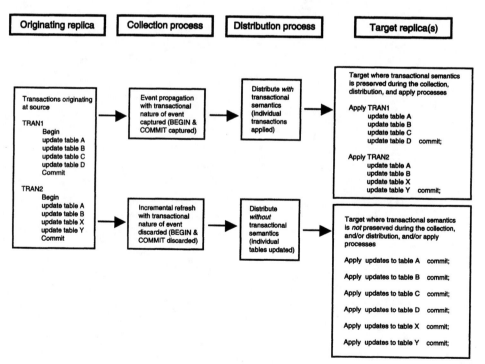

FIGURE 1.1   Preserving transactional semantics during replication.

tion, a user of the target data would always see a balanced account. Asynchronous replication, where transactional semantics is preserved, is generally a must where near-real-time updating of a target replica occurs. In these situations, the target site does not have the luxury of a "batch window" in which to apply all changes while users are off the system(s) and the replication service has sole access to the data.

From a data integrity perspective, asynchronous replication where transactional semantics is *not* preserved is suitable for use only when some sort of "batch window" exists for applying all the changes from all originating sources as a whole. With this type of replication the onus for the integrity of the data at target replicas falls totally on the scheduling of the updates for each target. Assume from Figure 1.1 that Tran1 and Tran2 share the same originating data source. If tables A, B, X, and Y are updated as one replication set at point in time M, and tables C and D are updated later at point in time N, during the time between M and N, users see all of the results of Tran2 and one-half of the result of Tran1. This may or may not be acceptable from a business perspective.

Another variation with the same result occurs where the target subscribes to all updates from tables A, B, X, and Y, in anticipation of receiving all the results from only Tran2 updating. Because Tran1 and Tran2 share the same originating source data, their users view all of Tran2 updating plus one-half of Tran1 updating, which may be a surprise for the target users. When transactional semantics is lost, there is no way of applying the results of just a single transaction.

A further complication of *not* preserving transactional semantics during the replication process is the potential for failed updates at a target replica due to referential integrity constraints defined at the target. For example, this type of violation occurs where a dependent row exists without its associated parent; think of a purchase order detail line without its associated purchase order header row, or a purchase order header for a customer that has not been inserted yet. These violations occur because the apply process commits updates to only one replica table at a time; it does not preserve a transactional whole across replica tables. In this situation, the table order within the apply process becomes critical. See Chapter 6 for the design issues associated with not preserving transactional semantics within asynchronous replication.

TIP

The designer(s) of a replication environment must have full knowledge of the originating transactions and the data sources they use. Only then can an architect define what makes a consistent whole for each target replica.

Preserving Transactional Semantics and Transactional Content for a Distributed Unit of Work

If the originating transaction was the result of a distributed unit of work, that is, one that updates multiple databases within the BEGIN and COMMIT scope, and the collection mechanism was a pull from the database log technique, transactional semantics and transactional content of the original transaction will not be preserved as a single unit across the replication process. Within the replication process, the originating transaction becomes multiple, separate transactions. The number of separate transactions equates to the number of separate database logs being updated. As each log pull mechanism individually captures the changed data from its designated log, it captures its own BEGIN and COMMIT statements. In order for the transactional semantics and transactional content of the originating transaction to be preserved across the distributed unit of work, the asynchronous replication software must be able to re-merge the information captured from multiple logs and then apply it at subscribing targets as a single unit of work. Because this replication process is occurring asynchronously across many components, there is no way to ensure that all transactional parts will arrive at the target replica in time to be re-merged and applied as a single, reunited unit. The apply component at the target replicas applies each transactional part as it is received. If all replication components are running and the network is transferring data without a significant lag, all transactional parts should be applied separately within a very narrow time frame; however, if this is not the case, the time before transactional consistency is achieved at the target replicas reflects the latency of the slowest replication leg. Figure 1.2 illustrates this problem. I know of no asynchronous replication product of the log pull variety that has the functionality to reunite the separate components of a distributed unit of work. Therefore, if the business requirement is to subscribe to all the updated information from an originating distributed unit of work, then either synchronous replication or an asynchronous messaging type of replication should be used.

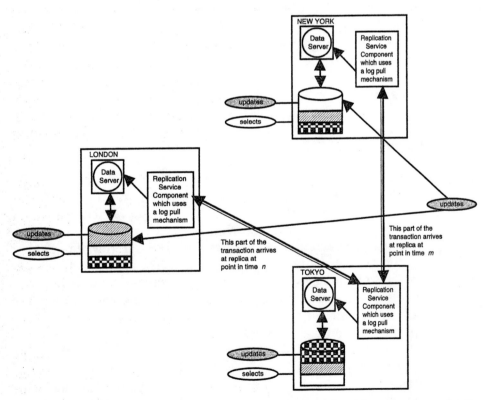

FIGURE 1.2 Preserving transactional semantics and transactional content for a distributed unit of work.

Process-to-process asynchronous replication

This type of asynchronous data replication is usually based on a publish/subscribe messaging paradigm. In this context, the processes involved in this asynchronous replication can be application programs or business or technical reusable services implemented within the middle tier of a multitier architecture. Process-to-process asynchronous replication has four separate and distinct components. The first component is the publish process, which is accomplished as part of the originating event. The second is the distribution process, which usually makes use of a store-and-forward paradigm. The third is the subscribe process by which those other processes (applications or services) interested in the event receive the message. The fourth is the apply process where the receiving process performs tasks dictated by business rules defined for the receipt of that particular message. An optional fifth component, a monitoring process for all the other processes, is also usually present. As with database-to-database asynchronous replication, there is no one standard way that these distinct processes should be implemented. Because the technology is even newer than database-to-database asynchronous replication, each vendor has implemented its own strategy. What is important for the current discussion is that all of the process-to-process approaches have the following characteristics:

- *They are implemented as middleware with simple APIs (application programming interfaces).* Because APIs are used by processes for sending and receiving messages, it is obvious that process-to-process asynchronous replication is not application transparent. The application code for new or legacy systems must contain calls to the *put* API to publish a message and to the *get* API to retrieve messages. In addition, the receiving process must contain code to handle the message it retrieves. This code reflects the business requirements for receipt of that particular message.
- *They support multiple message formats.* These formats could include fixed format (e.g., IBM COBOL records), delimited format (e.g., C null delimited strings), variable format, and self-describing messages.

- *They guarantee delivery within the distribution process.* This ensures that every message will be delivered only once.
- *They maintain some level of sequential integrity throughout the delivery process.* (See Asynchronous Replication Issues below.)
- *They provide publish/subscribe with transactional integrity.* In other words, they provide persistent storage for messages that is integrated with the transaction management of the sending and receiving processes. This is extremely critical; it ensures that messages are not committed to the delivery systems until the sender commits a transaction and that messages are not considered delivered until the receiver commits a transaction. This is called preserving the transactional state. Because messages are committed by the message delivery system when a sender commits a transaction that includes one or more messages, the delivery system state matches the sender's transactional state. Similarly, because messages are considered delivered when a receiver obtains one or more messages and commits a transaction, the message delivery system matches the receiver's state. The ACID properties of transactions are preserved at both sending and receiving processes. See Figure 1.3 for an illustration of what could happen if transactional integrity was not preserved during the send and receive process.

When to use asynchronous replication

As stated earlier, whenever the tight data consistency of synchronous replication (two-phase commit processing) is not demanded by the business requirement, then an asynchronous replication technique is best. This lowers the cost, improves concurrency within resource managers, and generally shortens the length of the originating database transaction.

Comparisons of OLTP and OLAP environments for asynchronous replication

To spare the OLTP environment the added stress of also serving as the OLAP environment, most firms establish separate data stores for decision support. These decision-support systems are architected to handle lengthy statistical queries that would otherwise compete for resources with the short transactional updates of OLTP environments. Currently if both OLTP and OLAP

CASE 1	CASE 2	CASE 3	CASE 4
Everything works well. No abort occurs.	Abort occurs after DB tran is committed, but before message is sent.	Abort occurs after message is sent, but before DB tran is committed.	Abort occurs after message is sent, but before DB tran is committed.
Program / Process	Program / Process	Program / Process	Program / Process
begin tran *update a* *update b* *end tran (commit)* *pub message*	*begin tran* *update a* *update b* *end tran (commit)* **Abort** pub message	*pub message* **Abort** *begin tran* *update a* *update b* *end tran (commit)*	*begin tran* *update a* *update b* *pub message* **Abort** *end tran (commit)*
Results: DB work is committed. Message is published.	Results: DB work is committed. Message is *not* published.	Results: DB work is *not* committed. Message is published.	Results: DB work is *not* committed. Message is published.

FIGURE 1.3 Outcomes with loss of transactional integrity between database updates and message infrastructure.

environments share the same physical data store, data can be locked by the longer query processing of OLAP users and therefore reduce concurrency for OLTP users. In addition, data physically designed to service the needs of OLTP environments is not optimally designed for decision-support environments. However, in the future as both hardware and software parallelism becomes more robust, physical sharing between both environments will become a more viable option.

Characteristics of OLTP environments include the following:

- *Relatively short updating transactions.*
- *High number of users sharing either the same physical data store or a replicate with real-time or near-real-time data consistency with primary sources.*
- *Highly normalized data structures (usually to third normal form). (See sidebar in Chapter 5.)* This avoids update and delete anomalies and usually provides adequate transactional perfor-

mance. An example of an update anomaly is where data has been denormalized so that both customer number and customer name are stored in the purchase order header record. In a normalized structure, customer name would be stored only in the customer record. An update transaction that changes the customer name in the customer record but not in the purchase order header record creates an anomaly.

Characteristics of OLAP environments include the following:

- *Complex queries that tend to summarize, consolidate, and apply complex calculations to data.* This includes the ability to drill down, roll up, slice, and rotate across and within multidimensional views of the data.
- *Small number of users sharing data structures with a data latency level that generally does not need to have real time or near-real time consistency with primary source(s).*
- *Denormalized data structures with precalculated values that reduce the number of joins across data structures.*

A replication service that is used in the OLTP environment has different requirements than one used in an OLAP environment.

With respect to data replication for OLTP environments, the following characteristics apply:

- *Near-real-time requirements for data consistency.*
- *Requirement for simple data transformational services.* Because data stores tend to be very normalized, only simple data transformational services are required.
- *High-availability requirement.* There usually is a high-availability requirement of near 24 × 7. Therefore there is generally no concept of a "batch window."

With respect to data replication for OLAP environments, the following characteristics apply:

- *Generally relaxed data latency requirements.*
- *Requirement for complex data transformational services.* Because data is usually merged from multiple primary sources,

extensive and complex data transformation is usually required.

• *Relaxed availability requirement.* There usually is the luxury of a batch window where all update activity to the replica can occur.

Considering the aforementioned characteristics, a delta propagation of events type of asynchronous replication is more appropriate for OLTP environments and a refresh type of asynchronous replication is more appropriate for OLAP environments. However, each case should be considered individually, and the best approach is the one that not only satisfies the business requirements but also integrates well into the infrastructure. Chapter 7 addresses more issues associated with using replication in an OLAP environment.

Important issues to consider when using asynchronous replication

Due to the asynchronous nature of this type of replication, the critical issues that should be addressed are more closely related to architecture than to physical infrastructure. With a full understanding of the underlying concepts associated with each issue, it should be relatively straightforward to design and implement an efficient asynchronous replication environment. These issues include the following:

• *Defining requirements for support of transactional semantics and/or transactional integrity.* With the refresh type of asynchronous replication, all transaction demarcation is lost. With database-to-database event propagation, full transactional integrity is usually preserved across the collection, distribution, and apply portions of the asynchronous replication. The only open issue is how distributed units of work are handled by the asynchronous replication service. With process-to-process event propagation, information about the originating event, which is either a software transaction or a subset or superset of software transactions, is received by a subscribing replica. The apply process reflects the business rules assigned to the receipt of that message. It could be a single software transaction or a workflow type of processing that spawns other software transactions. The critical issue here is that transactional integrity exits between the message queues and the sending and receiving processes.

- *Ensuring the appropriate level of sequential integrity.* With the refresh type of asynchronous replication, all transaction demarcation is lost. Therefore, all sequencing of the originating event is also lost. The refresh occurs in batches and brings the replica to a more current point in time, creating a more current snapshot. With both database-to-database event propagation and process-to-process event propagation, sequencing is an issue. Multiple publishers of events have numerous entry points into the queuing and distribution systems of the replication process. It is an asynchronous process with many distributed components. Networks may be slower at some publishers than others, individual collection or distribution components may be in a failed state or just slow due to lack of sufficient CPU resources. However, the assumption with event propagation is that the apply process always executes at each replica. Once an event is applied, it cannot be unapplied to alter its sequence with respect to other events. Therefore, the sequencing generally maintained is sequential integrity (originating sequence order) for all events published from each individual publisher. However, once events are part of the distribution process, they are applied in a first-in first-out queue at a replica. There is no simple way to ensure sequential integrity across all publishing sites for a given replica in an asynchronous environment.

- *Using conflict detection and resolution mechanisms.* Two models are used to distribute data and assign ownership when data is stored redundantly. The first is a master/slave model; the second is an update-anywhere model, sometimes referred to as peer-to-peer replication or symmetric replication. (See Chapter 2 for a complete discussion of the distribution alternatives.) What is important here is that in the master/slave model each individual piece of data has only one designated master (that is, an updatable replica) at any given time. Therefore, all update activity occurs at that designated master, and all update conflicts for that data element are avoided. With peer-to-peer replication, there is no designated master for any individual data element. Any replica can be used as the updatable source at any time. When asynchronous replication is used, the conflicts are determined after the fact and are resolved at the subscribing target locations. Rules are applied at a target to aid with the resolution. One rule might be to apply updates so that the target always reflects the most current data based on the time stamp of the originating changes. Another rule might be to apply updates so that the target reflects the update that occurred at the prioritized replica. Whatever rules are applied, the fact is that users of the data do not see a globally consistent state. Yes, compensating transactions can be issued to resynchronize all replicas, but other updating transactions were entered based on these earlier data values. This may or may not present a problem for a firm; it depends on the business requirements and associated risks for that firm. For an airlines reservation system, the result would be overbooked flights. The worst-case scenario for the airline is that it compensates the overbooked passengers with free tickets for future flights. For an investment banking system managing global risk, using compensating transactions could result in the firm being over exposed or possibly violating regulatory obligations. It is important to recognize that resolution schemes are complex, they cannot handle every possible conflict, and they present integrity risks to users. Weigh the alternatives carefully before implementing peer-to-peer asynchronous replication.

 WARNING

If used and managed correctly, asynchronous replication can greatly improve data availability and application performance in a distributed environment. If used inappropriately, it can corrupt the data to a point that repair becomes highly complex, if not downright impossible.

WHY SHOULD REPLICATION BE IMPLEMENTED AS AN ENTERPRISE SERVICE?

As defined earlier, a replication service provides a *complete* copy management facility in a distributed, heterogeneous resource manager environment. This is a tall order. It demands an architectural effort and the necessary support infrastructure. This can be accomplished from either a top-down or a bottom-up approach, but it does require strategic planning. If an enterprise service perspective is not used, it is very possible to win a few replication battles and yet lose the replication war. In other words, a firm might successfully implement replication for a small number of isolated applications but fail when it attempts to implement replication on an enterprisewide scale.

Using a service approach even on the first, small replication effort ensures that the following are addressed:

- *Replication remains open.* This means that the service is architected to allow multiple vendors' products and home-grown applications as part of the total solution.
- *Replication alternatives are scalable.* Here scalability is more than just the ability to run on bigger and better hardware. It is the ability to support a heterogeneous database environment with small and large volumes of data transfer across a heterogeneous network environment, with minimal impact on any of the resources involved. These resources are of the hardware, software, network, and people varieties.
- Replication is easily and consistently administered.

Chapter 3 presents an overview of vendor approaches for architecting replication solutions. In addition, it presents general requirements for creating and evaluating replication software.

Establishing a Technical Baseline

The initial implementation of a replication solution does not present the most challenges; the ongoing support truly tests the design and architecture of the complete replication infrastructure. To meet the challenge of building a robust replication infrastructure, understanding basic technical concepts is necessary. Establishing this technical baseline is the goal of this chapter.

OPEN SYSTEMS

Chapter 1 disclosed that most firms have an average of six distinct database environments. Firms want to link this heterogeneous environment into a coherent whole. Therefore, the replication service must be open. In this context, "open" means that the replication service allows multiple vendors' products as well as home-grown replication solutions. In addition, the interfaces among components should be based on industry standards so that replication solutions can become more like commodities, which can easily be interchanged.

TIP

New applications and services should be architected in such a way that they are not tied to any particular vendor's hardware or software platform. This approach views solutions as interchangeable commodities. Even if the goal of total "plug-ability" can not be reached, the closer we get to achieving it, the easier and cheaper future changes become.

CHARACTERISTICS OF DISTRIBUTED SYSTEMS

Distributed systems exhibit the following characteristics:

- *Remote components.* The components of the system are spread across space.
- *Concurrency.* Any number of the components can execute in parallel.
- *Isolation of failures.* Any component can fail independently of any other component.
- *Heterogeneous technology mix.* The environment usually contains a mixture of technologies that slowly change over time.
- *Mobility of component.* Resources, processing nodes, and users are physically mobile.
- *Asynchronous nature of events.* It cannot be assumed that related changes occur in a single instance of time.
- *Lack of global state.* The global state of a distributed system cannot be determined precisely.

LOGICAL UNIT OF WORK

A logical unit of work—a software transaction—is a sequence of one or more data manipulation statements that together form a unit of recovery. Data manipulation statements include insert, delete, update, and/or read statements. Within the logical unit of work, either all statements execute successfully or none of the statements execute; it is an all-or-nothing scenario. In other words, the logical unit of work brings the resource managers, from one state of consistency to another state of consistency. These database transactions exhibit the same ACID properties as do transactions in general. ACID, as you may recall, was identified as an acronym for atomicity, consistency, isolation, and durability. See Appendix B for a complete discussion of the ACID properties of transactions.

A software transaction or logical unit of work is said to be committed when all of its processing has completed successfully. With respect to resource managers, a transaction is committed when all data manipulation statements have executed successfully. In other words, all changes made by the transaction to recoverable data become permanent.

TYPES OF DISTRIBUTED DATA ACCESS

Ideally a user should be able to make a request for data and have that request resolved in a totally transparent fashion. The user should not need to know where the data permanently resides, what type of resource manager (database management system) is used to manage that data, what access language was required to navigate within the resource manager, or what network protocols were required. All of this should be hidden from the user. However, architects, developers, and system support personnel must be aware of the heterogeneous nature of the environment and must be able to interface with the appropriate middleware.

When data is distributed across network nodes, a mechanism for distributed access must be available across these nodes. Distributed data access is also an integral part of client/server architectures, where data and processes are distributed between clients and servers. There are four types of distributed data access. These types will be described in order of increasing complexity, and the relational model will be used as the basis for all illustrations. The relational model presents data as being organized into tables. Within a table, rows represent records of data, and columns represent fields in that record. There are no duplicate rows in a given table, and the order of rows and columns within a table is not significant. Each table reflects facts and values of the real world. All relational database management systems (RDBMS) use a standardized access language called SQL (structured query language). Using SQL simplifies the distributed access illustrations presented in Table 2.1 and Figure 2.1. However, the basic concepts are applicable across any type of resource manager.

The four types of distributed data access include remote request, remote unit of work (remote transaction), distributed unit of work (distributed transaction), and distributed request. Table 2.1 summarizes the characteristics of these various types of distributed data access. Figure 2.1 illustrates the same concepts in a graphic format.

As defined earlier, a logical unit of work is the work completed as a unit of recovery. It is the work that is completed between a pair of database commit points. It may or may not modify data in one or multiple database sites. It equates to a software transaction.

Remote request

A remote request is a method of accessing distributed data in which an application or user can read and/or update one DBMS using one SQL statement. The DBMS may be located anywhere, and the single SQL statement constitutes a single unit of work. Within a simple client/server environment, this equates to the client application issuing a single data request to be processed at a single remote server.

TABLE 2.1 Types of Distributed Data Access—table format

Type of distributed access	SQL statements per Unit of Work	DBMS per Unit of Work	DBMS per SQL statement
Remote Request	1	1	1
Remote Unit of Work	>1	1	1
Distributed Unit of Work	>1	>1	1
Distributed Request	>1	>1	>1

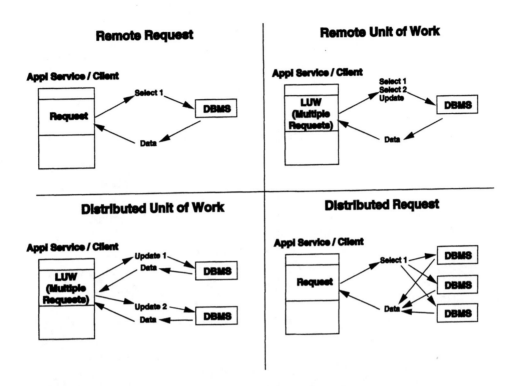

Note:
Where a DBMS is used within the illustration, an application server could be substituted

FIGURE 2.1   Types of Distributed Data Access—graphic format.

Remote unit of work/remote transaction

A remote unit of work (a remote transaction) is a method of accessing distributed data in which an application or user can read and/or update one DBMS using multiple SQL statements within a single unit of recovery. A remote transaction permits more complexity than does a remote request. It allows the transaction to contain multiple data requests; however, as with remote requests, all data must reside at a single DBMS. A remote transaction supports the ACID properties for that single resource manager. Therefore, if a failure occurs during a remote unit of work, the system backs out all changes associated with the transaction and returns that resource manager to its previous state of consistency. Within a client/server environment, this implies that the remote data is placed at a single server and accessed from a client workstation in a single logical unit of work.

Distributed unit of work/distributed transaction

A distributed unit of work is a method of accessing distributed data in which an application or user can read and/or update multiple DBMSs using multiple SQL statements within a single unit of recovery. The only restriction is that each individual SQL statement can access only a single DBMS. This distributed transaction capability allows a transaction to contain multiple data requests for data residing at multiple locations. A distributed transaction must support the ACID properties of transactions across all resource managers involved in the commit scope. Therefore, if a failure occurs at any location during the distributed unit of work, the system backs out all changes to all locations and returns each resource manager to its previous state of consistency. Within a client/server environment, this implies that the data that is distributed among multiple servers can be accessed from a client workstation within a single logical unit of work.

Distributed request

A distributed request is a method of accessing distributed data in which an application or user can read and/or update data in multiple relational tables that reside in multiple DBMSs within a single SQL statement. This is the most complex type of distributed data access. It is a distributed transaction in which each request can reference data residing at multiple locations. As with distributed transactions, all actions performed within the distributed request compose a single unit of work and, as such, must preserve the ACID properties. Within a client/server environment, this implies that the data can be distributed among multiple servers and can be accessed transparently from a client workstation in a single request.

TIP

Data should be accessed only via some sort of application programming interface (API). This ensures a layer of isolation for the data and will eventually allow DBMSs to become more like commodities, which can be easily interchanged. It is my belief that databases will never actually become true commodities because database standards lag behind new product features. To exploit the functionality of a particular DBMS, users must make use of non-standardized product features, thereby eliminating the option of easily replacing one vendor's product with another. This truly is a Catch 22.

TYPES OF DISTRIBUTED DATABASE SYSTEMS

Distributed computer environments are becoming the norm. In this type of environment, users share peripherals, data, and programs while the infrastructure provides system management across the plethora of network, hardware, and software components. Databases have been a part of this distributed evolution. A brief history of this database evolution follows. Early technical literature defines two types of systems for linking distributed database environments: federated database systems and distributed database systems. Because both function in a distributed arena, calling one option a distributed database system is, at best, confusing. However, these are the accepted terms, so they will be used here.

Distributed database management systems

By definition, distributed database systems should support the following functionality:

- *Single logical database that is physically distributed.*
- *Single database definition, that is, schema.*
- *Global multiphased commit protocol across all resource managers that is completely system supported.* This enables multiresource manager updates from within a single logical unit

of work (a transaction). As stated earlier, transactions are used to define an all-or-nothing block of work.
- *Global optimization of queries.*
- *Location transparency for all data access.* This enables applications and/or users to modify and read data without knowledge of where the data is actually physically located.
- *Coordinated recovery in the event of a system or disk failure at any site.*

These features should allow support for all four types of distributed data access—remote request, remote unit of work, distributed unit of work, and distributed request. Even though a high degree of homogeneity exists in a distributed database system, each resource manager must be able to function with total independence of every other resource manager.

Federated database management system

By contrast, a federated database system is simply a collection of autonomous database management systems (DBMSs). Each DBMS may support a different data schema, query language, and transaction management. The role of the federated database management system software is to mask all these differences from any application process or user.

A federated database system should support the following functionality:

- *Multiple database schemata residing on diverse platforms.*
- *Ability of each underlying DBMS to function with total independence of any other DBMS.* The middleware supports the federated environment.

Because the component database management systems are linked only to the degree specified by the federated middleware, the following functionality may or may not be supported:

- *Global multiphased commit protocol across all resource managers.* If this functionality is not supported by the federated middleware, then the transaction processing capabilities of the resource managers involved or application code must be used to ensure data integrity within a logical unit of work across the multiple resource managers.

- *Location transparency.* This insulates applications and users from knowledge of the physical location of data slices.
- *Common query language.*
- *Coordinated recovery in the event of a system or disk failure at any site.*

Due to the heterogeneous nature of federated database systems and the varying functionality supported by the federated middleware, full support for the four types of distributed data access may or may not be available.

Twelve Distributed DBMS Rules

In 1987, C.J. Date defined 12 rules of compliance for a fully distributed database management system:

Local autonomy. The sites in a distributed system should be autonomous, that is, independent of each other.

No reliance on a central site. A distributed database management system should not rely on a central site because this would create a single point of failure for the whole system. This central site would also pose a bottleneck with respect to performance and throughput.

Continuous operation. A distributed database system should never require downtime.

Location transparency and location independence. Applications and users should not need to know physical locations of persistent storage for data.

Fragmentation independence. For RDBMSs, tables can be divided into fragments and stored at different locations transparently to applications and users.

Replication independence. Data should be able to be replicated transparently to multiple computer systems within the distributed environment.

Distributed query processing. The performance of a given query should be independent of the location at which the query is submitted.

Distributed transaction management. A distributed system should be able to support the ACID properties of transactions. It should provide support for remote requests, remote units of work, distributed units of work, and distributed requests.

Hardware independence. A distributed database system should be able to operate and access data spread across a wide variety of hardware platforms.

Operating system independence. A distributed database system should be able to run on different operating systems.

Network independence. A distributed database system should be able to run regardless of the communication protocols and network topology used to interconnect the various system nodes.

DBMS independence. An ideal distributed database management system should be able to support interoperability between heterogeneous DBMS systems running different nodes.[1]

Date's rules of compliance set the stage for a strategic framework for delivering open, distributed computing solutions.

OSF/DCE perspective

The Open Software Foundation's Distributing Computing Environment (OSF/DCE) provides a strategic framework for a distributed computing environment. The Distributed Computing Environment (DCE) is a set of integrated services that works across multiple systems and yet remains independent of any single system. DCE software includes tools and services that function as a layer of software that masks the differences among different kinds of computers. Once DCE components are installed and configured on the computers within the network, the environment is ready to run distributed applications. Some of the services provided by DCE include the following:

---

[1]A. Berson, *Client/Server Architecture* (New York: McGraw-Hill), 425–8.

- *The ability to harness latent computing power.* DCE Remote Procedure Call (RPC) software allows distribution of applications across multiple computers. This distribution enables applications to use untapped computer resources wherever they exist in the network; it provides load balancing. In addition, DCE Threads allow programs to execute multiple remote procedures on multiple host computers in the network. This can greatly improve application performance.
- *The opportunity to increase resource availability.* By redundantly placing critical applications services and data on multiple host computers, availability is increased. This allows critical components to be available even when partial failures occur.
- *The ability to increase the collaborative capabilities of users.* DCE Distributed File Services (DFS) provides a single view of all files, both UNIX and non-UNIX, across all systems to all users. This makes sharing and collaborative work a reality.
- *The ability to track data and programs that might move within the system.* DFS has a database that stores the location of all files within the file system. When a file moves, DFS automatically updates the database with the new location. In addition, application clients can use DCE Directory Services to locate their associated servers.
- *The ability to accommodate heterogeneous data.* DCE RPCs mask the differences in byte ordering, data formats, and padding between data items by converting data to the appropriate form needed by clients and servers.
- *The support for versioning of application code.* When it becomes necessary to support new features within application code, programmers need only change the interface definition, assign a different version number, and recompile the client and server code. The version numbers ensure that each client finds the appropriate server code.
- *The ability to synchronize events.* DCE Time Services (DTS) runs on every host computer and keeps the associated host clocks closely synchronized.
- *The ability to provide a secure environment to all distributed resources.* DCE Security Services authenticates all DCE users

and servers to ensure all users are who they claim to be. In addition, it provides authorization capabilities to protect distributed resources from unauthorized use.

One of the design goals for DCE is to conform to standards where they exist. Therefore DCE Version 1 is compatible with the following:

- Domain Name System, as implemented in Berkeley Internet Name Domain
- International Telegraph and Telephone Consultative Committee X.500 Directory Services
- International Standards Organization's model for Open Systems Interconnection
- POSIX standard for thread implementation

With the advent of OSF/DCE, the emphasis has been on implementing federated database environments. This gives a firm the most flexibility because it does not restrict the firm by limiting its database usage to a single vendor family. In addition, it provides the most robust, standardized services currently available within a distributed environment. DCE is in only its first release, so there is still room for improvement. It is a good start, but acceptance within firms will take time.

DATA DISTRIBUTION ALTERNATIVES

Because a distributed computing environment supports the sharing of peripherals, data, and processes, there is no underlying requirement that data be stored redundantly. Therefore, data distribution alternatives include both options, storage without data redundancy and storage with redundancy. Options where no redundancy is allowed include centralized and fragmented models. Options where data is stored redundantly include variations of a master/slave model or the update-anywhere model.

Options with no data redundancy

When no redundancy is allowed, only a single copy of the data exists. Two distribution options are possible for this alternative: centralized and fragmented models.

Centralized model

The centralized model involves no data distribution. All data is stored in a single centralized resource manager. The use of the data can be distributed via local and remote access, but the data itself resides in one central location. See Figure 2.2.

General characteristics of the centralized model include the following:

- Only a single copy of the data exists.
- Ownership of and ability to update the single data source are shared.

The main advantage to this lack of redundancy is that the data is always consistent and current. Because no redundancy

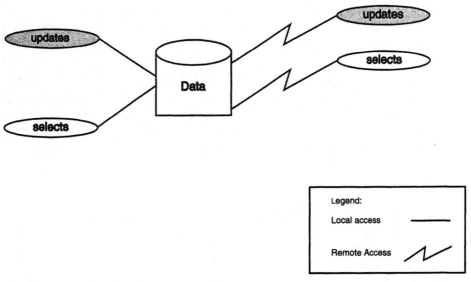

FIGURE 2.2   Centralized model.

exists, all users always see exactly the same data. In addition, the lack of distribution makes control, security, and maintenance very simple and straightforward. The biggest drawback to this model is that there is a single point of failure. If a failure occurs and the data becomes unavailable, all systems stop functioning. A further concern is the potential for high network usage, which could be costly if remote access is high.

Fragmented model

This option involves the distribution of the single centralized data source identified in the centralized model. The distribution is accomplished via horizontal and/or vertical partitioning. However, no data is stored redundantly with the exception of primary keys if vertical partitioning is implemented. In the relational model, horizontal partitioning divides a table by rows. The basis for the division is usually the value in one or more columns within that table. For example, in a banking firm, the partitioning column might be branch code with each branch "owning" and storing the data associated with the customers it serves. Vertical partitioning divides a relational table by columns. Continuing with the banking example, vertical partitioning of a customer table could have customer address information stored at a regional center and customer loan information stored at the branch that serviced that customer's loan request. Here the customer identifier column (primary key) would be stored in both the regional customer address table and the local customer table. As with the centralized model, the use of the data can be distributed via local and remote access, but only one copy of the data exists; it is partitioned across multiple distributed locations. See Figure 2.3, which illustrates a horizontally fragmented distribution model.

General characteristics of the fragmented model include the following:

- Only a single copy of the data exists, but data is fragmented (partitioned) across multiple locations.
- Ownership of and ability to update the single distributed source are shared.

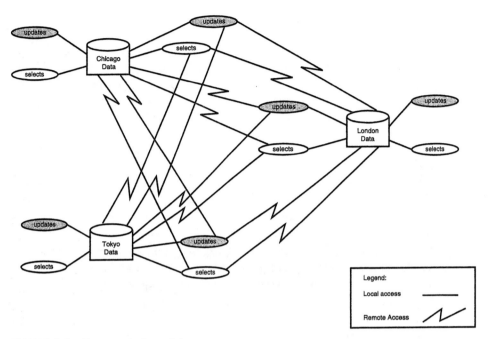

FIGURE 2.3 Fragmented model.

As with the centralized model, the biggest advantage is that the data is always consistent and current. Redundancy exists only where vertical partitioning has been implemented and primary keys are carried redundantly. If this is the case, some sort of reconciliation should be implemented to ensure the integrity across the vertical partitions. In this model, control, security, and maintenance are slightly more complex than in the centralized model because multiple locations are used for persistent storage. The issue of a single point of failure has been reduced but not eliminated. For example, the local branch, as identified in the above example, could complete a loan transaction even if the regional center was unavailable. The validation of the customer address information could occur later if this is acceptable to business users. Network usage is reduced with respect to the centralized model. However, remote access is still required.

Options with data redundancy

Two types of models for maintaining data consistency and assigning ownership exist when data redundancy is allowed. The first is a master/slave model; the second is an update-anywhere model, sometimes referred to as peer-to-peer replication or symmetric replication.

Master/slave model

As the name implies, a master/slave model has a designated master for each individual data element, sometimes called the primary source, which can be stored centrally or distributed. It can be partitioned within individual table(s) and distributed across multiple locations. In addition, the ownership of a primary source can be transferred between redundantly stored replicas as a factor of time. The critical issue is that at any one time every individual piece of data has one and only one primary source. This tenet makes life simple in a replicated environment because there is always a definitive source for data reconciliation and recovery purposes. All update activity for a particular slice of data always occurs against only one replica at any particular time.

In the master/slave model, the assumption is that all replication occurs asynchronously to the updating of the primary source. This means that there is some degree of latency before data consistency is achieved at any target (that is, any replica). Methods of achieving this asynchronous replication include either complete or incremental refresh or delta propagation of events. See Chapter 1, "Asynchronous Data Replication" for a complete comparison of the replication alternatives.

General characteristics of this model include the following:

- Multiple copies/replicas of the data exist.
- Ownership and ability to update are shared across the single primary source (the master).
- All non-primary replicas are considered read-only with data consistency being maintained by means of an asynchronous replication service.

Update-anywhere model

In the update-anywhere model, there is no designated master (primary source) for any individual data element. Any replica can be used as the updatable source at any time. In this model, replication can occur either synchronously or asynchronously. If synchronous replication is used, a two-phase commit protocol is used to ensure the data consistency across all replicas. In other words, the data across replicas is always consistent because all changes occur synchronously to all copies by means of a distributed transaction. If synchronous replication is used, all ACID properties as defined for transactional systems are preserved. In addition, concurrently running distributed transactions are serialized by a locking mechanism, just as if they were executing as local transactions.

If asynchronous replication is used for data consistency in this model, there is no isolation of transactions from a global perspective. The "I" of the ACID properties is violated. Each individual transaction at its point of execution does exhibit isolation; however, conflicting transactions execute in parallel without any guarantee that a transaction uses the most current state of the database before making an update. There is also no serial history of transaction execution. Therefore, identifying who changed the database state from state m to state $m+1$ is not always possible. Any and all update conflicts are determined after the fact and are resolved at the target subscribing replica locations. Maintaining data consistency with asynchronous replication in an update-anywhere model is very complex. Conflicts can and will occur even if the design tries to minimize them.

Two types of update conflicts can occur: intertable conflicts (conflicts between tables) and intratable conflicts (conflicts within a table). Intertable conflicts occur when related data is spread across two or more locations, usually as a result of poor data partitioning design that allowed the splitting of primary and foreign key references across sites. (See Chapter 5 for a complete discussion of this topic.) This type of conflict can occur regardless of whether data is stored redundantly. Intratable conflicts occur when data is stored redundantly across multiple locations and at all times every replica is considered an updatable replica.

In an asynchronous replication environment, both types of conflicts are detected only after the fact and repaired via manual operations or system-generated compensating transactions that undo previously committed transactions. Use of compensating transactions means that sometimes the updates of a transaction are not durable, the "D" of the ACID properties. Loss of durability creates a rippling effect in that the transactions that are subsequently undone were viewed by other transaction before the undo process occurs. Do these secondary transactions also require compensating actions to ensure database consistency? And so the chain of undo continues.

Using the asynchronous replication flavor of this model is like running a centralized database and turning off all locking mechanisms. It runs freely and provides great performance, but the integrity of the data is compromised. Some replication vendors have introduced libraries of routines that automatically issue compensating transactions, but the inherent flaws of this model still exist. Transactions are no longer isolated, updates may no longer be durable, and transactions may no longer be auditable. In addition, is it even possible to identify all potential conflict situations and have the appropriate routine available? What about the descendent transactions that viewed transactions that subsequently were undone?

When considering this model, carefully weigh the risks associated with persistent data inconsistencies. If the decision is to implement the update-anywhere model, try to keep the number of conflicts that can occur to a minimum. Use this model only with systems that have low update rates. Implement data distribution schemes that minimize the number of update replicas. Use database-enforced referential integrity. Notify the application when an update conflict has been detected so that an auditable reconciliation can follow.

 TIP

When using an update-anywhere model, all referential integrity (RI) constraints should be defined in the database. Because the asynchronous replication process can detect RI conflicts only when they are stored within the database, do not try to enforce referential constraints by means of application logic.

General characteristics of the update-anywhere model include the following:

- *Multiple copies / replicas exist.*
- *Ownership and updatability is shared across any of the replicas.* There is no concept of a master or a single primary source.
- *Data consistency is maintained either by means of synchronous replication (a two-phase commit processing across all replicas) or by means of an asynchronous replication service that incorporates a conflict detection and resolution mechanism.*

Keep in mind that the following models are *not* truly update-anywhere models. If a relational table is partitioned so that each partition is updatable only at a single designated replica, then this is not an update-anywhere implementation; it is an example of distributed primary fragments within a master/slave model. Similarly, if the ownership is transferred between replicas but at any one time only a single owner/update replica exists, then this is really just a more complex version of the master/ slave model.

TRADE-OFFS FOR CENTRALIZED VERSUS DISTRIBUTED APPROACHES

Many trade-offs are associated with data distribution decisions. From a user perspective, the more distributed the data placement, the better the performance and availability of their applications. However, if their application uses a replica that is not the primary, then the timeliness with which data consistency is achieved for that replica could be a concern. From an administration perspective, the less distributed the data placement, the easier the environment is to administer. A summary of the trade-offs associated with data distribution is outlined in Table 2.2.

More than one perspective can be used to weigh the trade-offs of distributing data:

- *Role perspective.* This approach looks at a user's demand for high availability and performance versus the administrator's desire for easy maintenance. The fewer copies, the easier the

TABLE 2.2 Data Distribution Trade-offs

	Centralized environment	Distributed environment
Data access costs	Costs can be high. Both local and remote applications access the central source. If remote query access is heavy, costs can be significant.	Costs are generally lower. Applications access data stored locally. However, depending on the replication approach used to maintain data consistency, communication costs can be an issue. An example of this would occur where complete extracts and refreshes are used with large volumes of data.
System dependability and its effect on data availability	A single point of failure exists. If a failure occurs at the central location, the entire system is disabled.	A failure at any node does not generally affect the other nodes.
Data Consistency with primary source	Data is always consistent because no redundancy exists and all access is to the primary source.	For replicas that are not the primary source, the timeliness of the data (i.e., its latency) is a factor of the replication approach used to maintain the consistency.
Application Performance	Performance is a factor of the network resources that are available.	Because data access is local, performance tends to be better than with a centralized data solution.
Workload balancing	Because all data resides at the same centralized location, there are fewer options available for load balancing.	Because many locations and CPUs are available within the distributed environment, there are many options available for load balancing.
Version control of system software and application code	Control is relatively straightforward and simple.	Control is much more complex due to the multiple copies that exist within the distributed environment.
Security	Security is relatively straightforward and simple.	Security is much more complex due to the multiple components that exist within the distributed environment.
Operational costs	Low. There is a consolidation of efforts at the centralized location.	High. Costs are a factor of the number of locations that must be supported.
Storage media costs	Low. Data is not stored redundantly.	High. Costs are a factor of how many redundant copies are maintained.

environment is to maintain; the greater the redundancy, the better the performance and availability of applications.

- *Technology and interoperability perspective.* The less data distribution that occurs across the fewer heterogeneous platforms, the simpler the entire environment is to manage. However, this perspective promotes a more restrictive environment and many times limits the options for innovative business solutions.

 WARNING

Do not distribute just for distribution's sake. The distributed computing model is not necessarily a superior model; it is just one of multiple models. If the nature of a firm's business does not lend itself to decentralization, then a distributed model should not be deployed. In these cases, it is better to enhance the network infrastructure to support data sharing via remote access than to ship data wastefully around the enterprise.

APPLICATION MODELS THAT USE ASYNCHRONOUS REPLICATION

The following is a sampling of design patterns that can be used when implementing asynchronous replication. The list is by no means exhaustive, but it will serve as a good starting point. Modify the patterns where appropriate in order to meet the full set of business requirements.

Simple one-way replication

The following design patterns illustrate simple one-way replication and use the master/slave model. The first is a one-to-many implementation where a single primary source replicates to multiple read-only replicas. The second is just the reverse, a many-to-one implementation. It is where multiple primary fragments replicate back to a single, consolidated read-only replica.

Master/slave model with non-fragmented primary and one-to-many replicas

The master/slave model with non-fragmented primary and one-to-many target replicas is simply one-way replication in which all update activity occurs at the master (the primary); the changes are subsequently asynchronously replicated to one or more target replicas. A target replica can be situated locally or remotely with respect to the master copy, and any replica can subscribe to all or only a subset of the changes that occur at the primary. The target replicas are read-only copies since all update activity occurs at the primary source. See Figure 2.4 for an illustration of the data flow for this model.

This model has multiple uses. It can be used for asynchronous replication of data between applications (interapplication replication) or within a single application (intra-application

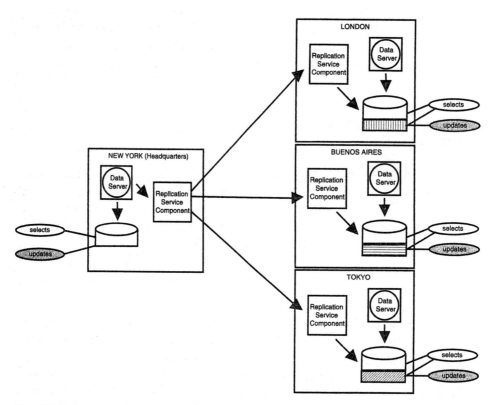

FIGURE 2.4 Master/slave model with non-fragmented primary and one-to-many replicas.

replication). An example of interapplication replication is the replication of centrally stored reference data to all distributed applications that need this read-only data for validation purposes. Many firms use this model to replicate reference data maintained by legacy systems in a mainframe environment to newer client/server applications, which would otherwise have to make remote calls to the mainframe for validation purposes.

During the apply portion of asynchronous replication, data mapping and transformation services can be invoked. Therefore, this model is applicable for replication between OLTP (online transaction processing) and OLAP (online analytical processing) environments. Currently most firms store OLTP and OLAP data redundantly in separate databases. One reason for this redundant storage is that decision-support systems usually require access to broad sets of data from multiple corporate sources. Most often data from these diverse operational systems requires some sort of data transformation. In other words, before arriving at an OLAP server, the data is repaired, merged, appended, rationalized, and/or summarized. Examples of this type of data enhancement include the following:

- *The altering of data types for situations where the data types between primary and targets do not match.*
- *The altering of data content to ensure that all OLAP servers (data marts) represent code values identically.* For example, within human resource data, ensuring that the gender code is stored as a single character with "F" representing female and "M" representing male.
- *The denormalization of data structures to improve query performance.* Summary totals can be created and the asynchronous replication service can update these new data elements in addition to the raw detail fields. For example, financial balances can be created that store monthly and quarterly totals in addition to the detail information.

Most replication services incorporate both mapping and transformational services so that the data schemata between primary sources and target replicas need not match and so that the data can be appropriately enhanced.

As middleware becomes more robust, it will become easier to perform parallel access to heterogeneous data stores and to perform dynamic transformation and summarization. Middleware will allow the amount of data redundancy to be reduced and permit designers to focus on finding the most appropriate mix of data centralization and distribution, practicing what I call judicious distribution.

Consolidation model

The consolidation model is the reverse of the master/slave model with non-fragmented primary and one-to-many replicas. In this case, multiple primary fragments replicate back to a single consolidated target. The fragmentation of the primary sources usually occurs via horizontal partitioning and is based on the value in one or more columns within the data. It is still simple one-way replication in that all update activity occurs at the master for that particular fragment and the changes are subsequently replicated asynchronously to the single replica. The consolidated target is centralized with the fragmented primary sources usually distributed across multiple remote locations. The single centralized replica is a read-only copy since all update activity occurs at the fragmented primary sources. See Figure 2.5 for an illustration of the data flow for this model.

Using this model generally involves rolling up distributed information from autonomous remote locations into a centralized headquarters. The important design aspect with this model is that each distributed primary fragment does not contain information redundant with that of any other primary fragment. In other words, the master/slave model of replication is still preserved.

 TIP

When implementing a consolidation model, the subscriptions used to request the updates from the primary sources should always contain the *"where clause,"* which identifies the fragmentation key and the column values for each source. Not only does this serve as good documentation, but it also prevents any up-

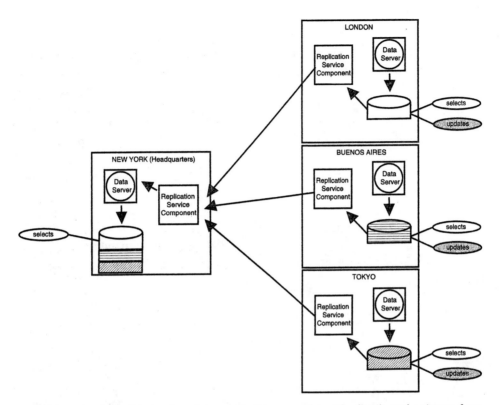

FIGURE 2.5 Consolidation model—master/slave model with distributed primary fragments and a single consolidated replica.

dates that occur outside the subscription range (which should not happen if appropriately designed) from being replicated back to the centralized target. It isolates the scope of an error should one occur.

Complex replication

The following sections address more complex design patterns. They are considered more complex because they involve two-way replication or require the migration of the primary source across multiple replicas. Migration of a primary source requires application code to point the updating application to the appropriate updatable replica.

Master/slave model with distributed primary fragments

This master/slave model with distributed primary fragments involves two-way replication with each location being both a sender (publisher) and a receiver (subscriber). Each location acts not only as a primary source for a particular horizontal slice of data but also as a target for all slices that are primarily sourced at the other location. The result is that each location has a complete replica, of which it updates only its particular primary slice. See Figure 2.6 for an illustration of the data flow for this model.

This model is generally used where update activity is restricted to the data slice that is locally owned but where querying and/or reporting requires a total view. The complexity of this model is not in its implementation, but in its maintenance.

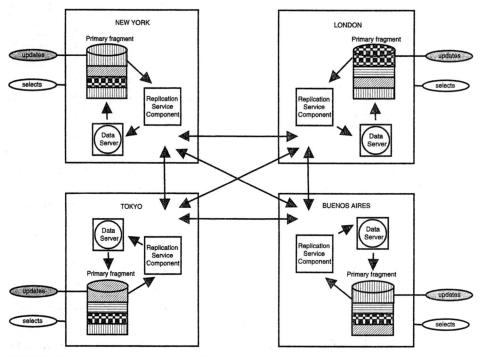

FIGURE 2.6 Master/slave model with distributed primary fragments and each primary also serving as a complete replica.

Recovery and reconciliation after a failure are complex because recovery occurs at a relational table level but reconciliation must occur at the row level across multiple primary sources.

TIP

When implementing a master/slave model with distributed fragments and when each primary also serves as a complete replica, the subscriptions used to request the updates from the primary sources should always contain the *"where clause,"* which identifies the fragmentation key and the column values for each source. As with the consolidation model, this serves the same purpose with respect to documentation and updating outside the subscription range. It isolates the scope of an error should one occur.

Within this distributed primary fragment model, if the ownership of a row is to be changed, it is best to maintain the master/slave model always. Therefore, the current owner should delete the row, and the new owner should insert the row. Each replica will receive the appropriate delete and insert via the asynchronous replication process. Some users of this model advocate a different approach. They recommend that the subscriptions should *not* contain any *"where clause"* that identifies the fragmentation key and column values used. For these advocates, a change of ownership entails only an update statement at the location of the current owner. Because the subscriptions have no *"where clause"* all data changes are replicated. In other words, a location is allowed to update, in this case insert, outside the realm of its defined ownership. Using this technique changes the master/slave model into an update-anywhere model. All the warnings and concerns identified for the update-anywhere model come into play.

Pass-the-Book model

In this model, multiple replicas exist and the ownership (update location) migrates across replicas based on defined criteria. Most often the migration criteria are based on times of day. General characteristics for this model include the following:

- *Each location has a designated time span when it assumes the responsibility of being the primary source.*
- *Each location must have subscriptions to all other replicas to receive updates during that replica's stint as the primary source.*
- *Application design must ensure that only one primary source exists at a time.*
- *If there is the luxury of a quiesce period before ownership migration, all changes still in queues can be applied.* If this is not possible, a conflict detection and resolution mechanism must be in place at each target.

A typical implementation of this model would entail the application incorporating a "site-info" table that identifies the current unique owner of the data. This table should reside at all replica locations and should be replicated. Updates to the "owner" column of this table are now replicated across all locations. To prevent the possibility of any slice of data having two owners, the current owner should give away ownership rather than allow ownership to be requested by multiple locations, perhaps simultaneously. In addition, ownership of all referentially tied data should be changed within the same unit of work (the same transaction). If the ownership column(s) are carried redundantly in the "site-info" table and within the data itself, change both the "site-info" table and the data column(s) within the same unit of work.

It is important to remember that this model uses asynchronous replication; therefore, if replication queues have not been cleared before the ownership column is updated there may be updates within the replication system waiting to be applied. These updates will either update a non-owner or fail due to an attempted update at a non-primary location. A further complication is that immediately following the change of ownership process, updates could arrive out of sequence. What happens depends on how the application is designed and coded or on what conflict detection and resolution mechanism is in place at targets. Figures 2.7 and 2.8 illustrate the data flows for this model.

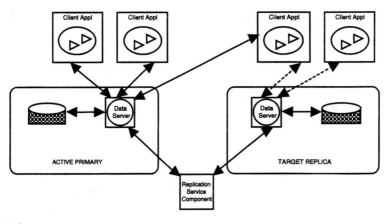

FIGURE 2.7 Master/slave model with migration of ownership—configuration 1.

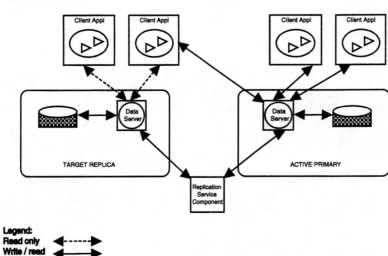

FIGURE 2.8 Master/slave model with migration of ownership—configuration 2.

Workflow Requirement for Dynamic Ownership of Data

Replication can be used to implement a workflow model. This model is characterized by dynamic ownership of data. A typical example is the manufacturing flow of data from the order processing department to the manufacturing area, to the shipping office, and finally to the billing department. It is important to note that when replication is used to implement this model, the data changes state, it does not change location. Therefore there is no requirement for an artificial fragmentation of the transactional data into the various physical locations where the data is actually used.

To implement this model a status column is incorporated into the data table(s) that identifies the current owner. Ownership is pushed from one location to the next by the value within that status column. Only the current owner of the row is allowed to dynamically push the row to the next owner by changing the value of the identifier column. In the manufacturing example cited above, the status column would change from OR ordering department, to MN manufacturing area, to SH shipping, and finally to BL billing.

To avoid any conflicts, the workflow application must ensure that only the current owner of the row has the privilege to update it, that the row never has more than one owner, and that sequencing conflicts can be resolved. By using a push model for changing owner, a new owner does not receive ownership until the current owner has relinquished it. Because a workflow system has a predefined sequencing structure (such as, to manufacturing, to shipping, to billing as in the previous example), sequencing conflicts can be resolved by applying this predefined order.

Use of replication to implement a warm-standby solution

Fault tolerant systems are used to ensure against a loss of service and data by providing redundant components and data. In this model, replication is used to maintain a warm-standby copy of a database that applications can switch to if a hardware or software disaster occurs at the primary server. When using a standby approach, business users experience only a small delay before the application can continue. With a warm-standby solution, the replication mechanism used to maintain data consistency is an asynchronous approach. Therefore, the standby data server has a state that lags behind that of the primary data server. Consequently, there is a very good chance that some transactions will be perceived as lost in the switchover process. By contrast, if a hot standby is maintained, no transactions will be lost. Hot-standby solutions can be implemented either via a software solution (synchronous replication with two-phase commit protocol across the databases involved) or via a hardware solution such as using RAID devices or mirroring disk activity. Some negatives are associated with using hot-standby solutions, including that application code may have to be modified to incorporate synchronous replication and that performance for the initiating application may be adversely affected as locks may be held for longer periods of time. When a hardware solution is used for implementing a hot standby, the databases of the primary and standby usually have to be in close proximity, which means that the solution is susceptible to site failures. In addition, software errors that cause disk data structure corruption such as page chain errors may be duplicated to the standby hardware solution.

With warm-standby solutions, the primary and standby data servers can be in geographically distinct locations connected via the WAN. This allows the system to survive site failures. In addition, if a delta propagation of events type of asynchronous replication is used, there can be no propagation of software errors such as corrupt page chains. Figures 2.9 and 2.10 illustrate a warm-standby implementation that uses database-to-database event propagation. Figure 2.9 illustrates the solution during normal operation, and Figure 2.10 illustrates the solution in recovery mode.

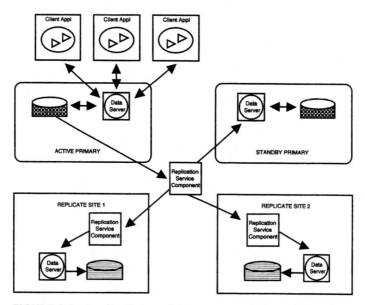

FIGURE 2.9 Replication model for warm-standby solution during normal operation.

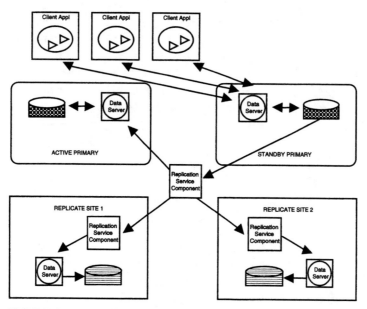

FIGURE 2.10 Replication model for warm-standby solution using standby primary.

One of the best alternatives for implementing a standby solution is to mix the hardware solution of hot standby with the asynchronous replication of warm standby. This combination will provide more fault tolerance than either option alone.

Vendor Approaches
to Replication

3

Many vendors have products that offer replication solutions. My goal here is to present an overview of some of the currently available replication alternatives and to provide a checklist for evaluating replication software. I will discuss solutions by IBM, Oracle, and Sybase, whose products take different architectural approaches to asynchronous replication. By no means should this be construed as an endorsement of any vendor's solution, nor should the lack of representation be considered a condemnation. I will concentrate on the internal architecture of each product, not on product features. I believe that if readers develop an understanding of the approaches used to implement asynchronous replication, they will be better able to match business and technical requirements to an appropriate replication solution.

As replication alternatives become more mature, product features tend to converge. In other words, replication solutions will become more like commodities. In addition, several firms do a very good job of comparing product features; among these are such companies as Gartner Group, Patricia Seybold Group, and Forrester Research. The only product feature truly required is the ability to replicate within a heterogeneous resource manager environment.

As articulated in Chapter 1, most firms have an average of six distinct database environments. In addition, firms generally do not pull out one database vendor and totally replace it with another. They will, over time, move toward a new database solution by having new users and applications adopt the new database technology, then migrate the legacy systems to the new database environment. This transition adds yet another database to the already diverse mix. Firms need to maintain data consistency across these heterogeneous databases. Therefore, the replication alternative must be able to support as primary sources and/or target replicas a very dissimilar group of DBMSs. Heterogeneous replication should not have to be reinvented with the addition of each new database alternative.

Within this chapter, I will address the three major areas of architectural differentiation: the role of the database engine, support for transaction-based or table-based replication, and the types of asynchronous replication models supported. Products such as Sybase's Replication Server and IBM's DataPropagator Relational (DPropR) bypass the database engine totally and rely exclusively on transaction logs to determine update activity. This approach minimizes the impact on production applications and transaction performance. Other vendors such as Oracle use database triggers that can be event- or time-based.

With respect to transaction-based or table-based replication, Sybase's and Oracle's offerings support transactional semantics across the replication process (see Chapter 1). IBM's DPropR uses table-based replication and subsequently does not support the concept of a user transaction within the replication apply process. This is probably why IBM's literature usually refers to DPropR as a copy management tool rather than a replication tool. It is oriented more toward creating copies of tables.

Both IBM and Sybase offerings advocate the use of a master/slave model. Remember from Chapter 2 that the master/

slave model propagates data from one primary source to *n* target replicas. These products allow the user to migrate the primary source across multiple locations, but only one location can have ownership at any given time. Oracle's offering allows the use of either the master/slave model or what it calls symmetric replication, which uses the update-anywhere model. Therefore, it allows any number of replicas to assume the role of the primary at the same time. As articulated in Chapter 2, this strategy is risky with respect to maintaining data consistency because resolving conflicts after data has been updated presents many challenges. Oracle's product resolves conflicting updates according to user-define rules.

The products discussed within this chapter will be presented in alphabetical order by vendor.

IBM

IBM offers multiple products within its replication and copy management alternatives; however, I will cover only three products—DPropR in great detail, and IBM/Transarc's Encina and Lotus Notes, in brief.

DataPropagator relational

DPropR supports data replication in a heterogeneous relational database environment. It uses the master/slave model and expects that every piece of data will have a single primary source at any given time. It does not preserve the transactional nature of the originating event throughout the replication process.

All replication through DPropR is asynchronous. It supports two types of replication: refresh propagation, which is the complete refresh of a target replica, and update propagation, which is the incremental refresh of a table (that is, only the changes captured since the last refresh are applied). With DPropR, propagating summarizations and aggregations is quite simple and straightforward.

Internal architecture of DPropR

DPropR is architected as two component products, a capture component and an apply component. These components perform as follows:

- *Capture.* The capture component grabs database changes that occur at a primary source and saves them in change data tables. IBM provides a capture component for the following members of the DB2 product family: DB2/2, DB2/6000, DB2/400, DB2/VM, DB2/VSE, and DB2/MVS. These capture products use an interface to the DB2 log, or journal in the case of DB2/400, to detect and save changes to tables that have been flagged for replication. DPropR interfaces to other tools to support replication from non-IBM data sources. For example, in an Oracle environment, the capture component uses update triggers to capture changes. Triggers run synchronously with Oracle transactions, and they can increase the elapsed time of each updating transaction.
- *Apply.* The apply component makes changes to the target replica tables. All of the IBM capture-supported databases plus DB2 for HP-UX are also supported by an apply component. DPropR and IBM's DataJoiner product can be used to support source and target tables in Oracle and Sybase.

DPropR is composed of three logical servers. These include what IBM calls the Data Server, the Copy Server, and the Control Server. The Data Server is located at the relational database designated as the primary source. It contains the primary source tables and several DPropR control tables. The Copy Server is located at the relational database designated as the target replica. It contains the target replica tables, the change data tables that store data received from the capture component before it is applied to the target tables, and a control table used by the apply component for routing information. The Control Server can be located at either the primary or target location and contains several DPropR control tables pertaining to the subscription and apply processes.

The apply component maintains data consistency by creating the initial data copy, performing periodic full or incremental refreshes at specified apply intervals, and responding to any gaps in replication by automatically performing full refreshes or by issuing messages that alert the user to the need for manual intervention. It works by applying updates accumulated in the copy table(s) to the subscribing target tables. Because a primary table can have multiple subscriptions, there could be many copy tables at various stages of receiving updates. The apply component keeps track of the latest updates to each copy table.

To be part of the replication environment, a table must go through a registration process—a request to publish—and a subscription process—a request for a copy. A subscription links a source table to a target table and has two essential steps. The first is a definition of a copy request, and the second is the delivery of the copy, which is performed by the apply program. During runtime, the apply program performs three tasks. The first task is either to execute the SQL associated with a subscription or to call a utility that will perform the apply process. If SQL was executed, the second task is to assemble the answer set and update the target tables. The final task is to update the internal control tables so that positions within the replication process can be maintained and so that pruning of the change data tables (copy tables) can occur. The change data tables created at registration have the potential for unlimited growth, as every row that is inserted, deleted, or updated in the base table is represented as a distinct row in the change data tables. Pruning controls the growth of copy tables by deleting rows that have been successfully applied.

Encina

IBM offers two products that support synchronous replication and asynchronous message queuing. One is IBM/Transarc's Encina and the other is CICS (Customer Information Control System). These products are TP monitors/transaction managers. They are pertinent not only for their support of two-phase commit processing across heterogeneous database management systems (that is, synchronous replication), but also for their ability to support a two-phase commit protocol between a DBMS and the TP monitor/transaction manger's internal queuing service. Encina's internal queuing service is called Recoverable Queuing Service (RQS); within CICS, it is MQ Series. This message-queuing middleware can be used to extend access to mobile workers or to support application services within a multitier, service-based architecture. In most current client/server applications, communications are synchronous. In other words, both the requesting application and the serving software are active at the same time. This works well for traditional DBMS transactional environments; however, with mobile computing or within a multitier, service-based architecture, the requirement is to support intermittent-connection transactions. In this type of environment, the applications must support asynchronous communications with the deferred delivery of messages or data and the guarantee of transaction delivery. With this type of communication, the requester software puts a message in a queue and then resumes its processing without waiting for the remote system to perform the requested activity. At present, most DBMS vendors have not fully integrated this asynchronous messaging technology into their DBMS product functionality. Therefore, developers building applications that require messaging must provide the functionality to link the DBMS with the message-queuing middleware.

Lotus Notes

Within Lotus Notes, replication is used to enable two replicas to exchange modifications, additions, and deletions. Replication can occur in one or both directions between replicas. Therefore, Notes supports an update-anywhere model. Notes differentiates between what it calls replicas and copies. All replicas of a particular database have the same replica ID, a unique number that Notes assigns to a database when it is created. The replica ID distinguishes a replica from a copy of a database that does not have the same replica ID.

A typical replication flow for server-to-server replication would entail the following steps:

- Server A initiates replication to Server B. This is accomplished either through a scheduling mechanism or through a direct request entered at the console.
- Security authentication occurs.
- Servers compare lists of databases to identify identical replica IDs.
- Date comparisons occur to determine if replication is required.
- Each server builds a list of objects that have been modified since the last replication. Items within the object list include documents, design elements, and access control lists.
- Transfer of the new documents and updates occurs.
- Administrative clean-up occurs.

Because Notes uses an update-anywhere model, the software manages conflicts using date comparisons. The databases themselves do not have record locking or file locking. Therefore, Notes keeps track of each document that has been edited by two or more users since the last replication. During replication, Notes saves all versions of an edited document and marks them for review. Two types of conflicts can occur, a save conflict or a replication conflict. A save conflict occurs when two or more users open and edit the same field of the same document at the same time on the same server. Notes treats the first document saved as the "main one" and all others as response documents. A user must manually add the changes within the response documents to the document saved as the "main one."

A replication conflict occurs when two or more users open and edit the same field of the same document on different servers between replications. When Notes detects a conflict during replication, it chooses the document with the most changes and designates it as the "main one." All others are marked as response documents. To resolve replication conflicts, users must add the information from the response documents to the main document and then delete the response documents. Notes replication supplies an automatic conflict detection mechanism, but all conflict resolution is a strictly manual process.

ORACLE

Oracle provides multiple mechanisms for data replication. The focus of this discussion will be read-only snapshots and symmetric replication.

Read-Only Snapshots

Read-only snapshots support a master/slave model and allow the user to replicate changes from the master table to any number of distributed databases. A read-only snapshot is refreshed from its designated master in a transactionally consistent manner at a time-based interval or on demand. The snapshot can be a full copy of a table or a subset of the table.

Snapshots are created by using the SQL command *CREATE SNAPSHOT*. As with table create statements, one can use the *CREATE SNAPSHOT* command to specify storage characteristics, extent sizes and allocation, and the table space or cluster used to hold the snapshot. Snapshots can be either simple or complex. In a simple snapshot, each row is based on a single row in a single remote master table. Therefore the defining query for a simple snapshot contains no distinct or aggregate functions, *GROUP BY* or *CONNECT BY* clauses, subqueries, joins, or set operations. If a snapshot's defining query contains any of the aforementioned clauses or operations, then it is a complex snapshot.

Internal architecture for read-only snapshots

When a read-only snapshot is created, the Oracle software creates several internal objects within the schema of the snapshot replica. These created objects at the snapshot location include the following:

- *A base table*. This base table is used to store the rows retrieved by the snapshot's defining query.
- *A read-only view of the base table*. This view is used whenever a user queries the snapshot. The view has the name provided in the *CREATE SNAPSHOT* statement.

Objects created at the master replica include a local view. Oracle uses this view of the master replica to refresh the snapshot. Oracle stores the result of this query in the base table of the target replica.

A snapshot can be either completely refreshed or incrementally refreshed. An incremental refresh is called a fast refresh. For simple snapshots, the designer can choose to create a snapshot log for the master table. Every time a change is made to the master table, Oracle uses a trigger to update this log. The changes captured in this log are used to perform a fast refresh of a simple snapshot. In other words, only the changed rows are used to update the target replica. By contrast, a complex snapshot or a simple snapshot without a snapshot log at the master must be refreshed using a complete regeneration from the master table.

A snapshot log can be used by multiple simple snapshots of a single master table. After an incremental snapshot refresh, any rows in the snapshot log that do not apply to any other snapshot of the master are removed.

Architecture for updatable snapshots

With Oracle replication, updatable snapshots can also be implemented. When this option is selected, two additional objects are created at the snapshot site. One is a table used to store the ROWID and the time stamp of rows updated within the snapshot. The other is an AFTER ROW trigger on the snapshot base table. It is needed to insert the ROWIDs and time stamps of updated and deleted rows into the updatable snapshot log.

When the snapshot is created as a replicated object, Oracle creates an additional trigger and associated package on the snapshot base table. This trigger is used to call the generated procedures at the master site to apply the changes. If the user has selected synchronous replication, then the trigger package makes the remote procedure calls. If the user has selected asynchronous replication, then the trigger package inserts the necessary deferred transactions into the deferred transaction queue at the snapshot site. With read-only snapshots, Oracle creates a read-only view of the underlying base table, while for updatable snapshots, this view is writable.

Symmetric replication

Symmetric replication supports an update-anywhere model. In other words, all replicas of the data can be updated, and updates are propagated to all other replicas. Full transactional integrity is supported so that updates made by transactions to multiple tables are applied at replicas transactionally. This ensures data consistency and referential integrity across the tables. In addition, both synchronous and asynchronous replication are supported. When synchronous replication is selected, the changes must be successfully applied to all replicas within the same transaction. When asynchronous replication is selected, the changes are applied to the local replica and then forwarded to all other subscribing replicas within a separate transaction at a user-defined interval.

Internal architecture for symmetric replication

Oracle's replication mechanism is trigger-based. When data is modified using any Data Manipulation Language (DML), that is, *insert, update, or delete* statements, the changes can be propagated using either row-level or procedural replication. If the designer selects row-level replication, the Oracle software generates triggers and stored procedures that are used to replicate each transaction. When a DML statement is executed at a local primary, the replication software fires the generated trigger that results in a call to a procedure in the generated package at each replica. The procedure applies the changes at the replicas. Row-level replication ensures that all changes to a table, whether directly from DML statements or from a stored procedure, are propagated to all target replicas.

When the designer selects procedural replication, then only the call to a stored procedure is replicated. The called stored procedure applies the updates to the designated tables at each target replica. When a procedure is replicated, the Oracle software generates a wrapper for that procedure. When the procedure is executed at the local primary, the wrapper ensures that a call is ultimately made to the same procedure at each target replica.

Whether row-level replication or procedural replication is selected the designer must also decide on whether the changes should be propagated synchronously or asynchronously. If synchronous replication is selected, then all changes must be applied at the local primary and all target replicas within the same transaction. The update at the local primary fires a trigger that calls a remote procedure that applies the same change at each target replica. A failure at any target replica or within the network infrastructure will cause a failure of the transaction at the local primary. The transaction will continue to fail until either the network problem or the target replica problem is corrected, or until the unavailable target replica is dropped from the replicated environment.

If asynchronous replication is selected, then deferred transactions are used to propagate and apply changes to target replicas. Deferred transactions allow calls to remote procedures to be processed using a store-and-forward mechanism. A local transaction initiates the execution of a deferred transaction by submitting the request to a propagation queue within its local environment. The local system forwards the deferred transaction to n replicas for execution within a separate transaction. The deferred transaction mechanism guarantees that the request to schedule delivery will be propagated. In other words, these deferred calls are added to the job queue at the local primary. Job queues are used to schedule events at designated intervals. Background processes periodically wake up, check job queues, and execute outstanding jobs.

Conflict detection and resolution

Oracle's symmetric replication supports either the master/slave model or the update-anywhere model for asynchronous replication. Designers must carefully weigh the trade-off of each alternative. If the business requirement is for totally consistent data at all replicas at all times, then the only alternative is synchronous replication. If the business requirement can tolerate some data inconsistencies for short periods of time as long as no update conflicts occur, then the appropriate model is asynchronous replication using the master/slave model. However, if the business requirement can tolerate temporary inconsistencies as long as they can be detected and resolved so that, over time, the replicated data converges to a consistent state at all locations, then it might be appropriate to use an update-anywhere model for asynchronous replication. Oracle's symmetric replication product detects that an update conflict has occurred and automatically invokes an application-specific conflict resolution routine to restore the replicated data to a consistent state.

Symmetric replication has a built-in facility for detecting conflicts. When changes are propagated by pushing the deferred transaction queue, this facility calls a procedure that was generated in the package at the target receiving location. The arguments to this procedure are used to detect conflicts. The arguments include the old values of each column in the row and the new value of each column. Obviously, inserted rows have no old values, and deleted rows have no new values. The procedure compares the old values of the row with the current values for the same row at the receiving location. A conflict is detected if there are any differences between these values for any columns in the row. If no conflicts are detected, the row at the receiving location is modified so that it contains the new values. If a conflict is detected, Oracle applies the appropriate conflict resolution routine, if available. All unresolved conflicts are logged into an error table at the receiving location. For row-level replication, users can designate one or more conflict resolution routines that are applied in a priority order. The routines are either Oracle-supplied or developed by the application development team. For procedural replication, users must supply a conflict resolution method as part of the replicated procedure.

A sampling of the Oracle-supplied resolution routines include the following:

- *Time stamp oriented.* Apply the data with the latest time stamp, or apply the data with the earliest time stamp.
- *Commutative resolution of additive updates.* Apply all data additively.
- *Priority based.* Apply the change from the location with the highest priority.
- *Minimum/maximum selection of updates.* Apply the minimum value when the column value is always decreasing, or

apply the maximum value when the column value is always increasing.

Keep in mind that many forms of conflict resolution cannot guarantee convergence if the replicated environment contains more than two masters.

SYBASE

Sybase's principal offering for support of replication is Replication Server. It has also acquired Complex Architectures with its Enterprise Messaging Server (EMS) product. Sybase is expected to market EMS for wireless data communications in the mobile client/server DBMS market and to integrate EMS into its product line. Because this integration effort is not expected until 1997, I will concentrate here on its Replication Server product.

Replication Server

Replication Server supports the replication of data and stored procedures in a heterogeneous database environment. It uses the master/slave model and expects that every piece of data will have a single primary source at any given point in time. It preserves the semantics of the transaction throughout the capture, distribution, and apply processes. If a distributed unit of work is executed it does not re-merge the transaction from multiple transaction logs (see Chapter 1, "Preserving Transactional Semantics for a Distributed Unit of Work").

To support the heterogeneous database environment, Sybase provides log pull mechanisms (capture functionality) for databases other than its SQL Server product. For those databases for which Sybase does not provide a log pull mechanism, users have to purchase a capture mechanism from another vendor if such a product exists or develop their own. Sybase does provide tools—a language and its Open Client and Client-Library/C routines—to aid with this endeavor; however, it is not an easy task. For the apply side of replication, Replication Server does a very good job of separating what is asked for (a function) from how it is implemented (a function string). This allows very easy replication to any relational target replica. This will become apparent after a brief discussion of the components within Sybase's replicating environment.

Internal architecture of Replication Server

Replication Server is architected as three services, a capture service, a distribution service, and an apply service. The principal components of this product include the following:

- *Replication Server (RS)*. Replication Server is a Sybase Open Server application that provides the distribution service and coordinates all replication activities. Its main responsibilities are to receive primary updates from databases using what Sybase calls a Log Transfer Manager or a replicating agent and distribute them to subscribing Replication Servers, and to receive data updates from other Replication Servers and apply them to local target replicate databases or forward them to other subscribing Replication Servers. In other words, it receives and distributes from primary sources, and it receives and applies to target replicas.
- *Replication Server System Database (RSSD)*. The RSSD is a Sybase SQL Server database that contains the RS system tables. Each RS has its own RSSD; however, the SQL Server that manages the RSSD can also store other client application databases. The system tables within the RSSD are used to store the data required by an RS to send and receive replicated data.
- *Replication Agent or Log Transfer Manager (LTM)*. A Replication Agent program or an LTM notifies an RS of actions in a database that must be replicated to other databases. The LTM for SQL Server reads the database log and transfers log records for replicated tables and stored procedures to the RS that is managing that database. A Replicating Agent is required for every database that contains either primary source data or stored procedures that are flagged for replication. Databases that receive only replicated data do not require a Replication Agent.

Replication Server uses a log pull as the capture mechanism, a store-and-forward distribution mechanism, and an SQL apply mechanism. The overall data flow is as follows:

- *An LTM reads the log of a primary database.*
- *The LTM forwards any transactions for tables and / or stored procedures flagged for replication to the RS supporting that database.*
- *The RS stores the transaction on its stable queue.*
- *The receiving RS performs subscription resolution.* This entails either discarding the transaction if no subscriptions exist for the data or determining which RSs have subscription for the data and forwarding the transaction to those RSs.
- *The RS supporting a target replica applies the transaction to the replicated database.*

The data apply process works as follows. Each database has a configurable connection to one RS by which it receives the data to be applied. Executor processes map the apply functions (that is, an insert, update, or delete function) to a function string class that uses the "SQL-speak" of the receiving database. For example, if the receiving database is a Sybase SQL Server, then it uses a SQL Server function string class that speaks T-SQL; if a DB2/MVS is the target replica, then DB2's dialect of SQL is executed using the DB2 function string class. For stored procedure replication the executor process causes the requested stored procedure to be executed with the parameters passed as part of the replication process.

General Requirements for Creating and Evaluating Replication Software

Table 3.1 provides a list of general requirements that can be used as a starting point for either building your own replication service or evaluating a vendor solution. The list is not completely exhaustive because every firm is unique and will have specialized requirements. Each firm should modify this list and assign weights to reflect its specific requirements.

TABLE 3.1 Checklist for Evaluating Replication Software

Architectural Requirements	
	The replication solution should be architected as middleware whose purpose is to provide data replication services. This will enable the software to integrate into a multitier architecture and permit the software to be easily "unplugged" and replaced by an alternative solution at a later time, if necessary.
	The solution should support location/distribution transparency. A database or process using the replication service should not need to know the location of any object.
	The solution should support a high degree of database and process transparency. The degree of application transparency is a major differentiater between database-to-database and process-to-process asynchronous replication.
	For vendor solutions that are of the database-to-database event type of asynchronous replication, ask the following questions:
	• How transparent are the interfaces to the resource managers involved in the replication process?
	• Do resource managers have to be altered to participate in the replication process? If yes, how easy is it to do and to undo?
	For vendor solutions that are of the process-to-process event type of asynchronous replication (messaging) ask the following questions:
	• How transparent are the interfaces to the application code (processes) that use the messaging service?
	• To what extent does application code have to be altered to participate in the replication process? How complex are these alterations? How easy is it to do and to undo?
	The replication solution should be industry-compliant. For example, the solution should use DCE security, DCE naming services, and the like. DCE is the Distributed Computing Environment, as defined by the Open Software Foundation (OSF). Because both new and legacy systems will be part of the replication environment, the solution should support replication to both XA and non-XA compliant resource managers.
	It should support the DCE Framework for security. This includes identification/authorization; reauthentication; auditing; encrypted communication; access controls; and password encryption,

expiration, and retry limits. Questions that should be asked include the following:

- How robust are the security implementations?
- Who can use the functionality of the replication software?
- What IDs and passwords are stored?
- Where are they stored? Are they encrypted?
- What IDs and passwords are used on the resource managers to alter the data?
- How is network security integrated with the replication software?

The replication solution should be fail safe (i.e., fail in a manner that protects other components in the environment).

There should be no inherent bottlenecks within the replication solution; for example, calls to a centrally stored repository that could create availability and contention issues.

Functional Requirements

The replication solution should be scalable. With respect to replication, *scalability* means the ability to replicate both small and large volumes of data across heterogeneous resource managers. Questions that should be asked include the following:

- Which resource managers can be used as primary sources?
- Which resource managers can be used as targets?
- Given the appropriate resources, are there any limits to the quantity of data that can be part of the replication process?

The solution should support or interface with data transformation and mapping services. This functionality handles cases where source and target data schemata do not match and where source data needs to be enhanced. Types of data transformation that should be supported include the following:

- *Altering of data types for situations where the data types between primary and target types do not match.* For example, a primary source could store the data in character format and a target stores that same data in a numeric format.
- *Altering of data content to ensure that all data target(s) represent code values identically.* For example, in human resource data, the gender code is stored at the primary source as character with "1" representing female and "2" representing male. At targets it is stored as character but with the letter "F" representing female and "M" representing male.

TABLE 3.1 *(cont.)*

- *Enhancement of data.* An example occurs where targets use denormalization to improve query performance. Summary total fields/columns are created at targets, and the replication service updates these new data elements in addition to the raw detail fields/columns. For example, financial balances are maintained during the replication process. These balances store monthly and quarterly totals.

For asynchronous data replication, there should be a scheduling mechanism. This is most applicable for targets but may also be applicable for primary sources depending on what mechanism is used to capture the changes.

There should be a friendly mechanism to describe the data and/or objects that are to be replicated.

There should be a friendly mechanism to subscribe to the data and/or objects that are available for replication.

The initialization process for targets should be simple and straight-forward. The initialization process is used to get a target in sync with its primary source(s).

The replication service should be well behaved and provide the quality of service specified in the business requirement. For example, it should provide guaranteed delivery and ensure that data is secure and not corrupted during the replication process.

There should be a log mechanism that records any failed replication effort.

For refresh type of asynchronous replication, the following requirements should be specified:

- Can any concurrent access be made available during the refresh process?
- What locking granularity is used during the load process? Possibilities for relational DBMSs include page, table, or row.
- How fast is the load process?
- Can the load process be restarted in cases of failure?

For database-to-database event type of asynchronous replication, transactional integrity should be preserved throughout the replication process. In addition, requirements should be defined with respect to an approach for applying a distributed unit of work as a single transaction at the targets. This requires the merging of extractions from multiple logs if a log pull mechanism is used. Decisions must also made with respect to what level of support should be given to transaction nesting.

For process-to-process event type of asynchronous replication, transactional integrity should be preserved between the update of the resource manager and the insert/removal of the message from the persistent storage used for queuing.

For event type of asynchronous replication, some level of sequential integrity should be preserved throughout the replication process. Options include using sequential integrity from each primary source individually or the merging of primary sources dictated by rules based on time and/or priority of primary source.

Some sort of meta-data repository should be available to designated users. This metadata should include the following:

- For each target, the identification of each data element's primary source
- For each target, a statement of the required data latency level with the designated primary source (i.e., the amount of time a target can be in an inconsistent state with its designated primary source before data consistency is achieved).

Administration Criteria

Systems Management

Configuration: The configuration process for the replication software should be simple and straightforward. It should permit dynamic reconfiguration (i.e., adjusting configuration parameters without the need to restart the system software). Support for some sort of configuration history is also a plus.

Monitoring: There should be a GUI (graphical user interface) monitoring tool for the entire replication environment. The replication monitoring tool should integrate with the existing monitoring infrastructure of the firm.

Performance monitoring: There should be a tool for performance reporting. The replication process should efficiently use existing resources. These resources include hardware, software, networks, and people.

Error management: There should be an error log.

TABLE 3.1 *(cont.)*	
	Control of the replication process should be supported from either a central hub or local sites.
	Shutdown: The replication software should handle emergency shutdown. Replication systems should be able to be quiesced and be started automatically after a shutdown.
Resource Management	
	Space management: The queuing mechanism for the replication process should efficiently use resources.
	CPU: The subscription resolution engine for the replication process should be efficient and error free.
	Network: The replication processes should be well behaved with respect to network utilization. For example, are network packets filled, and are packets secure? What protocols are supported?
	Access management: The access protocols that are supported should include recognized standards such as ODBC by Microsoft and/or some proprietary protocols such as Sybase's Open Client.
Change Management for Replication Software	
	It should be relatively easy to apply upgrades and "fixes" to the replication system software. The ease of upgradability depends on the number of components involved.
	Migration to new release levels of software should be straightforward and permit release level coexistence. Questions to ask include the following:
	• Must all components migrate to the new release level at the same time? • Can multiple release levels coexist within the same replication environment?
Change Management for Resource Managers Involved in the Replication Process	

There should be tools that aid with the altering of database objects. Questions to consider include the following:

- What tasks must be executed when the DDL (database definition language) of a primary source is altered? When the DDL of a target is altered?
- Are utilities provided that aid with the change process at a primary source? At a target?
- Is there a repository that can be used to identify all targets that receive replicated data from a particular primary source (change impact analysis tool)?

Recovery

There should be an automatic recovery mechanism that provides recovery after specific types of failures.

Replication components should fail safely (i.e., do not affect other components when they fail).

There should be a data reconciliation facility/tool. This can be used to validate the replication process and to resynchronize source and target sites after a failure.

Vendor/ Market Forces

The vendor should be viable. Questions that should be asked include the following:

- What is the financial health of the company?
- What is the size of the company?
- Is it public or privately held?
- What is the vendor's market share? How many licenses does this represent?
- What do industry analysts such as Gartner Group, Forrester Research and Seybold say with respect to this vendor?

Product price should be competitive with other replication products that have the same functionality.

The vendor selected should provide the appropriate level of product support. Questions that should be asked include the following:

- Is technical support available in the necessary worldwide locations? Is the support at the worldwide locations via persons located at those locations or via phone support to other locations?
- Is support available 24 × 7?

SUMMARY

As this chapter has discussed, multiple architectures are used to implement replication. Because of these differences, some products lend themselves more easily to certain types of replication. Any application with requirements for near-real-time replication and a strong requirement for data integrity should select a solution that preserves transactional semantics throughout the replication process and uses the master/slave model. As requirements are relaxed, more alternatives become available.

If the application under consideration is for OLAP processing with the merging of data from multiple sources, then a solution that focuses on table loads is preferable. It allows for data transformation services and a data quality review function to ensure that all sources have contributed to the consolidation effort before users are allowed access. Given the wide variance in application requirements, each of the replication architectures discussed has a legitimate place.

Section

II

Building the Replication Services

Application Partitioning and Placement Alternatives

Partitioning of application functionality and the subsequent decisions on data placement are the two key factors for implementing successful enterprise computing systems. These two factors offer the greatest benefits if performed properly; on the other hand, they carry the most risk if done poorly. Partitioning provides flexibility and opportunities for code reuse. Optimal data placement increases application availability and performance. This chapter addresses application partitioning alternatives; Chapter 5 presents a methodology for optimal data placement.

WHAT IS APPLICATION PARTITIONING?

Application partitioning is the breaking up of the functionality of an application into tiers or layers. However, there are multiple ways to view partitioning. One way is to view it from a hardware perspective; another way is from a physical software perspective; a third is from a logical software perspective. From a hardware perspective, tiers allude to the number and kinds of computers that participate in and add support for the application functionality. Using hardware tiers maximizes the capabilities of the various hardware devices involved (for example, using

PCs for application presentation functionality and midrange servers for database support). Depending on how the software partitioning occurs, multiple software tiers can execute on the same or totally separate and different hardware tiers.

The physical software perspective is concerned with where the application components execute. It does not address the how of the application partitioning, only the where. Physical software tiers make hardware tiers possible and help to maximize network usage.

Logical software partitioning concentrates on separating application functionality into components. These components reflect the three fundamental areas of application functionality:

- *The presentation portion of the application.* This portion defines the user interface logic.
- *The application logic or business rules portion.* This portion defines all processing logic.
- *The data management portion.* This portion defines data access logic.

Most often the components of these three tiers are further partitioned to provide greater flexibility and reuse. Once the tiers have been outlined, then appropriate interfaces between the components can be defined and implemented. These application components can exist solely within one computer, can be spread across multiple computers, or can be stored redundantly across multiple computers. The focus of this chapter is logical software partitioning and the subsequent placement of the application components.

Brief history of application architectures

Traditional mainframe applications that are implemented with a dumb terminal communicating with a mainframe host have one hardware tier, one physical software tier, and two logical software tiers. The presentation and application logic function as one logical software tier, and the data management as a second software tier. Both tiers execute on the host and interact with each other through data manipulation language (DML). The dumb terminal executes no application logic. Therefore, in the purest sense, this is not client/server computing because, by definition, in a client/server environment the client must execute some application logic beyond terminal emulation.

First-generation client/server applications implemented what is commonly called a two-tier application architecture. These early applications used data passing between the two tiers and synchronous processing, which means the components interacted in real time. The data-passing architecture had a high network overhead associated with the remote data management. Therefore, DBMS vendors introduced stored procedures, database triggers, and user-defined functions as ways to reduce network traffic. Stored procedures are small application programs that reside within the DBMS. Using stored procedures yielded the network efficiencies associated with message passing. Even though most of today's client/server applications still use this message-passing, two-tier approach, enterprises are discovering that this architecture is incapable of meeting the requirements of many types of applications. Future applications will use more message passing between three or more tiers, plus synchronous and/or asynchronous processing. Here asynchronous processing refers to a store-and-forward type of deferred processing. This multitier approach will bring the benefits of client/server computing to robust enterprise applications and will be an integral part of the second generation of client/server technology.

Two-tier software architecture

Two-tier software architecture is cooperative processing where two logical software tiers interoperate by exchanging data or messages. Within this framework, the first tier is composed of presentation and business logic, which jointly reside within one process space. The second tier is the data management layer, which is the resource manager or DBMS component. If data passing is employed then some sort of DML is used to interoperate between the two tiers. If message passing, not data passing, is used, then DBMS stored procedures are used as the interface. Application programs do not interact directly, but they do interact indirectly by sharing a common database or file. This type of configuration is usually very limiting and lacks flexibility. The physical software decision, the "where," is limited to either one or two physical tiers. When the majority of the business logic resides on the client, it is commonly called a "fat" client.

Three-tier software architecture

By contrast, three-tier data-passing configurations offer more flexibility because they insert a data access layer between the business logic and the DBMS. This data access layer can be an off-the-shelf gateway or user-developed code. This layer insulates the business logic from the DBMS. The business application code uses an application programming interface (API) to communicate with the DBMS. This allows changes to the DBMS as to its location or database schema and changes to the server platform without subsequent changes in the other two tiers. An API should exhibit the following characteristics:

- *It should be extensible.* It should be able to support future modifications and enhancements, yet still be backward compatible.
- *It should be well defined.* Its behavior and parameters should be documented.
- *It should provide user transparency.* It should insulate the application developer from details of the infrastructure. This implies ease of use.
- *It should exhibit consistent behavior as defined.*
- *It should offer support for transporting data and objects.* Even if the original implementation does not support object transport, the API should eventually be able to offer support for distributed object technology, such as remote methods.

Three-tier message-passing applications usually have a first tier composed of presentation and some application logic. This tier communicates with the second tier, application business logic, via message passing. The second tier communicates with the data management tier via data passing. The main advantage of using a three-tier configuration is that it makes possible the independent changing or replacement of any of the three components—presentation, business logic, or data management—without having to modify the other two components. Three-tier architectures are not new; users on the mainframe have been using this type of architecture for at least 10 years.

Multitier software architecture

A multitier software architecture implements what is called a service-based architecture. In reality, it is just a more partitioned flavor of the three-tier architecture. Here the application logic tier is further partitioned into very modularized technical and business services. These modularized, reusable services use program-to-program communication via message passing. With message passing the developer specifies the format and content of the message and the infrastructure handles the delivery. The messaging infrastructure can be supported by a variety of alternatives. A sampling of these alternatives include a low-level interface such as Advanced Program-to-Program Communication (APPC) or sockets, a remote procedure call (RPC) facility, a vendor-supplied message middleware, or a distributed transaction processing (TP) monitor. The important aspect of the tiered approach is that a requesting service communicates with a servicing program that then executes its defined behavior. It can return the desired results or, if its behavior dictates, no reply is needed.

Trade-offs between two- and three-tier architectures

The main advantages of using a two-tier message passing architecture include the following:

- *Simple and efficient approach.* DBMS stored procedures are easy to use. In addition, tools and design practices are well known and available.
- *Non-complex vendor environment.* Usually only one or possibly two vendors are involved in the total solution—a DBMS provider and a development tool provider in most cases.

The principle disadvantage is the functional limitation and inflexibility of the DBMS stored procedure mechanism. For example, a stored procedure is limited to one DBMS.

By contrast, multitier architectures are more flexible and vigorous because the application logic does not run under the control of a DBMS. Control is usually provided by the native operating system, a TP monitor, or some other flavor of middleware. The main advantages of using a three-tier or multitier architecture include the following:

- *Ability to develop a more robust application.* Within the three-tier environment, it is possible to invoke other heterogeneous server application programs and access data residing in other heterogeneous resource managers. In a two-tier environment, this is usually very difficult. For example, it is not easy to access a Virtual Storage Access Method (VSAM) file from within a Sybase stored procedure.
- *Improved component manageability.* The components that make up the application logic, that is, the middle tier, are visible to standard monitoring tools and utilities. When business logic resides within the resource manager or client, they can not be easily monitored by system support software.
- *Opportunities to optimally place processing components.* Data access functions can be placed close to resource manager(s). Presentation functions can be placed on the user's workstation. Business logic can be placed on the most appropriate hardware and software platforms. For example, specialized servers can be employed for complex mathematical calculations (a calc server) or for the sharing of business rules (a rules server). These types of placement decisions should be based on the technical and resource requirements of the process as well as its frequency of use.
- *Improved load-balancing capabilities.* TP monitors and optimal placement decisions can provide this capability.
- *Improved component availability.* TP monitors and other types of middleware products provide failover capabilities to backup servers.
- *Lessening of the impact of change.* This includes data isolation, where changes to the data model or database structure are hidden from the presentation and business logic portions of the application and DBMS independence, where one DBMS is to be replaced by another or where the application must be ported to a different DBMS.
- *Improved opportunity for code reuse.* Once a library of reusable processes has been created, the development effort for applications should be shortened. In theory, developers should be able to 'shop' through development libraries and find the

processing components needed to build their application. Building becomes an assembly operation with all subcomponents precoded and thoroughly tested; however, this can occur only when all components have been well documented and all libraries carefully managed.

The disadvantages associated with three-tier architectures include the following:

- *Complex management.* Three-tier architectures have many more application modules than two-tier scenarios. This adds complexity to both the production and development environments. With respect to the development environment, library documentation and management become important issues. Administration is required to prevent overlaps in code functionality, which defeats the objective of code reuse. In the production environment, software distribution, monitoring, and version control present many challenges. These challenges are directly proportional to the number of modules and the number of distributed locations involved.
- *Possibility of a performance hit.* The increase in cross-program traffic could have a negative impact on performance.
- *More complex development environment.* Because functionality can be reused, best practices should be incorporated into code development. Each process must be well behaved. In other words, each process must perform all functions as defined, and none that are not, and adhere to its published interface. In addition, each process must be cataloged within a library so that it can be found when needed.
- *More challenges associated with defining the architecture.* More design decisions must be made. For example, functional partitioning schemes and placement alternatives must be evaluated.

Until recently, multitier architectures have been more difficult to implement because of the lack of robust tools. However, the situation is changing rapidly. Program generators are becoming available that will aid in the development of service modules for use in the middle tier. In addition, the middleware that supports communications between tiers is becoming more robust and readily available. This middleware includes such options as RPCs, messaging systems, message-queuing systems (store-and-forward mechanisms), distributed TP monitors, and object request brokers (ORBs), which provide distributed object middleware.

In summary, the following recommendations apply. For many routine applications, a two-tier architecture is simpler, faster to develop, and less expensive to run. However, if the application falls into any of the following categories during any time of its life expectancy, a multitier architecture should be used:

- It decomposes into more than 70 application logic components.
- It uses heterogeneous data sources.
- It has a workload of more than 40,000 transactions per eight-hour period.
- It has more that 400 concurrent users.
- It is strategic in nature with a life expectancy of more than three to five years.

Two important issues that should also be considered are the amount of anticipated code reuse and the criticality of the time-to-market factor. If there is little opportunity for code reuse and time-to-market is a critical factor, then the most rapid development method is the best choice. This suggests a two-tier architecture. Being the first on the block with a new product, for example, a customer banking service, could very easily pay for itself. Once the initial financial rewards have been reaped, then a decision regarding a more robust multitier implementation can be made. In addition, if the life expectancy of the application is short, a throwaway approach may be warranted. When addressing architectural paradigms, there are two distinct options to consider. One stresses the advantages of reuse, and the other recommends a totally throw-away approach. Both paradigms have merit.

 TIP

For every application, weigh carefully the trade-offs between rapid development and a quick time-to-market versus the potential long-term benefits of implementing reusable application services.

Guidelines for logical software partitioning

As stated earlier, logical software partitioning divides the application into the three fundamental structures of user interface logic, business logic, and data access logic. These demarcations represent fuzzy lines with respect to their acceptance and total implications; however, an architect must start the "cutting" process somewhere. Generally the first cut should separate the user interface from the rest of the application. The user interface portion has the least potential for reuse. In addition, this separation allows the business logic and enterprise data to be centrally managed, secured, and shared. These management and security issues are significant for strategic applications.

The second major divide should separate all data access logic from the business logic tier. This separation allows resource manager independence. Care should be exercised here because even though this functionality may be small the number of components that can be generated is large. To prevent the proliferation of redundant access modules, best-practice rules that identify policies for encapsulation and reuse should be followed.

The third and most complex division is within the business logic tier itself. Here the flow should be as follows:

- *Identify all business transactions.* The input to this is the process model. A business transaction is composed of multiple interdependent and dependent tasks.
- *Decompose each business transaction into software transactions.* Software transactions identify the logical units of work, as defined in Chapter 1. A software transaction represents the interdependent tasks that must be completed as a whole. The most important rule to follow here is that all changes of state (update activity) that are interdependent *must* be executed within the same software transaction. This ensures that the ACID properties for these interdependencies are preserved. An example of this is a banking transaction where the debit activity and the credit activity must be executed within the same logical unit of work.
- *Identify "decisions reached" and "constraints enforced."* These can be shared across applications by using a shared rules server.

- *Identify the dependencies between the software transactions that compose the business transaction.* This identifies the work flow characteristics between the software transactions that make up the complete business transaction. Execution of dependent business processes (those that are not interdependent but are still part of the single business transaction) may be deferred. Business transactions that have these workflow characteristics are called long-lived transactions. By identifying the dependencies that exist between the software transactions that compose the long-lived business transaction, it is possible to establish which software transactions can execute in parallel and which must be serialized. For all dependent transactions, it is imperative that the parameters required for the deferred task be stored transactionally as part of the initiating transaction. In other words, there must be a two-phase commit protocol between the commit to the resource manager and the writing of the data parameters for the deferred transaction to a transactional queue. This is the only way to ensure that the deferred transaction is executed if and only if the initiating transaction is committed. Because a deferred transaction executes asynchronously to the originating transaction, a compensating transaction must be used to undo the committed transaction should an error be discovered within the deferred transaction that demands this undo action. Therefore, all the warnings identified for conflict detection and resolution schemes within asynchronous replication come into play (see Chapter 1). As a general rule, deferred processing should be used only where the business rules demand it and where temporary inconsistent states within the enterprise can be tolerated.
- *Identify components that have potential for reuse.*

Once these tasks have been completed the data interfaces for the software transactions can be identified.

GUIDELINES FOR PARTITION PLACEMENT

When operating within a distributed environment, using network resources efficiently is critical. Moving excessive amounts of data not only is costly, but has a negative impact on all network users.

Therefore, applications should be designed and partitioned so that they behave as good WAN citizens. An example of this is data access calls that perform a high degree of filtering at the database server, thereby minimizing the amount of data returned to the requesting service or client. In addition, when possible it is best to have the requesting service and the resource manager connected via a LAN rather than a WAN. This topic is further clarified within the distribution methodology in Chapter 5.

General guidelines for placement of application functionality are dependent on the number of tiers chosen for the application architecture. If a two-tier architecture is selected, the following guidelines apply:

- *User interface logic should be placed on the client.*
- *For performance reasons, processes that access database resources should be implemented as database stored procedures.* An additional benefit of this is that subsequent changes to the data access calls are isolated from non-data access application logic.

For multi-tier architectures, the following guidelines apply.

- User interface logic should be placed on the client.
- All data access should be accomplished through APIs to resources managers.
- Services that have a high degree of data access should be placed near the data server that stores the required data.
- Services that have a high degree of reuse should be optimally placed to provide the highest degree of sharability or be stored redundantly.

In the future, more tools will be available to create the application business logic as tiered services. These tools, such as CORBA-compliant Distributed Smalltalk (CORBA is an acronym for Common Object Request Broker Architecture as specified by the Object Management Group), will allow any service to be invoked through its defined methods. In addition, these object services can be optimally located and relocated based on performance requirements without causing any changes at clients or servers.

Service-level Agreements

Within a multitier architecture, each service must offer precise statements regarding its behavior, its interface, and its quality of service. A *behavioral statement* defines its functionality, that is, it specifies what the service does. An *interface statement* describes preconditions and post-conditions, and identifies the input and output data requirements. A *quality of service statement* defines those characteristics of the service that are technology dependent. These include such variables as performance, availability, reliability, security, and transactional semantics. This list is by no means exhaustive, but does represent what could be called 'core' requirements. The following is a brief discussion of some of these variables:

- *Performance*, which includes response time, throughput, and general overall capacity, can be difficult to predict because it is very dependent on all of the resources involved. These resources include network bandwidth, CPU cycles, types of disks and the like. Regardless of the complexities, the user of the service must be aware of the expected best and worst case behavior under various conditions.
- *Availability*, specifies the likelihood that the component will be accessible during a specified period of time.
- *Reliability*, specifies the likelihood that the component will not fail during a given execution. In reality, this is a measure of software and hardware quality.
- *Security*, which describes the level of security supported by the service, includes variables such as authentication, authorization, nonrepudiation, level of confidentiality, and degree of data integrity. Authentication is the process of having every user, host, or application server prove it is who it says it is. Authorization or access control is the process that ensures that authenticated users have the necessary permissions to use designated resources. Nonrepudiation is the process of ensuring that any authenticated and authorized user cannot deny that it used a designated resource. The level of confidentiality

ensures that sensitive data is not disclosed to any un-authorized users. The degree of data integrity is the process of ensuring that sensitive data is not changed in an unauthorized manner.

- *Transactional semantics,* describes the transactional guarantees provided by the service. A service can be invoked either from within or outside a software transaction. It can support transactional nesting, that is, the spawning of subtransactions, or the updating of persistent storage.

Each service also has variables that are specific to its intended functionality. For example, if a service provides data replication functionality, data timeliness would be one of the variables addressed within its quality of service statement. Users of the replication service would need an agreement as to the degree of data latency that they can expect when they subscribe to this service.

All of these service-level requirements should be part of a contract negotiation whereby a consumer and a provider agree to what quality of service can be expected. Generally these service properties can be expressed as variables and measured empirically. However, due to the complexities of services and the underlying resources they use, it is best to consider service-level variables with a probabilistic assertion. For example, when addressing data timeliness for a replication service, the agreement could stipulate that the service will maintain a data latency level of less than 1 minute 90 percent of the time.

The combination of these statements represent a contract between the service and its clients, that is, it becomes a service-level agreement (SLA). SLAs identify specific levels of service that should be met across application components. They specify promises about how a given component will work, and what quality of service can be expected. Each component within a multitier architecture should have a specific SLA associated with it. In addition, each service must be constructed in such a way that it abides by all properties described within its SLA.

Data Distribution Methodology

5

There are few short cuts when practicing good design techniques. The important payback of a strong design effort is the lack of unwanted surprises when deep into the coding and implementation phase of an application's life cycle. In a distributed environment, surprises can be much more costly to correct. If a good design methodology is followed, the resulting system will be able to scale either up or down and will be adaptable to changes in technology.

Currently most firms are eliminating centralized databases and moving to a more distributed database environment. However, most main production databases still remain centralized, and there is renewed interest in evaluating the benefits of centralization. Therefore, the underlying tenet of this distribution methodology is the practice of judicious distribution. As identified in Chapter 2, the benefits of practicing judicious distribution are the ability to achieve the desired availability and performance gains while controlling associated administration costs and complexities.

When distributing data, the objective is to create a distributed database system that exists at many locations yet is based on one, integrated enterprise model. The necessity for an integrated enterprise model is critical because data and processes do cross business units. The long-term strategy must be based on coordinating database design across multiple application systems so that data and processes in one system are available to users of other systems.

DISTRIBUTION APPROACH

Building a distributed database environment is a process of matching the needs of the business users to the realities of the physical infrastructure and available technologies. Compromises need to be made between the service level requirements of the business and the costs associated with building the physical infrastructure necessary to support those demands. Therefore, this methodology is presented less as a rigid workplan and more as a set of major decision points. It cannot be mindlessly applied, but it should be used as a road map to ensure that all major questions have been asked.

Nine-step workplan

In order to make intelligent distribution decisions, developers and architects must exercise due diligence in gathering the necessary facts, however time-consuming this might be. The challenge is to find the right mix of doing thorough analysis and proceeding aggressively to meet what in all likelihood are non-negotiable deadlines. Because both are important, making educated guesses is acceptable.

The decisions required within this workplan are tightly aligned to the application partitioning and placement alternatives addressed in Chapter 4. In general, the following tenets merge the two chapters:

- *The user interface should be at the lowest architectural level.* In most cases, this translates to the user's workstation.
- *The physical distribution of application logic should reflect the results of determining data placement.* To reduce network traffic, processes that use data should be placed near the data they use.
- *It is generally easier to replicate processes than data.*

The distribution workplan is composed of nine tasks. Some are primarily fact-gathering exercises; others are true decision points. After identifying the nine tasks, the remainder of this chapter concentrates on describing the objectives, inputs, approaches and suggested deliverables for each task. The tasks required to formulate a strong distribution scheme include the following:

1. Prepare an application distribution profile.
2. Prepare a physical infrastructure profile.
3. Create referentially tied data recovery groups.
4. Prepare a process-to-data use profile.
5. Integrate global data usage with the process-to-data use profile.
6. Create a data placement scheme.
7. Validate the placement scheme against existing constraints, capacities, and technologies.
8. Validate the placement scheme against service-level requirements.
9. Implement distribution scheme.

Figure 5.1 illustrates the flow of the workplan. It identifies the inputs to each task and the suggested deliverables. In addition, it depicts the interrelationships among the tasks.

Prepare an application distribution profile

The objectives of this task are to do the following:

- Describe the distributed nature of the application
- Start solidifying the network requirements

Input

The input to this task includes the following:

- *Knowledge of the application requirements and potential deployment locations.*
- *Functional decomposition diagrams.* Depending on the application development methodology being used, the name of the

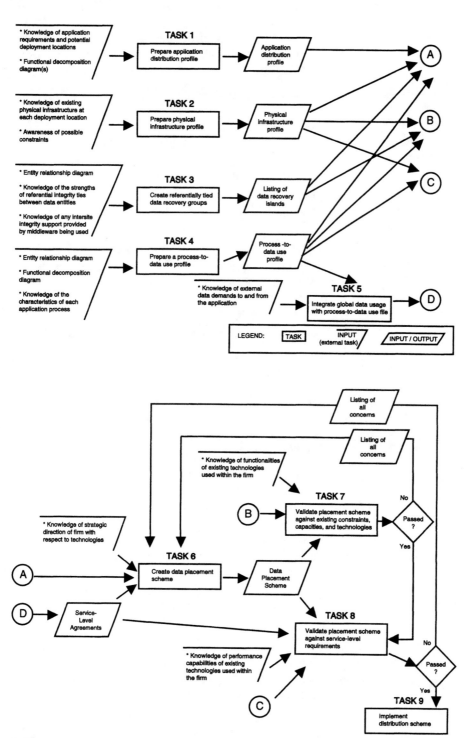

FIGURE 5.1 Data distribution workplan.

input might change, but the contents are the same. A functional decomposition diagram is a structured layout where high-level business functions are hierarchically decomposed into application processes. The decomposition is generally at a level that represents either a manual process or a computer software module. For an OLAP application, this would represent the querying and reporting requirements.

Approach

The approach includes two types of tasks. The first identifies logical categories of deployment location, users, and processes. The second assigns quantitative values to the logical categories. The required tasks include the following:

- *Identifying logical location types for the application.* Logical location types represent categories of deployment sites for the application. A banking example could include such location types as branch offices and back office hubs, while a manufacturing example could include regional centers and warehouse sites.
- *Identifying logical end-user types for the application.* Logical end-user types represent major roles performed by users of the application. A banking example could include such user types as traders and research analysts, while a manufacturing example could include procurement managers and shipping clerks.
- *Identifying business transactions and/or major processes that are executed by logical end-user types.* These equate to the major business functions, as identified on the functional decomposition diagram.
- *Assigning quantitative values to the location types.* This task assigns anticipated values to the number of users and processes execution rates by location type.

Generally an implied hierarchy exists across logical location types. An example of this hierarchy is exhibited in the location types of corporate headquarters, regional centers, and branch offices. The major functions performed at each location are distinct. Therefore, it follows that a similar set of business transactions and, by implication, data must be available to each instance of a particular location type. The network configuration and physical data structures for the firm should be designed to support this organizational structure.

TABLE 5.1 Application Distribution Profile

Application Name: _____

Location types	Locations	User types and anticipated numbers	Business transactions with anticipated execution rates
Regional sales centers	Brooklyn, New York	Sales Managers (3)	Consolidated reporting (15/daily)
		Marketers (30)	Sales capture (10,000 daily)
	Denver, Colorado	Sales Managers (1)	Consolidated reporting (5/daily)
		Marketers (4)	Sales capture (1,000 daily)
	London, England	Sales Managers (3)	Consolidated reporting (5/daily)
		Marketers (30)	Sales capture (7,000 daily)
Warehouse sites	Newark, New Jersey	Procurement manager (1)	Order placement (50/daily)
		Shipping clerks (6)	Order fulfillment (4,000 daily)
	Naperville, Illinois	Shipping clerks (5)	Order fulfillment (3,500 daily)
	Walnut, California	Shipping clerks (5)	Order fulfillment (3,500 daily)
	Lisbon, Portugal	Procurement manager (1)	Order placement (50/daily)
		Shipping clerks (6)	Order fulfillment (7,000 daily)

Suggested Deliverables

The suggested deliverable is a matrix that represents the information identified above. A sample application distribution profile is illustrated in Table 5.1.

Prepare a physical infrastructure profile

The objectives of this task are to do the following:

- Document the physical resources available at each potential deployment location
- Identify any potential distribution constraints

To determine the viability of distributing data and/or processes to a given location, it is important to have a thorough understanding of all the resources and constraints of that possible deployment site.

Input

The input to this task includes the following:

- Knowledge of the existing physical infrastructure at each potential deployment location
- Awareness of any possible constraints that exist within the environment

Approach

The approach includes questioning infrastructure support personnel and querying any existing electronic or hard-copy documentation. For each potential deployment location, topics to explore include the following:

- Network connectivity—both WAN and LAN
- Hardware resources and their available capacity
- Software resources and their available capacity
- Security levels supported
- System availability requirements currently supported
- Administrative support and their associated skill levels
- Any and all potential constraints that could influence the use of any site as a deployment location

Based on anticipated quantity of data and/or number of potential concurrent users, identify any platform constraints. In addition, identify any constraints regarding availability or reliability of a particular platform. One example of this type of constraint might be that an application requirement calls for a 7 × 24 availability, but the platform is currently available only for 12 consecutive hours. Closely tied to hardware and/or software exposures are security exposures. If security requirements limit access to a particular data source to a particular location or location type, then store that data at that location or location type. In addition, identify any possible administrative constraints that might exist at a particular location or location type. One example of this might be that the skill set required for database backup and recovery is unavailable, and bandwidths are such that remote administration is unreliable.

TIP

The only copy of a physical data store that must be shared across locations should not reside at a location where hardware, software, security, and/or administrative exposures exist.

Suggested Deliverables

The suggested deliverable is a matrix that represents the information identified above. A sample physical infrastructure profile is illustrated in Table 5.2.

An outcome of this analysis is the identification of any potential capacity issues. The sooner capacity issues are brought to the attention of the infrastructure planning and support groups, the more lead time is available to correct these situations. Enhancing the physical infrastructure is expensive in terms of both time and money.

Create referentially tied data recovery groups

The objectives of this task are to do the following:

- *Identity data recovery groups.* Data recovery groups are grouping of data entities that, due to their referential integrity constraints, or other business constraints should be recovered together to maintain data consistency.
- *Identify potential opportunities for implementing data partitioning by physical location.* The data keys to be used for partitioning should also be identified.

An important component of a distribution scheme is to ensure data integrity. Integrity must be preserved not only during normal update activity but also during administration activity such as recovery from failures. The major emphasis of this task is the grouping of primary data sources. Remember that primary

TABLE 5.2   Physical Infrastructure Profile

Application Name:

Location/ Location type	Network connectivity (WAN & LAN)	Hardware resources (e.g., servers)	Software resources (e.g., OS, DBMS)	Security level code	Availability level code	Administrative support and constraints	Additional constraints and concerns
Brooklyn, New York/ Regional sales	T1 line—London 128 kB—Denver Token Ring	Sun SPARC 1000	UNIX Solaris, Sybase SQL Server 11	High	7 × 24	Full support	
Denver, Colorado/ Regional sales	128 kB—Brooklyn Token Ring	Sun SPARC 51	UNIX OS 4.1/3, Sybase SQL Server 4.9.2	Medium	14 hours/day 7 AM–9 PM local time	Full support	
London/ Regional sales center	T1 line—Brooklyn Ethernet	Sun SPARC 51	UNIX OS 4.1/3, Sybase SQL Server 4.9.2	High	7 × 24	Full support	
Newark, New Jersey/ Warehouse site	128 kB—Brooklyn 64 kB—Naperville 64 kB—Walnut Token Ring	Sun SPARC 51	UNIX OS 4.1/3, Sybase SQL Server 4.9.2	Low	12 hours/day 7 AM–7 PM local time	Full support	
Naperville, Illinois/ Warehouse site	64 kB—Newark Token ring	Sun SPARC 51	UNIX OS 4.1/3, Sybase SQL Server 4.9.2	Low	12 hours/day 7 AM–7 PM local time	Limited UNIX and	Remote help from Brooklyn
Walnut, California/ Warehouse site	64 kB—Newark Token Ring	Sun SPARC 690	UNIX OS 4.1/3, Sybase SQL Server 4.9.2	Low	10 hours/day 8 AM–6 PM local time	Limited UNIX and SQL support,	Remote help from Brooklyn
Lisbon/ Warehouse site	64 kB—London Ethernet	Sun SPARC 690	UNIX OS 4.1/3 Sybase SQL Server 4.9.2	Low	9 hours/day 8 AM–5 PM local time	Very limited UNIX and SQL support,	Remote help from London

data sources are the recipients of all transactional activity. Distribution locations for primary sources and replicas will become apparent as developers work through these tasks and decide on the use of one of the application models presented in Chapter 2.

Input

The input to this task includes the following:

- *Entity relationship diagram (ERD).* This model is a logical view of the data required to support the application's functionality. It is produced as a normal part of application development.
- *Knowledge of the strengths of the referential integrity ties (logical relationships) between data entities.*
- *Thorough understanding of any intersite integrity support provided by the middleware being used.*

When performing logical data modeling for distributed systems, it is helpful to capture additional meta-data (characteristics with respect to entities, relationships, and attributes) and incorporate them into a standard dictionary package. These additional characteristics are extremely useful in making the data placement decision. Table 5.3 presents a summary of these meta-data requirements. The more accurate and complete the information, the more likely the creation of an efficient distribution scheme.

Approach

The approach entails partitioning the entity relationship diagram into subsets so that, to the greatest extent possible, no subset contains primary-to-foreign key references to another subset. The goal is to eliminate or at least minimize the number of model partitions that might have these cross-subset references. Currently there is very little middleware support for intersite integrity within a distributed environment. Most intersite integrity support must be provided from within application code or coordinated through external procedures. For example, database administrators now manually coordinate backup and recovery procedures across locations within a distributed environment.

Begin this partitioning task by logically grouping entities,

TABLE 5.3   Summary of Meta-data Requirements

Model component	*Meta-data characteristic to capture*	*Comments*
Entities	entity name	
	primary key column(s)	
	brief description	
	business guardian/owner	The guardian represents that business unit responsible for defining both business rules and technical requirements.
	anticipated volume	Includes both anticipated row size and number of rows.
	anticipated growth	
	attribute list that identifies all foreign keys	
	confidentiality tag	Either includes a statement or assigns a tag that indicates the level of access given to users of the entity due to its level of sensitivity.
	criticality tag	Either includes a statement or assigns a tag that indicates the degree of strength of the entity within the business in regard to disaster recovery.
	availability	Includes a statement regarding the "window" of the entity's use and by whom.
	periodicity	Includes a statement regarding the possible cyclic usage of the entity.
	retention	Includes a statement regarding how long the data stored in the entity should be preserved.
	purge criteria	Includes business rules that identify how deletions are to take place.
	policy triggers	Includes a listing of situations that will cause an automatic call to a specified procedure when a particular event takes place.
Relationships	relationship name	
	entity 1 name	
	entity 2 name	
	cardinality of entity 1	

TABLE 5.3 *(cont.)*

Relationships	optionality of entity 1	
	cardinality of entity 2	Expands cardinality to include the maximum number of occurrences and the typical number of occurrences on the "many" side of the relationship. (Typical number of occurrences does not necessarily equate to the average number of occurrences.)
	optionality of entity 2	Expands optionality such that if one side of the relationship is optional, then states the typical frequency that the relationship exists expressed as a percentage of "owner" entity having "member" entities.
	exclusivity	
Attributes	standard name	
	business name	
	description	
	format	
	confidentiality tag	Either includes a statement or assigns a tag that indicates the level of access given to users of the attribute due to its level of sensitivity.
	global "where used" list	Includes a listing of what processes use this attribute.
	"contained in" list	Includes a listing of other entities that contain this attribute.

then listing all entities or entity groupings that belong together within a matrix. For example, list together the entities associated with customer information, order information, and those used strictly for reference. Each entity or logical entity grouping should appear only once within the matrix. As you identify ties across the grouping, use the following recommendations to determine assignment within the matrix:

- *Entities with strong referential ties should be listed within the same group on the matrix, that is, they should be stored and recovered together.* An example of entities with strong referential ties include purchase order header and purchase order detail. They exhibit a strong parent-to-child integrity relationship and belong to the same logical entity grouping.
- *Entities with medium referential ties that are highly volatile should be listed within the same group on the matrix, that is, they should be stored and recovered together.* High volatility means a high frequency of update activity. Medium ties exist across logical entity groupings. An example of entities with this type of tie include the foreign key reference between part/product table and purchase order details.
- *Entities with medium referential ties that are not highly volatile need not be stored and recovered together.* Not being highly volatile means that update activity occurs very infrequently. These entities have the potential to be either denormalized or replicated. One example of entities with this type of tie include the foreign key reference between purchase order header and customer table.
- *Entities with weak ties are good candidates for replication to where-used locations.* Examples of entities with weak ties are the relationships between the transactional data of the application and the read-only reference data used for data validation on insert and update processing. These entities would include state code table, currency code table, and any other list validation tables.

Keep refining the list until all entities have been assigned to a group. Generally the groups represent tightly tied transactional data that must be recovered as a set, weakly tied reference data that can be replicated to all processing locations, and a small set of entities with medium ties to other strongly tied groups. For medium tied groupings where the foreign key references are not volatile, consider either denormalization or replication to where-used locations. In addition, identify columns that could be used to partition data across locations. For example, if this is a banking application, a branch code column could be used for this partitioning.

Entity Modeling and Normalization

Entity modeling techniques are used to build logical data models. Logical data models translate into a physical database design, however, the physical database design generally does not mirror exactly the logical data model. Logical models are modified to meet performance requirements of user processes and technical limitations of hardware and software components. Much literature is available on entity modeling; however, because denormalization techniques are addressed, I thought it prudent to offer illustrations of levels of normalization.

At least seven levels of data normalization are possible, but normalizing down to third normal form is all that is required in most situations. The three normal forms are as follows:

* *First normal form—an entity is in first normal form if each attribute of the entity occurs only once and there are no repeating groups of data.* To bring an entity to first normal form, remove all repeating groups of data and place them into their own entities.
* *Second normal form—an entity is in second normal form if it is in first normal form and if each attribute is dependent on its entire primary key.* An entity is not in second normal form if one or more of its attributes depends on only part of the primary key. Obviously, this rule is applicable only if the entity has a primary key composed of more than one column.
* *Third normal form—an entity is in third normal form if it is in second normal form and if no attribute of the entity is dependent on another non-key attribute.* This type of dependency is called a transitive dependency.

Data denormalization is the process of deliberately violating data normalization techniques. An example of data denormalization is the redundant storing of the customer name in the purchase order entity. Customer name is correctly stored in the customer entity, but due to performance demands it might also be stored in the purchase order entity. Storing it redundantly eliminates the need to do two table reads when displaying order information. Another example of data redundancy is the storing of derived data.

Whenever data denormalization or redundancy occurs, update and delete anomalies may occur when data is modified in one but not all of its stored locations. The result is that users get inconsistent views of data depending on which tables are used to satisfy a query. When data denormalization techniques are employed, update and delete processes should also be modified to incorporate changes to all redundantly stored locations. In some respects, replication can be considered a denormalization technique.

When considering data denormalization, the following factors come into play:

- Amount of change activity of the redundant or derived columns
- Complexity of the process(es) used to prevent update and delete anomalies
- Complexity of reconciliation procedures if denormalized structures are stored at different locations
- Replication alternatives used across distributed locations

 TIP

Data denormalization, like data distribution, should be used judiciously. For every gain in query performance, there is an additional complexity in maintenance.

Suggested Deliverables

The suggested deliverable is a matrix that represents entity groupings or an ERD with circles that represent recovery islands. In the introduction to this chapter, I mentioned that these tasks are less of a rigid workplan and more of a set of major decision points. This task is a prime example of that tenet. After completing this task, the user should find that the following decisions should be resolved:

- *Identification of all reference data.* If possible, at this time also identify a primary source for each piece of reference data. These read-only reference tables will invariably be replicated to all locations where the application's transactional data will be primary sourced.
- *Identification of data denormalization opportunities.* Data denormalization and redundancy can be used to resolve some distribution conflicts when distributing across recovery groupings. However, preventing update and delete anomalies can be particularly complex if the denormalization occurs across primary source fragments that reside at different locations. In addition, replication complexities can arise due to denormalization decisions. It is best to minimize denormalization across primary sources.

Prepare a process-to-data use profile

The objectives of this task are to do the following:

- Identify data use across processes
- Highlight "heavy hitter" processes

A process-to-data use profile is sometimes referred to as a process-entity model or a CRUD matrix. This matrix relates application processes to the entities that they create (C), read (R), update (U), or delete (D). Besides being necessary to support process and data distribution decisions, a CRUD matrix is also helpful for clustering processes into reusable application services.

Input

The input to this task includes the following:

- *Entity relationship diagram (ERD).* This is the same model used in the previous task.
- *Functional decomposition diagram.* This is the same input model as used in Task 1.
- *Knowledge of the characteristics of each application process*

Both of the diagrams mentioned above should be part of a firm's normal application development methodology. Most development methodologies also require the production of a CRUD matrix.

Approach

The approach entails producing a CRUD matrix and then flagging what will be considered "heavy-hitter" processes. To produce a CRUD matrix, list all entities across the top of the matrix and all application processes down the matrix's left side. In the grid portion, identify the effect of the process on the listed entities. Table 5.4 illustrates a subset of a process-to-data use profile.

For most application systems, there exists an 80/20 rule. Generally, 20 percent of the processes in the system perform 80 percent of the work. The purpose of this task is to identify that 20 percent. Subsequent placement tasks will concentrate on meeting the requirements of these so called "heavy hitters." Because placement decisions require compromises, it is best to compromise in favor of critical processes and not in favor of noncritical processes that occur only infrequently.

To qualify as a "heavy-hitter" process, one or more of the following requirements must be met:

- *High frequency of execution.*
- *High visibility within the business.*

TABLE 5.4 Process-to-data Use Profile (CRUD matrix)

Entity => *Process*	*Customer*	*Customer account*	*Order header*	*Order detail*	*Product*	*Invoice*
Order entry *	R		CRUD	CRUD	R	
Credit approval *	R	R	RU	R		
Price approval			R	R	R	
Order acknowledgment			R	R		
Order fulfillment *			RU	RU		
Order invoice *	R		RU	R		CRU
Payment received		RU	RU			RU

*identifies "heavy-hitter" processes

- *Critical service-level requirements.* For example, a very fast response time might be required.
- Requirement for large amounts of data and/or complex processing.

Simply stated, "heavy hitters" are the critical processes within the application. On the CRUD matrix, flag with an asterisk any process that should be considered a "heavy hitter".

Suggested Deliverables

The suggested deliverable, a process-to-data use profile, is a matrix that represents entities used by each process within the application. The matrix also incorporates the highlighting of those processes considered to be "heavy hitters." A sample process-to-data use profile is illustrated in Table 5.4.

Integrate global data usage with process-to-data use profile

The objective of this task is to do the following:

- Integrate global data usage with the application's process-to-data use profile
- Negotiate service-level agreements

The integration of the application's data perspective with that of the firm as a whole is important because, in a distributed environment, data is a sharable resource and flows across business lines. In other words, it has global use. During this task data flows into and out of the application are identified, and appropriate service-level agreements are negotiated.

Input

The input to this task includes the following:

- Process-to-data use profile created in the previous task
- Knowledge of the external data demands to and from the application

Approach

The approach for this task involves meetings with application development teams and data guardians that either "own" the data to which the application needs access or require access to the data that your application creates and/or modifies. The organizational groups involved in this effort might differ across firms due to differences in organizational structure; however, in all cases the same task must be accomplished.

The role of data guardians is critical to this effort. Most firms have either a single data administration group or multiple application-oriented data administration groups that assume the responsibility for data guardianship on behalf of true business guardians. This guardianship role generally entails the following:

- *Responsibility for coordinating the business rules associated with each data construct.*
- *Responsibility for coordinating the administrative rules used to support each data entity.*
- *Responsibility for ensuring the security of the data within their domain.* For example, the data guardian would decide on the appropriateness of storing a replica at a site where the operating system and/or the DBMS might be less robust than desired.

It is with the appropriate business and system data guardians, development team members, and architects that the following should be negotiated with respect to the data needed as *input* for the application:

- *Identification of what data is required.*
- *Identification of the primary source for each piece of data.* Always receive data from the primary source. If data is received from a source somewhere along the replication chain, the timeliness of the data decreases, and the likelihood that the data has been in some way corrupted increases.
- *Identification of the typical change rate for each piece of data.* If the change rate fluctuates to a very great extent, it might be necessary to implement either a manual or automatic warning system that alerts downstream replication nodes when a higher than normal change has occurred. If this type of warn-

ing system is required, it should be negotiated as part of the service-level agreement.

- *Agreement on the service-level requirements.* Service-level requirements identify specific levels of service that should be met across application components. In other words, they specify promises about how a given component will work and what quality of service can be expected. Service requirements address such service variables as performance, availability, reliability, data timeliness, and security. See sidebar in Chapter 4 for a discussion of service-level agreements. All service-level requirements should be part of a contract negotiation whereby a consumer and a provider agree to the quality of service that can be expected. Generally, these service properties can be expressed as variables and measured empirically. However, due to the complexities of services and the underlying resources, it is best to consider these variables with a probabilistic assertion. For example, the replication service will maintain a data latency level of less than three minutes 90 percent of the time.

Once the service-level agreements are acceptable to all involved parties then the most appropriate replication alternative can be selected. If database-to-database asynchronous replication is selected then only the replication infrastructure must be modified. If synchronous replication is chosen then the application that supports the primary data source must be modified to incorporate a distributed unit of work to the receiving databases. If process-to-process asynchronous replication—messaging—is selected, then both the sending and receiving applications must incorporate calls to the appropriate APIs to put or get the message. Data guardians should be involved in defining the message content.

 TIP

Any and all data errors or business rule violations should always be corrected at the primary data source.

With respect to the data that is required as *output* from the application, the appropriate data guardian(s), development team members, and architects should decide on the following:

- *Identification of what data is required.*
- *Identification of the number of processes and/or databases that require some sort of event notification.*
- *Identification of the typical change rate for each piece of replicated data.* As with the input data identified above, if the change rate fluctuates to a very great extent, it might be necessary to negotiate an agreement with respect to either a manual or an automatic warning system that alerts downstream replication nodes when a higher than normal change has occurred. Once again, the results of this negotiation should be incorporated into the service-level agreement.
- *Agreement on the service-level requirements for all applications involved.* Once again, service-level agreements of all core requirements should be negotiated.

As with input data, once the service-level agreements are acceptable to all involved parties then the most appropriate replication alternative can be selected.

Suggested Deliverables

The suggested deliverables are completed service-level agreements between appropriate data guardians, developers, architects, and infrastructure support personnel that identify all requirements for those application teams that either supply data to or receive data from the application under discussion. The critical aspects are that all involved groups agree on what the requirement is, what their task is in bringing it to fruition, and what quality of service will be provided in the production environment.

Create data placement scheme

The objective of this task is to integrate all of the knowledge assembled thus far and to formulate a first-pass data placement scheme.

The placement scheme addresses not only the intra-application data flows—those internal to the application—but also all interapplication flows—those associated with external primary sources and target replicas. This first-pass placement scheme becomes a strawman that in future tasks will be validated with respect to existing constraints, capacities, technologies, and service-level requirements.

Input

The input to this task includes the following:

- Application distribution profile (output from Task 1)
- Physical infrastructure profile (output from Task 2)
- Listing of data recovery islands (output from Task 3)
- Process-to-data use profile (output from Task 4)
- Service-level agreements (output from Task 5)
- Knowledge of the strategic direction of the firm with respect to preferred technologies

The tasks thus far have concentrated on data collection and analysis. This task is the first major decision point.

Approach

The approach entails using as input all of the information accumulated with respect to the application requirements, capacity and constraints of the existing infrastructure, and expected service-level requirements to formulate a data distribution scheme. If there have been any areas in the tasks completed thus far where the information collected has been incomplete or not totally clear, now is the time to clean up those loose ends. This is especially important for any constraints that may have been missed when creating the physical infrastructure profile. The more complete the information is, the better the chance of developing a valid distribution scheme.

The distribution scheme should first address the transactional data created and modified by the application. Employ the following steps:

1. *Identify viable locations for distribution.* Use the application distribution profile (Task 1) and the physical infrastructure profile (Task 2) to aid with the identification process.
2. *Solidify the selection of an application model.* If one has not already been selected, decide on the use of one of the application models presented in Chapter 2. Keep in mind that the

models are just templates and can be adapted as well as adopted. For example, if a distributed primary fragment model is used, the smaller and less technically robust locations could use remote access to a more stable location. See Chapter 9 for more details on application model selection.

3. *Distribute the data groupings identified in Task 3.* Use the following guidelines to aid with the placement process:

- Place data near its points of maximum use.
- If the same data entity instance will be updated from multiple locations, consider centralizing that data.
- If the same data entity type (but not instance) will be updated from multiple locations, consider vertical partitioning.
- If the data entity already resides at the location, consider sharing the existing copy.

Remember that the more timely the requirement for data consistency, the fewer the number of distributed locations there should be for that data. The reverse also applies; the less timely the requirement for data consistency, the greater the number of distributed locations there can be.

Once the transactional data has been placed, the next task is to decide on the placement of the read-only reference data used by the application. If the latency requirement of the read-only reference data is zero, that is, real-time access, then the application should access the existing primary source for that data via a remote request. If the latency requirement is for near-real time, that is, between a few seconds and a couple of hours, then replicate the reference data to the where-used locations via database-to-database or process-to-process asynchronous replication. If the latency requirement is greater than eight hours, then replicate the reference data to the where-used locations via complete or incremental refresh type of asynchronous replication or a scheduled delta propagation of events.

After placing the transactional and reference data, the next step is to identify the target locations that will be receiving data from this application. If possible, identify all the placement decisions graphically. Show the locations, the data that will be stored at each location, and the network bandwidths that currently connect the location nodes.

Once the graphical representation is complete, perform a rough estimate of the data flow volumes across the bandwidths connecting the location nodes. This should be only a paper analysis to give rough estimates. Include in the estimate the following:

- *Transactional data flows.* For the "heavy-hitter" processes highlighted on the process-to-data use profile, estimate the peak traffic flows between nodes. This entails estimating the amount of data sent from or returned to the process on a typical execution. Multiply this by the typical number of executions that will occur during what are considered peak times.
- *Replication data flows.* For the asynchronous replication tasks that provide data to or replicate data from the location, estimate the typical data flow that will occur at peak times between nodes. This entails estimating the change rate for primary data sources—those that your application has no control over—and the send rate for the "heavy-hitter" processes. Add this value to the value calculated for transactional data flows.
- *Error factor.* To adjust for estimation errors and to incorporate a fudge factor, multiply the above value by a factor of 2. Use a factor of 2.5 or 3 if you are at all uncomfortable with the values used for estimation. This final value should be the minimal network traffic that the physical infrastructure can support at peak times.

Suggested Deliverables

The suggested deliverable is a graphical representation of the data flows within the application (intra-application) and across other applications (interapplication). This data placement scheme also incorporates rough estimates of peak network traffic. This representation will be used as input to the next tasks.

Validate placement scheme against existing constraints, capacities, and technologies

The objective of this task is to ensure that the existing physical infrastructure can support the proposed data distribution scheme.

If it can, then the distribution scheme is workable and we can progress to the next task, a performance validation. If it cannot, then we must either modify the distribution scheme or correct and remove the existing constraint, enhance the capacity of the existing physical infrastructure, and/or improve the functionalities of the existing technologies.

Input

The input to this task includes the following:

- Data placement scheme showing a graphical representation of the data flows within and across the application (output from Task 6)
- Physical infrastructure profile (output from Task 2)
- Listing of data recovery islands (output from Task 3)
- Process-to-data use profile (output from Task 4)
- Knowledge of the functionalities of the existing technologies used within the firm

Approach

The approach is a methodical review of each deployment location with respect to any and all constraints, possible capacity limitations, and any lack of support for specific technological requirements. After all areas of concern have been identified, a cost-benefit analysis will help in deciding whether to correct for the limitation or to consider a different distribution scheme.

When evaluating a deployment location with respect to any constraints, use the physical infrastructure profile and the data placement scheme as input. Areas to validate include the following:

- *Ensure that the anticipated availability and reliability of a particular platform is supported.*
- *Ensure that the anticipated security level is supported.* If the security requirements are at a relational column level rather than at the table level, consider vertically and/or horizontally partitioning the table(s). Although this will solve the security issue, the major negative is the potential for degraded performance when attempting to merge (relational *union* for hori-

zontal partitions or *join* for vertical partitions) the partitions into a consolidated view.
- *Ensure that the appropriate level of administration support is available.*
- *Ensure that any other constraint listed on the physical infra-structure profile can be resolved.*

When evaluating a deployment location with respect to any capacity limitations, use the physical infrastructure profile and the data placement scheme with rough estimates of peak network traffic as input. If a significant growth in application volumes is anticipated and this factor was not considered in Task 6, incorporate a growth factor into this validation exercises. Areas to validate include the following:

- *Ensure that no platform limitations exist.* Validate that the anticipated quantity of data and number of concurrent users can be supported by the available platform(s).
- *Ensure that no database limitations exist.* Validate that the anticipated quantity of data and required data types can be supported by the DBMS. In addition, validate that the number of concurrent users can be supported by the DBMS.
- *Ensure that the network bandwidths between location nodes are sufficient to support the anticipated traffic.* Because this capacity limitation probably involves the most resources in terms of time and planning to correct, do a diligent effort to ensure that the network capacities are adequate. Network planning personnel are invaluable in the execution of this task. They bring a broader, cross-application perspective to this task.

When evaluating a deployment location with respect to availability of appropriate technologies use the physical infra-structure profile, process-to-data use profile, listing of data recovery islands, and the data placement scheme as input. Areas to validate include the following:

- *Support for distributed units of work.* The distribution scheme being evaluated might require support for a distributed unit of work (two-phase commit protocol) across databases and/or locations. The existing technologies within the firm might not provide this capability. Generally, using distributed units of work across locations connected by WAN resources should be avoided. See Chapter 1 for a discussion of the potential restrictions.

- *Support for the appropriate replication alternative.* The replication alternative(s) selected should provide the required functionality from a technology perspective. For example, if the requirement is for near-real-time data replication on a 7 × 24 availability basis, the replication alternative should support transactional semantics across the complete replication process. Evaluate the replication selection not only from a functionality perspective but also from the perspective of capacity and potential constraints.

Suggested Deliverables

The suggested deliverable is a listing of all concerns associated with the distribution scheme under consideration. The listing identifies any and all constraints, capacity limitations, and technology limitations associated with the distribution scheme under consideration. The user of this methodology must now decide whether to return to Task 6 and create an alternative distribution scheme or to pursue the appropriate avenues within the firm to correct for the actual or perceived shortcomings.

Validate placement scheme against service-level requirements

The objective of this task is to ensure that the proposed data distribution scheme and the existing physical infrastructure can meet the performance requirements agreed to within the service-level agreements. If they can, then the distribution scheme is workable and implementation can begin. If it cannot, then we must modify the distribution scheme, enhance the existing physical infrastructure, or negotiate for modification in the service-level agreements. Whereas the previous task concentrated on physical constraints, this task concentrates on performance requirements.

Input

The input to this task includes the following:

- Data placement scheme showing a graphical representation of the data flows within and across the application (output from Task 6)
- Physical infrastructure profile (output from Task 2)
- Process-to-data use profile (output from Task 4)
- Service-level agreements (output from Task 5)
- Knowledge of the performance capabilities of the existing technologies used within the firm

Approach

The approach is a methodical review of each deployment location with respect to all anticipated performance requirements. After all performance concerns and/or service-level violations have been identified, a cost-benefit analysis will help in deciding whether to enhance the physical infrastructure to meet the performance requirement, negotiate a more relaxed service-level requirement, or consider a different distribution scheme.

When evaluating a deployment location with respect to performance requirements use the service-level agreements for the "heavy-hitter" processes highlighted on the process-to-data use profile, the technology components identified in the physical infrastructure profile, and the data placement scheme as input. The goal is to ensure that the performance requirements decided on as part of the service-level agreements are attainable. With respect to data distribution, this would include such quality of service items as meeting response time requirements for transactional processes, attaining required data latency levels during any replication process, and ensuring required levels of reliability.

Suggested Deliverables

The suggested deliverable is a listing of all concerns associated with the distribution scheme under consideration. The listing identifies any and all violations of the service-level agreements. The user of this methodology must now decide whether to return to Task 6 and create an alternative distribution scheme, to modify service requirements and renegotiate the service-level agreements, or to pursue the appropriate avenues within the firm to correct for infrastructure shortcomings.

Implement distribution scheme

With the distribution scheme selected and validated, it is now appropriate to continue with the application development effort. As the development life cycle progresses, it is important to measure the success of the distribution scheme and refine and tune it. Chapter 9 presents an implementation plan for applications that anticipate using replication.

The methodology presented within this chapter should be used as a tool to expedite the development of distributed applications. If the tenets set forth in this methodology are followed, not only will the necessary data be available but it will be available in an efficient manner and with the appropriate level of latency. Most firms conduct their business at multiple locations; therefore, access to remote data is essential. To keep a competitive edge in the marketplace, firms cannot afford to suffer from the "I can't get that information from here" syndrome.

ADDITIONAL BENEFITS OF USING THIS DISTRIBUTION METHODOLOGY

The objective of this methodology is to define an approach that will assist application developers and technical support staff in meeting strategic and tactical goals for distributing both data and processes. If the tenets defined within its content are followed and the suggested deliverables are produced, the merging of the deliverables across application development areas will generate an informal repository. This inventory of data, process, hardware, software, and network resources can be used to reap the following benefits:

- *A catalogue of available data and process components to be employed within a reuse strategy.*

- *A where-used inventory of processes and data to be used by change management personnel.* This will ensure consistency of code and data definition changes across replicated locations.
- *An evolving logical network framework.* This framework helps network support staff be proactive in anticipating changes in the business, to project future network growth areas.
- *A where-used inventory of hardware and software components to aid with the change management function at a systems level.*

Designing and Configuring Databases for Replication

Databases and other types of resource managers provide persistent storage for data. As such, they are a key component of the replication process. Failure to design efficient databases can lead to performance problems, lack of flexibility, poor scalability, inefficient network usage, and overall escalating costs. In addition, poor design techniques usually lead to poor data quality. This chapter addresses database design and configuration issues that will provide insight into the decisions necessary to implement an efficient data replication environment.

DATABASE DESIGN CONSIDERATIONS

Designing databases in a distributed environment is significantly more complex than designing databases in a centralized environment, largely because of the need to consider network resources, data partitioning schemes, redundant data placement alternatives, and replication approaches. The following design considerations are meant to give the reader a background on the trade-offs associated with each issue. Because in most cases there is not a right or wrong answer, the deeper the understanding of the trade-offs, the more effectively the solution can be adapted to resolve the business problem.

Issues associated with deciding whether to preserve transactional semantics within replication

In Chapter 1, I discussed the trade-offs associated with preserving the transactional nature of the originating event during the collection, distribution, and apply processes of asynchronous replication. Choices associated with asynchronous replication will have an effect not only on database design alternatives but also on the quantity of effort involved in the design process. Chapter 1 stressed that the more near-real time the asynchronous replication approach is, the more important the preservation of transactional semantics becomes. This translates into using either a database-to-database communication type or a messaging type of asynchronous replication when near-real-time data consistency is required. These asynchronous replication update approaches exhibit the same transactional behavior as a single OLTP software transaction. The target replica is always in a transactionally consistent state before and after each asynchronous replication event. This simplifies the database design effort.

Transactional consistency is not preserved if an incremental table refresh approach is used. When a batch incremental refresh approach is used with a low-frequency refresh interval, a very significant analysis and design effort is required. For example, when an incremental table refresh is used with a scheduled refresh interval of one minute, the sequence in which tables are refreshed must be determined so that referential integrity at the target replica is preserved. This occurs because the apply process commits updates to only one replica table at a time. Therefore, the onus to ensure that the target database never contains referentially inconsistent data falls totally on the designer. An example of this type of violation happens where a dependent row exists without its associated parent—a purchase order detail line without its associated purchase order header row, or a purchase order header for a customer whose data has not been inserted yet.

Determining the apply table order will help to prevent referentially inconsistent states. The parent subscription must run at a higher priority than the dependent subscriptions when the changes to the primary replica are restricted only to *insert* and *update* activity of non-key columns. For *delete* operations, the dependents must be deleted before the parent. Interesting design challenge, since the table order for insert and update is in direct opposition to the table order for delete processing.

Therefore, some advocates recommend that referential integrity should not be implemented on target replicas. If the target replica can be updated only via the asynchronous replication process, this is a viable option as long as one of the following is true:

- *Transactional semantics are preserved during the replication process.*
- *A batch window is used to apply all updates to all tables within any given target replica.* The result of this effort is a consistent data snapshot at a target replica.
- *It is acceptable for users to view data that is referentially inconsistent.*

 TIP

In my opinion, incremental refresh types of asynchronous replication work best when there is a batch window for applying all updates to all tables within a specific target replica. This ensures that the target replica is in a transactionally and referentially consistent state before users are permitted to access the data. It also simplifies the design process.

Schema differences at publishing and subscribing locations

In a data replication environment, the database schemata between publishing and subscribing locations do not have to be identical. In fact, it is imperative that the data structures of each replica be designed to meet the performance requirements of their particular set of users. For example, a relational DBMS used for OLTP may have its data structures highly normalized; however, when that same data is used for decision support, the implementation might use a ROLAP (relational OLAP) solution. Here an OLAP tool is used to simplify front-end query access, and a relational database is used for the back-end data server. To meet the performance requirements of the query users, a star or snowflake database schema may be required. The critical factor is that the replication service should be able to handle these schemata differences.

As stated in the replication evaluation criteria in Chapter 3, the replication solution should support or interface with data transformation and mapping services, which correct for differences in database schemata. They handle data type mismatches, data content repairing, and denormalization enhancements; however, depending on the complexity of the transformational and mapping services required, different replication alternatives are more appropriate.

Synchronous replication can perform any DML or logic operation within the bounds of its logical unit of work. Therefore, with respect to transformation and/or mapping, there are no limitations. However, there are issues regarding performance, the amount of time locks are held, and the availability of all required resources. For the refresh type of asynchronous replication, there are also no restrictions. During the period between the extract from the primary sources and the refresh of a target, any number of transformational services can be invoked to massage the data into the format required for input at any target. However, with the refresh type of replication, the timeliness of the data as the result of the refresh process might not meet the demands of the users. In addition, the database is usually unavailable during the data load process.

When using the messaging type of asynchronous event propagation, there are also no restrictions. The publisher of the event builds the message and incorporates within the message the data elements needed to apply the results of the event at all subscribing locations. During the apply process at a target, the subscribing process can perform any and all desired transformations and mappings. When using a database-to-database type of asynchronous replication, some restrictions do apply. For low to moderate types of transformations and mappings, the most common case, there are no restrictions. However, complexity grows when the data needed to perform the transformation and/or mapping is not available at the target replica, either because it is not persistently stored there or because it is not being made available within the data being sent via the asynchronous replication process. For example, if a log pull type of mechanism is used, only the data rows that were modified will be available at a target. The apply process can call a database-stored procedure and perform DML and logic as appropriate, but if the extraneous data required for transformation is not available to the stored procedure the apply process becomes massively complex. In these situations, either store the data needed to perform the transformation at the designated target or use a different asynchronous replication approach.

Using specialty and proprietary databases as targets

Most resource managers used within an OLTP environment are traditional database management systems; as such, they support full transaction functionality. For these DBMSs, any type of asynchronous replication alternative is appropriate. If a synchronous replication alternative is desired, then either the DBMS's TP lite functionality or a distributed TP monitor (a TP heavy solution) is available.

When replicating between OLTP and OLAP environments, an important issue is the type of resource manager used as the back end for the OLAP tools. If a traditional RDBMS is used (one that can also support OLTP processing), then the same alternatives as identified in the previous paragraph are appropriate. However, if a specialty or proprietary resource manager is used as the back end, then the replication alternatives may be limited. In many instances, specialty and proprietary resource managers are stripped of their transactional support functionality to provide fast load capabilities. For example, they may not support any logging, may lock only at the database level, and/or support only one writer. In these situations, only a refresh type of asynchronous replication should be used. See Chapter 7 for a more thorough discussion of replication within an OLAP environment.

Use of database partitioning

An important design consideration is to identify database partitioning alternatives at both primary and replicate locations. Database partitioning divides a single database into multiple databases, which may or may not be distributed.

Database partitioning at a primary source

Database partitioning at a primary source has the greatest potential benefit when a log pull mechanism of capture is used. The log pull mechanism is a continually running process that extracts committed transactional information from the database log and sends it to the distribution mechanism of the asynchronous replication service. When this partitioning approach is used with a relational DBMS, the tables of a database are separated into groups. One group contains those tables or data that will be flagged or have the potential to be flagged for replication. The other group contains tables or data that will definitely not be part of the replication process. This partitioning is performed to reduce the amount of log data that the log pull mechanism has to scan. This is a useful technique when a great deal of update activity occurs within the database (a large log) and only a very few tables are flagged for replication.

Strong negatives are associated with this design alternative:

• *Partitioning within a database is complex.* Tables should not be separated so that referential integrity constraints cross databases. In other words, a primary key and all of its foreign key references should always be within the same database. This allows declarative referential integrity to be enforced. This means that the database itself manages the defined referential integrity constraints. A further complication of a poor partitioning scheme is the potential for changing a local or remote unit of work into a distributed unit of work. This occurs when a transaction updates only within a single database pre-partitioning (remote unit of work), but updates across multiple databases after the partitioning (distributed unit of work). See Chapter 2 for a further discussion of types of distributed data access. Distributed units of work complicate the coding effort and add complexity to recovery scenarios. In addition, if a target replica needs the result of a distributed unit of work, a log pull mechanism should not be used because the replication process has no functionality to reunite the disjointed pieces of the separate log pull mechanisms.

- *Database administration and recovery become more complex.* Recovering two databases with separate logs to the exact same point in time is much more complex than just recovering one.

- *Database security is more complex.* Issues include how to handle data views that cross databases, who owns the database view, where the user IDs reside, and how to handle a database stored procedure that resides in one database but must access data in multiple databases.

- *Some flexibility is lost.* A relational table or piece of data may not be currently flagged for replication, but that does not mean that a demand for a replica will not occur in the future. When the demand for a replica does occur, should the partitioning scheme be re-addressed? Should the non-replicated database now carry replicated data? Remember: This was the very situation we were trying to avoid with the original database partitioning effort. Therefore, artificial partitioning can create a rigid architecture that makes future maintenance efforts complex.

In my opinion, the risks and loss of design flexibility associated with the negatives of database partitioning at a primary source far outweigh the potential gain of less work for the log pull mechanism. I would recommend not using this technique.

Database partitioning at a target replica

Database partitioning at a target replica is also a design alternative. Partitioning at target replicas will have an impact on database recovery scenarios and on the degree of data access transparency for application code. The trade-offs here reflect the replication and database administrator perspective versus the application developer perspective. For administrators, if the target replica is partitioned so that every primary source replicates into its own target database, recovery and data reconciliation are simpler to handle. For the application developer, data access is more complex with the addition of each new database.

The issues that should be considered in this design decision include the following:

- *Number of primary sources supplying data to the target replica.*
- *Number of tables per database.* Some data servers allow recovery only at a database level. If the service-level agreement for database recovery demands a short allowable outage, then the more tables that reside within the database, the longer the amount of time for the recovery process.
- *Number of replication connections used to update the target.* Some vendors' asynchronous replication products provide only one connection per database for the updating replication process. If multiple databases are used, then multiple connections can exist. This can increase throughput; however, be warned that the data stream flowing across each connection should be totally orthogonal, otherwise the integrity of the data will be jeopardized. Orthogonal means that the data streams do not modify the same data. In other words, each data stream modifies only its designated portion of the data.
- *Characteristics of the recovery scenarios performed.* Orthogonal databases can be recovered independently of each other. In addition, if multiple databases are used and recovery is at a database level, recovery time is reduced. However, having multiple databases also makes database recovery to a point in time very difficult because synchronization within multiple logs to the very same moment is not easy.

I have found that the following partitioning scheme works well and strikes a good mix among the trade-offs. Most applications are composed of two general types of data, transactional data that is the meat of the application data and reference data that is required for read-only validation. This reference data is usually supplied by legacy systems. Therefore, two databases are created at each target replica. One is for read-only reference data that is supplied by application systems outside the scope of the application being developed; the other is for the transactional data required for the application being developed. By its very nature, this partitioning scheme should create orthogonal data groupings—that is, a software transaction for one group does not update into the other. This will eliminate the possibility of creating distributed units of work at replicas acting as both a primary and a target. In addition, it allows for two delivery data streams that are also orthogonal—one replication data stream from reference data suppliers and one from within the application transactional data itself. This allows greater throughput.

Deciding between data and stored procedure replication

Some vendor-supplied replication products allow users to replicate both relational table data and database stored procedures. The replication of stored procedures is sometimes referred to as *function replication*. Use of stored procedure replication is important because it allows two significant features: a method of encapsulating many data changes within a single replicated function and a technique for allowing a primary target to execute a stored procedure that does not modify data directly.

The ability to encapsulate many data changes within a single replicated function can improve replication performance and decrease network costs. For example, relational technology allows set-level processing. Therefore, if a primary replica executes a SQL statement such as

*update employees set salary = salary * 1.1*

the result is that every row in the employee table is updated (every employee receives a 10 percent increase in salary). If table replication is used, each target replica would receive a new updated version of every row. If the employee table is large, the network traffic is significant; however, if function replication is used, only the stored procedure name and the parameter of 1.1 is sent. Every target replica would have the required stored procedure and would execute it with the sent parameter(s). The result is an increase in performance and a decrease in network traffic.

The second significant feature of stored procedure replication, the ability to allow a primary target to execute a stored procedure that does not modify data directly, enables the target replicas to implement data modifications as they deem necessary. In other words, it can be used as a database-to-database triggering mechanism. In reality, the asynchronous replication of stored procedures is a flavor of application transparent messaging. With messaging, the originating process formulates a message that is composed of a message header with information about the message itself used for distribution purposes, and message content with parameters used to process the message at the receiving replicas. The message header information would include such data as technical details concerning message delivery and a complete description of the sender. It would identify who the sender is, what the message is about, where the sender is on the network, when the sender sent the message, and why the message is being sent. The message content would contain the actual data values specified for this message type in complete compliance with the designated business rules.

The sending process calls an API to pass the message (the message header and content) to the message distribution service. The receiving process calls an API to receive the message and subsequently performs the necessary processing of the message content. With stored procedure replication the stored procedure name equates to the message name. The replication service fills in other portions of the message header either when it pulls the stored procedure execution information from the log or when its internal resolution and distribution processing occurs. At the target replica, instead of an application process receiving the message and applying the necessary business rules to process the message content, a database receives notification that it should execute a stored procedure with this specified name and these input parameters. The stored procedure resides within the domain of the target database, and it executes by applying the business rules using as input the sent parameters.

Stored procedures originating at a primary replica

This type of function replication results in a one-to-many replication effort. The function is first performed in the primary replica. After execution, the replication service forwards the necessary replication information to target replica(s) where the function is also executed. With this type of replication, the primary replica acts as the initiator. Figure 6.1 illustrates one-to-many stored procedure replication.

This apply type of function replication provides a means of replicating operations that may be difficult to express through table replication. Typically with this type of function replication, the stored procedures in the primary database and the replicate databases perform the same operations, but it is not a requirement, nor is it enforced by the replication software. It is the responsibility of the application developer and production support staff to ensure the content consistency of the stored procedures across distributed databases if this is the business requirement.

Stored procedures originating at a target replica

This type of function replication results in a one-to-one replication effort with a possible one-to-many subsequent replication effort. Here the function is first performed at a target replica.

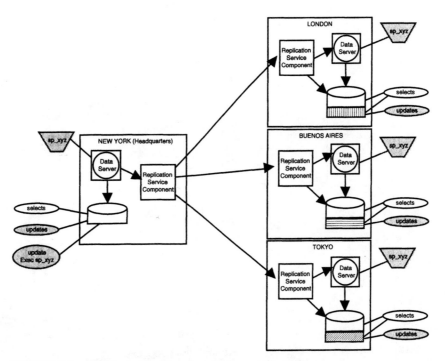

FIGURE 6.1   One-to-many stored procedure replication.

After execution, the replication service forwards the necessary replication information to the primary replica where the function is also executed. With this type, a target replica acts as the initiator. Figure 6.2 illustrates one-to-one stored procedure replication.

This request type of function replication provides a means of delivering a transaction from a target replica back to the primary database. For example, a client application at a remote target replica may need to make changes to the primary data. After the change occurs at the primary replica, the data is subsequently replicated back to the target database and any other subscribing target replica(s). This type of stored procedure replication preserves the master/slave model of asynchronous data replication. Typically with this type of function replication, the stored procedures in the primary database and the replicate databases are very different. The stored procedure at the repli-

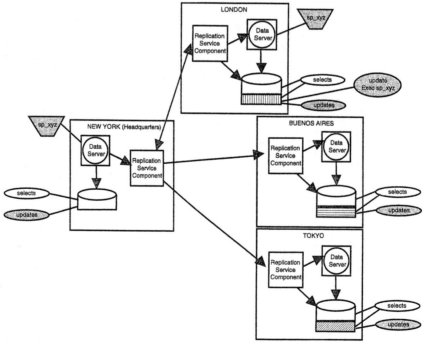

FIGURE 6.2 One-to-one stored procedure replication.

cate database usually does nothing or simply indicates that a pending update is forthcoming from the primary replica. This pending update information can be in the form of a message sent to the client or a flag on the local rows awaiting the update. It is the stored procedure at the primary database that performs the primary data modifications. During the asynchronous table replication back to the target initiator, the required data rows are modified, and if any pending row status was set, it would be updated to its actual status.

An example of this type of stored procedure replication could be implemented with the distributed primary fragment model. For an investment bank, each local branch owns and updates its own partition of a distributed primary fragment model. Periodically a trader may create a deal that would require an insert into a slice of data that he or she does not own. Note that the only type of DML activity that is allowed for this transaction is an insert into a non-owned partition. The transaction could use stored procedure replication with the originating event at the target replica. The locally executed store procedure could do nothing, or it could insert the required row into the non-owned partition in a pending status. This would allow the local trader to view the deal and its status throughout the asynchronous replication process without using a remote query. The stored procedure at the primary source for the fragment would do the official insert and all target replicas would receive the results via asynchronous replication from the primary source. The asynchronous replication apply process would be defined to either insert the row or, if the row already exists in a pending status, validate the data and change the pending status to actual. This scenario allows the trader originating the deal to see the result of the trade locally throughout the replication process and yet in theory still preserves the master/slave model. In essence, the trader uses asynchronous function replication to trigger a remote unit of work at a designated primary source. In theory, it can be argued that this approach does not violate ownership lines because inserts in a pending status only affect the local replica and database views can be used to show only actual versus pending deals. A more separatist version of this scenario would be to have a pending deal table locally where these deals are inserted. The apply process at target replicas would first check the pending table. If a row exists for this deal, it would delete that row and do the corresponding insert into the actual fragmented table. For the local trader to view both pending and actual deals, a relational view could be used that unions the two tables.

Index considerations

For the database-to-database type of asynchronous replication, there is an assumption that a unique index exists at each target replica. This requirement is based on the fact that the replication apply process assumes row uniqueness. Typically row uniqueness is achieved by creating a clustered or non-clustered unique index. Regardless of replication concerns, it is generally a good design practice to have a unique index on all tables within an RDBMS.

 WARNING

The use of the database-to-database type of asynchronous replication can produce unpredictable results if a unique index is not available at each target replica.

In ideal situations, the primary key columns and the unique index that defines these columns are identical between the primary replica and all target replicas. However, in some situations where data access patterns are significantly different across replicas, it may be necessary to create different indexes to achieve the required level of performance. Care must be taken in these situations to ensure that sufficient uniqueness exists, to avoid replication failures due to duplicate row conditions.

A similar situation can occur when addition indexes are created at a target replica that do not exist at the primary replica. Update activity can fail at the target replica due to uniqueness conditions that are not enforced at the primary replica.

Use of database triggers at primary and target replicas

Care should be used when implementing asynchronous replication and using the same database triggers at both the primary and target replicas. Data updates executed by database triggers on data that is also flagged for replication at a primary replica will be replicated like any other modifications. At a target replica, these database triggers will be fired by the updates executed by the replication apply process. Therefore, if the same triggers reside at both the primary and target replicas, the updates executed by the triggers on the primary replica will be executed twice at the target replica(s), first by the trigger itself and then by the replication apply process. The example in Table 6.1 illustrates the problem and thereby clarifies the discussion.

As a general design recommendation, the target replica should receive all data modification via the replication service. Do not implement database triggers at the target replica. By not mixing asynchronous replication and triggers at target replicas, the problem of duplicate modifications can be avoided.

Updating primary keys

Care should be used when updating primary key values at a primary replica with relational set-level processing. If multiple rows of a relational table flagged for replication are updated in a way that could create duplicate keys of another row, duplicate row errors could result at target replicas. The example in Table 6.2 illustrates this situation.

The following update statement is issued at a primary replica where *pkcol_a* is the primary key

```
for TBL_1
  Update TBL_1
    set pkcol_a = pkcol_a + 1
```

TBL_1 has three rows with *pkcol_a* values of 1, 2, and 3.
The log pull mechanism retrieves the log information and sends the following SQL statements to the target(s):

TABLE 6.1 Trigger Use at Primary and Target Replicas

Primary Database Replica	Target Database Replica
Database objects:	*Database objects:*
Table *TBL_A* (id int) with Trigger *TRG_A* on delete	Table *TBL_A* (id int) with Trigger *TRG_A* on delete
Table *TBL_B* (id int) is a history table for *TBL_A*	Table *TBL_B* (id int) is a history table for *TBL_A*
TRG_A inserts into *TBL_B* rows deleted from *TBL_A*	*TRG_A* inserts into TBL_B rows deleted from *TBL_A*
TBL_A flagged for asynchronous replication	
TBL_B flagged for asynchronous replication	
Transaction:	*Transaction:*
delete TBL_A where id = 1	*Begin tran*
Delete trigger *TRG_A* fired	*delete TBL_A where id = 1*
(insert TBL_B Select * from deleted row)	Delete trigger *TRG_A* fired
	(insert TBL_B Select * from deleted row)
	insert TBL_B (id) values (1)
	Commit tran
Results of transaction at TBL_B:	*Results of transaction at* TBL_B:
Row inserted with id = 1	Row inserted with id = 1 (result of *TRG_A*)
	Row inserted with id = 1 (result of replication of *TBL_B* from primary replica)
	Note: Second insert will fail if a unique index exists on column "id"

TABLE 6.2 Possible Errors with Certain Types of Relational Set-Level Processing

	Before primary key values	After primary key values
Before and after results at the primary replica		
	1	2
	2	3
	3	4
Before and after results at a target replica		
	1	4
	2	4
	3	4

```
Update TBL_1
   set pkcol_a = 2 where pkcol_a = 1
Update TBL_1
   set pkcol_a = 3 where pkcol_a = 2
Update TBL_1
   set pkcol_a = 4 where pkcol_a = 3
```

The replication mechanism treats each row as an independent update. Therefore, at a target replica the first and second rows are updated three and two times, respectively. If a unique index exists on the primary key columns at target replicas, which is generally the case, the additional updates will cause errors. If no unique index exists on the primary key columns, duplicate rows (rows with identical primary keys) will result.

To prevent this type of relational set-level errors from occurring with asynchronous replication, have a unique index across primary key columns at target replicas and use either a message-based type of replication or a replicated stored-procedure. When using stored procedure replication with the database-to-database type of replication, the stored procedure behaves like a store-and-forward messaging system. The name of the stored procedure equates to a message identifier, the lists of parameters perform identical tasks, and the receiving stored procedure executes the apply process just as the receiving process would in a messaging system.

Types of Software Transactions

In earlier chapters, transactions were classified as either business transactions or software transactions. Remember that a business transaction equates to a business event. A business transaction can be composed of multiple software transactions. A software transaction is a recoverable unit of work and changes the persistent state of the firm's data from one consistent state to another. Software transactions exhibit the ACID properties. (See Appendix B for a discussion of ACID properties.) Software transactions can further be classified as local or distributed, flat or nested.

No matter how software transactions are classified, the critical design aspect for implementing transactions is deciding on transaction demarcations. In other words, what business logic should be wrapped within a software transaction's **begin** statement and **commit** statement? From a business perspective, this question is important because it identifies what the business user views from the resource manager as a recoverable whole. For example, in banking, a debit and a credit compose a recoverable whole. A business user would not want the database to be in a state where the debit was visible without its associated credit. This translates into making both the debit and the credit that compose the business transaction part of the same software transaction.

Contrasting local and distributed transactions is very straightforward. A local transaction is one that executes only within a single machine. When local transactions are used within an application, coding and recoverability are simple and direct. Failures are easy to detect. Concurrent transactions are isolated and can easily be followed through the resource manager's locking mechanism. The resource manager generally logs data changes ahead of any writes to the database. Logging ensures recoverability. A distributed transaction is a transaction that executes across multiple machines. A distributed transaction requires all of the functionality needed to support a local transaction, but with the added complexity of using more than one resource manager. Transaction demarcation still plays its critical design role. Locking with distributed transactions is more involved than with local transactions because there is no global locking mechanism across resource managers. In addition, the ACID properties characteristic of software transactions must be preserved. In other words, the "all or nothing" semantics must be enforced across resource managers. If a hardware, process, communication, or resource manager failure occurs, all the work completed on behalf of the aborted transaction must be automatically rolled back. A distributed transaction equates to a distributed unit of work. (See Chapter 2 for a more detailed comparison of units of work.) When implementing distributed transactions, the following functionality should be available:

- A mechanism for identifying within the environment other processes collaborating within the transaction
- A protocol to propagate transaction state, including transaction ID, to all the processes involved.

- A protocol to coordinate the commitment of update activity across multiple, possibly physically separated processes.
- Security and appropriate execute authority across the involved processes.

Transactions can also be classified as either flat or nested. A flat transaction is the simplest kind of transaction in that it has only one level of control. Multiple actions, such as calls to other application services or multiple data modifications performed within its single scope of control, may occur, but all actions are either committed or rolled back as if they were one action. By contrast, a nested transaction is composed of a hierarchy of transactions. The top level transaction is called the *root node*. Other internal nodes or branches are called *subtransactions*. When transaction nesting is used, subtransactions may be aborted without aborting the parent transaction.

Figure 6.3 illustrates a flat transaction.

Application pseudo code:

```
start transaction {
      DML statement
      call applsrv1 with parameters (A, B)




}
onCommit {
      perform X
}
onAbort {
      perform Z
}
```

Legend
DML   = data manipulation language
              (include **insert, update, delete,** or **select** statements)
applsrv = application service within a tier architecture

FIGURE 6.3   Example of a flat transaction.

For flat transactions it is important to note the following:

- *In addition to being flat the transaction can also be classified as local or distributed.*
- *Any number of calls to application services or DML statements can be placed between the transaction* **begin** *and* **commit** *statements.*
- *Logic flow will execute the* **onCommit** *clause (if required by the transaction manager being used) if the transaction completes successfully.* If the clause is not required, the flow will continue after the **onAbort** clause.
- *Logic flow will jump to the* **onAbort** *clause if the user or the transaction manager aborts the transaction.* If the transaction is not aborted the **onAbort** clause will be bypassed.

Figures 6.4 and 6.5 illustrate two different examples of transaction nesting. The first example illustrates nesting within a single

Application pseudo code:

```
start transaction {
    DML statement(s)
    start transaction {
        DML and application logic
        }
        onCommit {
            perform M
        }
        onAbort {
            perform N
        }
        DML or application logic
    }
    onCommit {
        perform X
    }
    onAbort {
        perform Z
    }
```

Legend
DML   = data manipulation language
            (include **insert**, **update**, **delete**, or select statements)
applsrv = application service within a tier architecture

FIGURE 6.4   Example of a nested transaction within a single application program.

Application pseudo code:

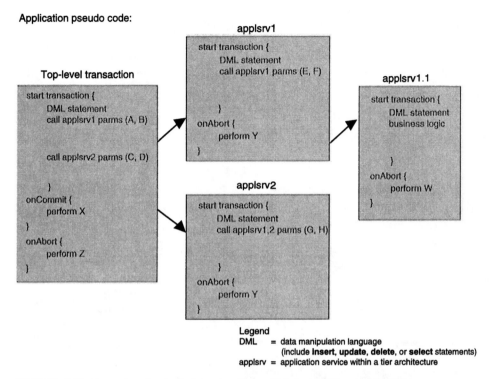

FIGURE 6.5 Example of a nested transaction within a multitier architecture.

application program, and the second illustrates the use of nesting within a multitier architecture using application services.

For nested transactions it is important to note that multiple start transaction statements are executed after the original start transaction from the root node. When nested transactions are used, it must be clear to the implementers how locks acquired by one resource manager on behalf of a specified application service working for a designated transaction conflict with locks acquired by the same resource manager on behalf of another application service working for the same transaction or for a different transaction. Different resource managers support different approaches and rules regarding these issues. In essence, this translates into knowing if and how the resource manager supports the following:

- *Commit rule.* If subtransactions can be committed or aborted independently, are their changes made permanent only when the parent transaction commits? In addition, when a subtransaction commits, are the results of its work visible to its parent transaction?

* *Abort rule.* If a transaction aborts, are all of its subtransactions also aborted?

* *Visibility rule.* Do all changes by a subtransaction become visible to its parent when the subtransaction commits? Are all of the objects locked by a parent transaction accessible to its child transactions? Are all of the objects locked by a parent transaction not accessible to its sibling transactions? Are changes made by a subtransaction never visible to its siblings?

Because no definite standards regarding transaction nesting are available, the application developer must find out how the resource manager and/or transaction manager of choice handles these nesting situations. Depending on the resource manager being used, it is possible to lock oneself out of one's own nested transaction. This does not mean that nesting should not be used. On the contrary, using transaction nesting allows developers to implement complex business rules, such as making it possible to avoid aborting the whole transaction when only one or more of the actions within the transaction fails.

Transaction nesting within replicated stored procedures

Most vendor-supplied asynchronous replication products do not support nested transactions within replicated stored procedures. (See sidebar for a discussion of transaction nesting.) Therefore, in the following stored procedure, different results will occur when the stored procedure is flagged for replication versus when it is not flagged for replication.

```
Create Proc SP_1 as
Update TBL_A
Insert TBL_B
Begin tran
   Delete TBL_C
```

```
    Insert TBL_C
    if @@error != 0
       rollback tran
    else
       commit tran
Return
```

Table 6.3 illustrates the results of the stored procedure when it is flagged for replication and when it is not. Notice that the difference occurs when the effects of the nesting come into play, in this case when an error occurs.

The differences occur because when the stored procedure is flagged for replication, its execution is implicitly enclosed within a *begin* and *commit* transaction. Care should be exercised when using transaction nesting because DBMS vendors do not support this functionality with standard approaches. Therefore, it is important to totally understand the implementation of transaction nesting within both the DBMS and the replication software.

Additional concerns when replicating stored procedures

Flagging a stored procedure for replication usually has the consequence of implicitly enclosing the execution of that stored procedure within a *begin/commit* transaction boundary. Therefore, a replicated stored procedure should execute only statements that are allowed within a transaction. The allowable statements

TABLE 6.3 Transaction Nesting Within Stored Procedure Replication

Results when stored procedure is not *flagged for replication*	Results when stored procedure is *flagged for replication*
A duplicate key in TBL_C creates an error	A duplicate key in TBL_C creates an error
Results:	*Results:*
Update TBL_A committed	Update TBL_A rolled back
Insert TBL_B committed	Insert TBL_B rolled back
Delete TBL_C rolled back	Delete TBL_C rolled back
Insert TBL_C rolled back	Insert TBL_C rolled back

vary across different DBMSs. The onus of identifying these allowable statements falls on the application designers and developers. A small sampling of these types of statements usually include the relational *select into,* any form of *truncate table,* and sometimes the data definition language statements (DDL) of *create* and/or *drop.*

An additional concern is lock contention. Because the execution of a replicated stored procedure is generally wrapped as a transaction, be aware of the potential for lock contention. Locks on the modified data pages will be maintained during the execution of the entire stored procedure.

A further example of this occurs when an RPC is executed from within a replicated stored procedure. The potential for lock contention exists. The following simplified example will result in a deadlock when the stored procedure is flagged for replication. The example uses Sybase OpenServer.

The OpenServer registered procedure is *SP_2.*

```
Create Proc SP_2 as
   Update TBL_B
   Set ....
   from TBL_A, TBL_B
   where TBL_A... = TBL_B
   Return
Create Proc SP_1 as
   Update TBL_A
   Exec OpenServer ....SP_2
   Return
```

The execution of *SP_2* from within *SP_1* is accomplished via a different thread to the Sybase data server. When *SP_1* is not flagged for replication, there is no lock contention problem: When the call to *SP_2* is executed, all locks associated with the first update in *SP_1* have already been released. However, if *SP_1* is flagged for replication, the execution of *SP_1* will be implicitly wrapped within a transaction, that is, a *begin* and *commit.* The locks acquired by the first update in *SP_1* will be held until the final *commit.* The update in *SP_2* will be locked out by the first update. A classic deadlock condition has occurred. Care should be used when designing such nesting situations. Thorough application testing should uncover any of these situations not identified and eliminated during the design effort.

Data types and their replication implications

Vendor replication products support replication of all the traditional data types, such as character, and such numeric types as small integer, integer, float, and the like. They also generally include data type conversion functionality so that replication can occur within heterogeneous database environments. However, an area of concern with respect to database design is how to handle the replication of long text and image as well as user-defined data types. Designers should reference the vendor's manuals for clarification on the data types supported within the replication process.

Long text and image data types

Because text and image data types are large by nature, their replication entails more overhead than that associated with traditional data types. Care should be used when deciding to replicate these large data types since a large amount of network resources can be consumed. Some asynchronous replication products allow multiple replication options for these large types of data. For example, replicate the complete relational row including the text and image data types, replicate all data types within the row except the large data types, or replicate only the large data types when the current value of the text or image has changed. If these options are not available within the replication product being used, it may be useful to vertically partition the table so that the text and image fields reside in their own table. This isolation prevents excess network usage when the whole relational row is always part of the replication process.

User-defined data types

Many data servers support user-defined data types. It is generally best to convert these user-defined data types into their underlying system types and use these system data types within any replication processing commands.

Time implications

In a globally distributed environment, time and time synchronization can be issues. To measure latency accurately within a replication environment, the time on all data servers and replication components must be synchronized to a high degree. This synchronization can be provided in a number of ways. One way is through DCE Time Service (DTS), which synchronizes host clocks in LANs and WANs. If DCE is not used, this synchronization is also provided under UNIX by Network Time Protocol (NTP). One of these time services or an equivalent should be installed on all host machines because this clock synchronization enables distributed applications to determine the sequencing, duration, and scheduling of events independently of where they occur.

Another database design consideration is to incorporate an accurate time stamp column on all tables involved in the replication process. This column should contain the data and time when the row was last modified. This column is useful when resynchronizing data during a recovery process. It is also used in incremental data extraction for use with incremental data refresh technology. The extraction process can be instructed to pull only data that has been modified since the last extraction process.

It may also be beneficial to incorporate two time-related columns. One reflects the time on the local server; the second reflects that time as Greenwich Mean Time (GMT). This design technique simplifies time comparisons across time zones.

Handling unique key generation across multiple primary fragments

In a master/slave model with distributed primary fragments that require globally unique identifiers, this functionality must be either designed into the database schema or embedded within the application. Options include the following:

- *Adding column(s) to a unique local identifier to designate ownership or origination.* With this solution the primary identifier is a composite key. Each primary replica assigns a unique sequence number as the identifier and then concatenates to that column one or more columns that make that sequence number unique across all primary replicas. An example of this in the banking industry occurs when the combination of branch code column and the sequence number column form a unique combination.

- *Assigning ranges of numbers or character combinations that are specific to each primary replica.* With this solution an assignment scheme is used to designate a unique range of identifiers to each primary replica. An example of this in a manufacturing environment is where the range 100000 to 399999 is used for parts originating from the San Francisco plant, and the range 400000 to 799999 is used for parts originating from the Chicago plant. Although this scheme works, there are two negatives. The first is that the range assignment may become too restrictive and a plant may run out of numbers. A second negative is that the identifier column is no longer atomic, that is, it carries more than just a single piece of data. It stores the unique identifier and also carries the value used for identifying plant origination. This makes it a poor choice. A better solution is to revert to the first solution and use a unique sequence number and the column of plant origination. This preserves the atomic nature of all data elements.

- *Using an external mechanism for unique key generation across all primary replicas.* If this solution uses a mechanism where all primary replicas must go to one location to retrieve their unique identifier, a bottleneck can be created that will hinder the performance of originating transactions. In addition, some procedures must be in place to handle situations when the identifier assignment location is unavailable.

DATABASE CONFIGURATION CONSIDERATIONS

Database configuration parameters help to ensure that the replication environment is architected to provide the best possible service. As with the database design consideration, the following configuration considerations are meant to give the reader a background on the trade-offs associated with each issue.

Release levels of software

Most vendor-supplied replication software requires the most current release of the software involved within the replication process. This includes such software as operating systems, data servers (especially if it is to be used as a primary replica), database gateways, and other middleware components. Getting release-level requirements as soon as possible is wise. It generally takes time to upgrade any type of system software because upgrades must be scheduled across multiple application systems.

Sort orders

Care should be exercised when using asynchronous replication between databases or data servers with different sort orders. By definition, a sort order defines the collating sequence used when data is sorted. If different sort orders are used, problems can arise in the apply process. Problems can also arise if the subscription requesting asynchronous replication includes a string comparison.

TIP

Some asynchronous replication products have developed functionality to aid in handling sort order issues. However, it is up to the user to determine whether differences in collating sequence will be an issue. In general, it is always best to make all the sort orders of the databases or data servers involved in the replication process the same.

Character set support

Differences in character sets between primary and target replicas can also be an issue. Most database-to-database asynchronous replication products perform character set conversions of data and identifiers between primary and target replicas, usually with some restrictions. For example, single-byte character set data cannot be converted to multibyte character set data and vice versa. For character set conversion to take place, the necessary conversion tables must be available to the replication middleware. In general, all data servers within a replication environment should use the same or compatible character sets.

Log parameters

When using a log pull type of capture process for asynchronous replication, log parameters become important. Equally important is the option for executing the capture process against either the active or an archived log. It is the responsibility of the replication architect to perform a thorough analysis of any and all effects of the chosen replication capture process on active or archived logs.

For example, some data servers permit scheduled log truncation procedures to be executed whenever a database checkpoint occurs. For a primary replica, this is not a good parameter to have turned on. If, for whatever reason, the log pull mechanism is unavailable for a period of time or cannot forward the captured information to the replication distribution process, the database log will fill up even if there is no database update activity because the *truncate log on checkpoint* command writes to the log.

The log pull mechanism generally establishes a secondary truncation point in the database log. It identifies the point in the log where the pull process is currently active. Behind the secondary truncation point, the capture process has completed its reading efforts. In front of that point are the transactions waiting to be read. Log truncation should occur only behind both truncation points. If the secondary truncation point in the log cannot be moved, the data server is prevented from truncating the log and as a result the log fills up. Different vendor capture solutions handle this condition in different ways. The log size not only should reflect the transaction activity but also should have enough additional space to allow for a capture process outage. Having a more than sufficient log size will make the recovery process easier.

DATA DELIVERY CONSIDERATIONS

As noted in Chapter 1, the event type of asynchronous replication maintains some level of sequential integrity throughout the delivery process. However, sequencing issues can arise if a target replica receives update activity from multiple sources.

Using multiple primary sources to a single replicate

If a target replica receives updates from multiple primary data sources, these updates will be applied as separate units of work. Vendor-supplied asynchronous replication products generally do not assign sequencing (ordering) across primary replicas because any publishing replica could become unavailable for a period of time. If the replication distribution process had to wait for all publishing replicas to respond before distribution could occur, target replicas would experience long latency periods. Therefore, the distribution process portion of a replication service distributes updates on an as-received or a scheduled basis.

A specific example of this in the database-to-database communication type of event-based asynchronous replication occurs where the primary data for a software transaction is held in multiple databases. The software transaction updates data in multiple databases within the same unit of work, that is, it performs a distributed unit of work. If a log pull mechanism is used as the capture technique, each database has its own log pull capture process that sends its portion of the transaction to the distribution process independently. If one of the capture mechanisms is down for a period of time, the target replicas receive only a portion of the total software transaction until the failed capture mechanism is again functioning. If this is not acceptable, then either synchronous replication should be used or the data should be distributed in such a fashion that the transaction is not required to perform a distributed unit of work.

The same issues exist with a messaging type of event-based asynchronous replication. Some re-sequencing of messages can occur at the receiving replica's queue; however, if a publishing replica becomes unavailable, the replication distribution process does not wait until it is brought back online. It continues to distribute updates on an as-received basis.

Advanced Replication Topics

Thus far, the concentration of this book has been on replicating in an OLTP environment, with new applications and without concern for the integration of multiple replication solutions. However, firms have both OLTP and OLAP environments, have both new development efforts and legacy systems, and will require the integration of synchronous and multiple asynchronous replication alternatives. This chapter addresses these advanced replication topics.

RETROFITTING LEGACY SYSTEMS INTO THE REPLICATION PARADIGM

Legacy systems are any systems currently in production that were not initially designed with replication in mind. During the course of any application's life cycle, it may become necessary to roll the application and/or its supporting data under the replication umbrella. Use of either synchronous or asynchronous replication techniques should be available to accomplish this task.

Legacy systems and synchronous replication

Rolling the data that supports legacy systems into a synchronous replication environment is more of a technology issue than an application issue. The resource manager that supports the legacy data must be able to cooperate with other resource managers within a distributed unit of work. Generally the cooperation is via a TP monitor/transaction manager since these products support robust distributed units of work within either a homogeneous or heterogeneous database environment. Therefore, this technology is sometimes referred to as "TP heavy." If the proprietary functionality of the existing resource manager is used to support the distributed unit of work, it is referred to as "TP lite" since resource managers don't offer the same full range of functionality as do TP monitors / transactions managers.

If the legacy system is the system chosen to initiate the distributed unit of work, then obviously the code for that legacy system must be opened and modified to handle this new functionality. If the code is of a high quality, this is a reasonable task; however, if the code is not of high quality, the coding and testing efforts can become complex, labor-intensive, and time-consuming.

Legacy systems and asynchronous replication

When retrofitting legacy systems into a firm's asynchronous replication initiatives, once again the age of the system is not as critical as the quality of the application code involved. If the code is at a quality level such that opening it up to add interfaces to asynchronous replication services will not create unanticipated surprises, then any asynchronous replication approach can be used. However, if the quality of the code is at question, then the more application transparent the replication solution, the more easily and quickly the implementation can be achieved.

The asynchronous replication solution that is the most application transparent is the database-to-database communication type. Most of these asynchronous database-to-database asynchronous replication alternatives assume that the resource managers involved in the replication effort are of the RDBMS type. If this is the case, these solutions generally use a log pull mechanism or a trigger based approach to capture the database changes at the primary replica. At target replicas, the apply portion communicates directly with the database. The apply portion also handles most types of data transformation and mapping. This means that existing application code need not be modified. Therefore, this is a relatively painless solution as long as a vendor-supplied log pull mechanism is available for the primary replica's resource manager and the target replicas are conventional RDBMSs. Coding one's own log pull mechanism for a resource manager not currently supported by the vendor is probably not a task most firms would want to tackle; however, modifying or creating one's own apply mechanism is not a difficult task.

If relational DBMSs are not part of the replication environment, then a messaging type of asynchronous replication is a more appropriate choice. Some vendors do have capture facilities for non-relational DBMSs, but generally these products support only DBMSs within that vendor's 'family' of DBMS products. A messaging solution is also appropriate if a transparent capture facility is not available. Remember: with this approach the primary (publishing) code is modified to call an API that puts the messages into the message queuing and distribution service. Target replicas pull their messages from their receive queue and apply the appropriate replication rules while processing the message. If the application code at either the primary or target replicas is weak, code modifications can create problems. Based on the quality and quantity of application code that must be modified, the messaging solution can take longer to implement, test, and move into production than a more application transparent approach.

REPLICATING IN A HETEROGENEOUS DATABASE ENVIRONMENT

This book stresses implementing replication as a firmwide service so that it can very easily fit into a heterogeneous database environment. Recall from Chapter 4 that a service-based architecture uses multiple tiers that separate the user presentation logic and the resource manager access logic into independent tiers. What remains in the middle tier is either application business logic or technical services. Replication qualifies as a technical service.

The more that replication can be implemented as a service, the more easily it will be to integrate it into a heterogeneous database environment. Most vendor alternatives for the database-to-database type of asynchronous replication provide functionality for use in heterogeneous database environments; however, the concentration of their efforts are for the well-known RDBMSs. If the heterogeneous database environment uses lesser-known RDBMSs, asynchronous replication vendors generally supply tool kits that can be used to assist a firm in coding its own capture functionality and/or apply portion. Coding one's own log pull capture facility is a sizable effort, but modifying the apply portions to accommodate non-supported RDBMSs is generally well within the scope of any firm's expertise.

If a firm has a wide mix of relational and non-relational resource managers, probably the best alternative is an asynchronous message solution. Because messaging is not application transparent, it fits well into this type of heterogeneous resource manager environment. Depending on the vendor solution chosen, the firm may have the responsibility for developing APIs for the "put" of the capture process and the "pull" of the apply process, for defining and modifying message structures, and for outlining the business and replication rules for handling the receipt of messages. If the modifications are architected well, a firm should be able to generate a good deal of code reuse.

USING REPLICATION IN DATA WAREHOUSING ENVIRONMENTS

Maintaining data consistency between operational systems and decision-support systems in a global warehousing environment presents many challenges. In addition to the challenges identified for replicating in the OLTP environment, there are also issues involved with maintaining multiple degrees of latency between consistency points across the various OLAP data stores, merging and transforming both internal and external data sources, handling complex differences in schemata, and using proprietary resource managers that may not support the same functionality as traditional DBMSs.

In Chapter 1 OLTP and OLAP environments are compared with respect to asynchronous replication. In addition to understanding the differences between the two environments, it is important to understand the business drivers for OLAP within a firm and the different types of OLAP tools currently available.

Knowledge workers demand information about anything, anywhere, anytime

With the current advances in technology, the objective of most information systems is to provide information about anything, anywhere, anytime. It is important to differentiate between information and data. Data is the raw details about the events that have occurred and are scheduled to occur within a firm. Information adds meaning to the raw details. To provide users with the information they require, data must be analyzed and synthesized into information. This requires the ability to do the following:

- Access and combine information from numerous and diverse data stores.
- Create multidimensional views of data.
- Summarize, consolidate, and apply complex calculations to data within these stores, including the ability to drill down, roll up, slice, and rotate across and within dimensions.

Blurring the line of demarcation between OLTP and OLAP

As stated in Chapter 1, firms are becoming flatter and putting more control in the hands of the business user, as evidenced by the decentralization of business functions to a widening set of locations. The new information users have more complex and integrated applications at their disposal. Figure 7.1 illustrates this integration of applications and data.

The mix of user applications include transactional systems (OLTP), decision-support systems (OLAP), business integration systems, and personal productivity/workgroup systems. Transactional systems are the core systems that capture and maintain detailed, accurate information about the business. Decision-

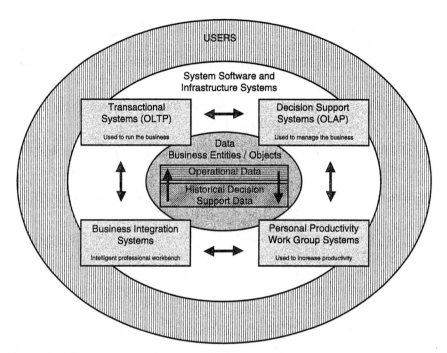

FIGURE 7.1 Integration of user applications and data.

support systems are generally more strategic in nature. They are used to make critical decisions that ultimately control the enterprise's ability to compete in the market place. Business integration systems are a newer type of application that generally spans multiple departments and crosses organizational boundaries. They usually are the result of automating complex, manual processes. Such systems have been made possible by the availability of greater computer power and more sophisticated software. Business integration systems include rule-based management systems, complex trend analysis (i.e., data mining), and data visualization. The final type of user application is personal productivity/workgroup systems—off-the-shelf, PC-based packages that make the individual more productive. They include such software as word processors, spreadsheets, graphical packages, mail-based applications, and document management and publishing systems. All these applications require data.

From a user and application perspective, the line between current operational data and historical data has become blurred.

Is there a need for separate data stores for OLTP and OLAP environments?

Because the line between current operational data and historical data is now blurred, one might ask, is it possible to use the same physical data store(s) to support both OLTP and OLAP systems? The basic production relational database management system (RDBMS), when used for OLAP in a two-tier client/server architecture, falls short of providing the data manipulation necessary to meet user requirements for data analysis and information synthesis. Major reasons for this are the limitations of Structured Query Language (SQL) and the poor-comprehensibility and efficient access of data stored in a normalized relational form.

OLTP production data is often stored in very normalized relational databases, designed by database administrators to provide optimum data storage with minimum data integrity problems for rapid processing of transactional systems. However, these normalized structures are not designed to be comprehensible by end users, therefore, they are not particularly easy for composing the complex queries of OLAP users. Therefore, witness the advent of non-traditional database management systems and specialized OLAP tools that aid with the complex querying process.

In all likelihood, data will always need to be stored redundantly for decision Support Systems. OLAP systems require access to very broad sets of data, usually from multiple corporate sources. Most often the data from these diverse operational systems requires data transformation and distribution to OLAP servers. Before arriving at a server, the data is repaired, merged, appended, rationalized, and summarized. As middleware becomes more robust, it will become easier to perform parallel access across heterogeneous data stores and to perform dynamic transformation and summarization. The amount of data redundancy needed will lessen, and designers will be able to concentrate on finding the most appropriate mix of data centralization and distribution.

A brief history of the OLAP tools will clarify the issue of data sharability.

Brief history of OLAP tools

Information access tools have come a long way since early report writers and spreadsheets. Originally OLAP vendors supplied their users with databases. Some were based on their own proprietary resource managers; others were based on relational DBMSs supplied by other vendors. Along with these underlying databases, OLAP vendors supplied tools to conduct analysis and repositories for meta-data and storage of user-defined calculations that were usually built using their front-end tools. The environment was very limiting and closed.

The current trend within the OLAP industry is to decouple the tools from the other components. This allows vendors to present their products as front-end tools to other vendors' DBMSs. This is extremely important for it pushes the OLAP environment into a multi-tier architecture. The tiers of this architecture include (1) the resource manager, usually an industry standard, relational DBMS or a proprietary, multidimensional DBMS, which acts as the data store; (2) the application server layer, which performs the analytical processing functions and interacts directly with the database(s) and (3) the client, Presentation layer. The application server layer is truly the heart of OLAP. It maps the multidimensional business views to the physical databases. In addition, it contains a repository that holds the definitions of the dimensions, hierarchical structures used as consolidation paths for data, formulae used in query calculations, and database access information. The final layer is the client, which is the presentation layer and which may also perform some analysis and administration. Complimenting this multitier OLAP architecture is a technical service layer that prepares the data for the OLAP database engine. This layer performs such functionality as transformation, distribution, and replication. Implementing the transformation, distribution, and replication as part of a service-based environment keeps the OLAP environment very open. It also paves the way for more interoperability between the OLTP and OLAP environments.

In general, OLAP tools can be classified in three general categories:

- *M-OLAP—Multidimensional OLAP.* These tools use a proprietary database as the resource manager with an OLAP front end. M-OLAP tools currently are available in two- or three-tier architectures. A multidimensional database (MDDB) stores data in structures that offer an alternative way of organizing summary data. Through the use of cross-indexed hierarchical structures, data is organized into dimensions and measures, by time.
- *R-OLAP—Relational OLAP.* These tools use a relational database as the resource manager with an OLAP front end. R-OLAP tools currently are available in either two- or three-tier architectures. To achieve the desired performance from the relational engine, these tools recommend using specialized data schemata, such as a star or a snowflake schema.
- *Desktop OLAP.* These tools use a relational database as the resource manager engine with a weak OLAP front end. Desktop OLAP tools use only a two-tier architecture and always have a "fat" client.

It is important to understand that OLAP tools and list type of query- and report-generating tools do *not* provide identical functionality. OLAP tools provide multidimensional analysis, including both multidimensional data presentations and the ability to do calculations across all the dimensions of the application's data. This involves more than just the cross-tabulation functionality provided by relational query tools. In addition, OLAP tools are not limited to the data volumes that can be held in the memory of a desktop PC. They can perform sophisticated calculations and presentations on large volumes of data. To aid with this process, most OLAP tools have a built-in knowledge of the hierarchical structure of the data.

MDDBs provide fast query response but are proprietary in nature, a factor that can have a negative impact on a firm's operational support infrastructure and can limit replication possibilities. Using an RDBMS and just implementing denormalization technique is only a short-term tactical solution. In the long run, it will yield an inflexible decision-support system that is skewed toward particular applications. However, coupling a relational star or snowflake schema with an OLAP middleware tool gives the query user a simplified, multidimensional view of the physical data model. It uses meta-data to simulate the multidimensional views.

As RDBMS vendors incorporate more robust engines and exploit all forms of parallelism, it is my belief that the time will come when RDBMSs can give the same query performance as MDDBs. Does this mean that eventually the need for MDDBs will diminish? I believe the answer is no. The complex querying demands of sophisticated analysts can never be meet by the SQL language. Therefore, I believe firms will use a spectrum of OLAP tools. At the light end are simple desktop OLAP tools; in the middle are R-OLAP tools that may or may not share the same physical RDBMS; and at the heavy end is the sophisticated M-OLAP environment for truly complex data analysis. Figure 7.2 illustrates a typical architecture used for an OLAP environment.

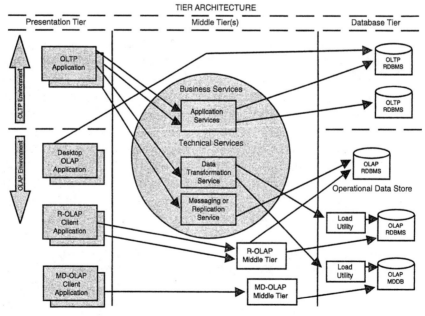

FIGURE 7.2 Architectural overview.

The illustrated architecture uses a tier approach and stresses the building of services—in essence, the middle tier. Within the middle tier are multiple business and technical services. The business services support reusable business functions that are called from within the application code. The technical services represented in the illustration are those reusable services used to support the OLAP environment.

Within this architecture, data from multiple OLTP systems is used to build the warehousing environment. Desktop OLAP tools, which use a two-tier architectural approach, can query either OLTP or OLAP data stores; however, in Figure 7.2, to avoid the complexity of multiple crossed lines, only the querying of OLTP data stores is shown. The R-OLAP and M-OLAP tools are illustrated as using a three-tier architectural approach. These tools store the meta-data used for complex query transformations either within the middle tier or within the back-end DBMS.

A replication service is only one of multiple architectural layers and services that can be used to support an OLAP environment. Figure 7.3 illustrates these multiple layers.

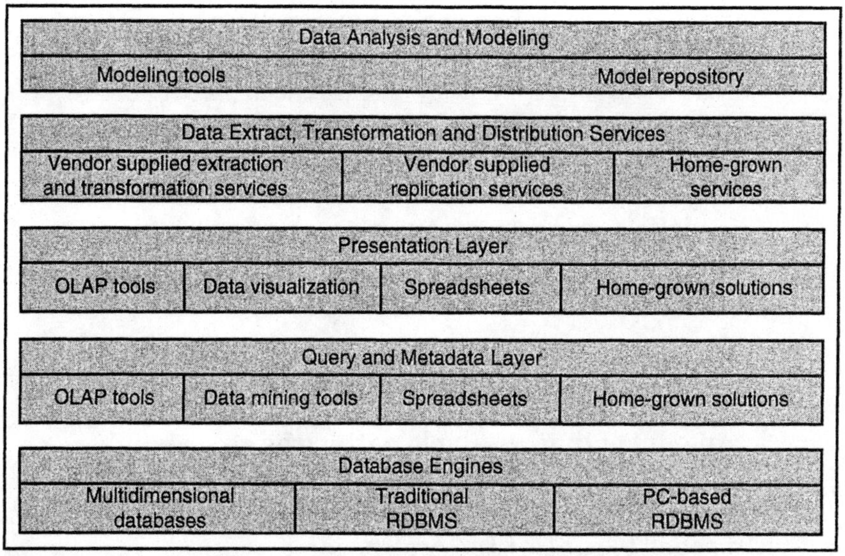

FIGURE 7.3 Architectural layers within an OLAP environment.

Replication challenges in the OLAP environment

As identified earlier, additional challenges are associated with using replication in OLAP environments. These include the maintaining of multiple degrees of latency between consistency points across the various OLAP data stores, the merging and transformation of both internal and external data sources, the handling of complex differences in schemata, and the use of proprietary resource managers that may not support the same functionality as traditional DBMSs.

Maintaining multiple degrees of latency between consistency points across the various OLAP data stores

Within an OLAP environment, various user groups need different degrees of data latency. Some users need to query and analyze near-real-time data; others need consistent snapshots that represent close of day or close of month replicas of OLTP environments. Depending on the latency demands of the users, different asynchronous replication solutions may be more appropriate.

For users that need near-real-time data consistency with OLTP systems, the most appropriate asynchronous replication approaches are either of those for delta propagation of events. These users employ what are called operational data stores. R-OLAP tools work best in these cases because the relational DBMS used as the back-end database engine provides full transactional support of event propagation.

For creation of consistent data snapshots, either a scheduled delta propagation of events or a complete or incremental refresh can be used. The selection should be based on the following:

- Functionality that can be supported by the back-end database engine
- Amount of time available within the batch window
- Amount of transformation and mapping services required
- Amount of resources—network, CPU, storage, and personnel—needed to support the replication process

Merging and transforming both internal and external data sources

In OLAP environments, data stores usually contain data that is the result of merging and transforming data from both internal and external sources. Firms generally have more control over internal data sources than external ones. When external sources are used in OLTP environments, they are usually the result of some sort of market feed, such as the broadcasting of pricing data for financial trades. In OLAP environments, this external data is merged with the internal recording of the business transaction and becomes part of a historical representation of the complete event. If the data merging takes place as a separate service that is isolated from the replication process, then in all likelihood the transactional nature of each event is discarded. Whenever a loss of transaction semantics occurs, the best asynchronous replication approach is a complete or incremental refresh. However, keep in mind that the refresh type of replication is not desirable for OLAP operational data stores because they require near-real-time data to be of use to query users.

Handling of complex differences in schemata

If the schemata differences between the OLTP and OLAP data stores are such that their complexity goes beyond the transformation and mapping capabilities of the vendor's asynchronous replication alternative, then separate transformational services should be invoked. As stated previously, when these services are invoked, in all likelihood the transactional nature of each event is discarded. This loss of transaction semantics dictates that a refresh type of asynchronous replication be used. Once again, this limits the use of this data store as an operational data store.

Use of proprietary resource managers

The use of proprietary databases in a replication environment presents its own unique set of issues. As stated in Chapter 6, most specialty and proprietary resources managers are stripped of their transactional support functionality in order to provide fast load capabilities. For example, they may not support any logging, they may lock only at the database level, they may support only one writer. In these situations, only a refresh type of asynchronous replication should be used.

TIP

Until proprietary database engines can support the traditional transaction management we have come to expect with DBMS, the event type of asynchronous replication should be avoided. That limitation equates to not allowing proprietary databases to be used for what the OLAP industry refers to as "operational data stores"—data stores that maintain near-real-time data for use with OLAP tools.

A further complication with proprietary databases is the need to perform multiple transformations to get the data in a format acceptable to the proprietary load utility. This can be costly in terms of both time and computer resources. It involves the following tasks: extracting and merging data from multiple sources, enhancing of the data to build the necessary hierarchical summary points, and finally loading the data. These tasks further contribute to making a near-real-time replication solution an impossibility. Near-real-time replication needs the preservation of transactional semantics, only moderate transformations, and a resource manager that can share resources with a constant stream of query users.

Trade-offs associated with a centralized warehouse versus multiple data marts

Implementing a warehousing environment can be done in several ways. Some approaches advocate a top-down, corporate-centric information system; others stress a more conservative, bottom-up, application-centric approach. The bottom-up approach uses application decision-support systems as building blocks to achieve a global warehousing environment. Whichever approach is used, decisions must be made regarding where the data should reside. Data placement can vary from a single central warehouse from which all users, both local and remote, access information, to many distributed data marts that are accessed only locally.

Trade-offs characterize any data distribution decisions. The advantages of a centralized data source for warehousing are as follows:

- *Data viewed by all decision-support users is identical.* Because only a single warehouse exists, the data is totally consistent and has the same degree of latency (timeliness) for all query users.
- *Maintenance and security are relatively simple and straightforward.*
- *The replication strategy is simple.* The replication alternatives used to populate the warehouse deal directly with the primary data sources within the OLTP environment.

The disadvantages to this centralized data approach are as follows:

- *Existence of a single point of failure.* When a failure does occur, all decision-support systems are unavailable to users.
- *Heavy network use.* Because query requests come from both local and remote users, a large remote user base can result in very high network costs.

The advantages of a more distributed data environment for warehousing include the following:

- *Avoidance of a single point of failure within the OLAP environment.* A failure at one node does not interfere with usage at other nodes.
- *High level of performance and availability for all decision-support systems.* Because query users access local data, the time and costs associated with remote access is avoided.

The disadvantages are as follows:

- *Data viewed by all decision support users is* not *identical.* The amount of latency before data consistency is achieved with the

designated primary source(s) is a factor of the replication service used for that target OLAP replica.
- *Administration and security are more complex.*
- *Replication costs associated with maintaining data consistency across all distributed OLAP replicas.*

The data distribution challenge for warehousing is to achieve the optimal mix of centralization and distribution, what I call judicious distribution. This mix should optimize for local use of data, yet centralize for ease of maintaining consistency.

Interoperating with other strategic initiatives

In Chapter 1 the various types of replication were classified as synchronous or asynchronous. The asynchronous approach was further broken down into complete refresh, incremental refresh, or delta propagation of events. Most firms incorporate multiple replication alternatives due to different data latency requirements at various target replicas. In addition, firms use these various technical options for their other inherent, specific features. For example, they may use TP monitors and transaction managers for load balancing and/or to manage distributed units of work to resource managers that may or may not be part of the total replication effort. Due to this mixing of tools and functionality an integration strategy that addresses these interoperability issues is critical.

Integration of synchronous and asynchronous replication in a tier approach

A tier or hubbed approach to replication integration is a good solution when different replication alternatives are used for specific replicas. Different replication alternatives are used across different replicas in such a way that no replica receives replication directives from more than one type of replication alternative. This solution works well for globally shared data. In addition, it illustrates a cost-effective approach for building a firm's network infrastructure. Figure 7.4 illustrates this network infrastructure.

With this approach, the hubbed locations are connected with more robust bandwidths. The tiering from each hub uses less expensive network resources. Each second-tier location is connected to only one of the hubs. The replication characteristics of this model are the following:

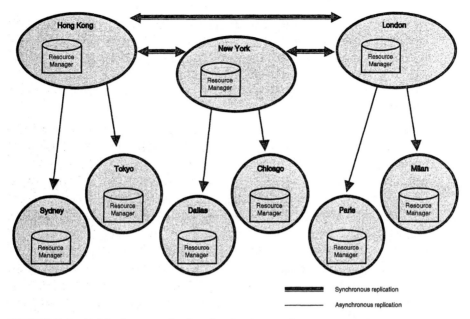

FIGURE 7.4 Hubbed approach of replication integration.

- *Synchronous replication (distributed units of work) used across hubs.* Using synchronous replication across the hubs is workable because the number of hubs is kept small and their network infrastructure is robust. With this model, each hub also serves as a backup for the other hubs. Should a true disaster occur, any second-tier location can be switched to an alternative hub.
- *Asynchronous replication used from hubs.* Each hub acts as a primary source for a designated set of second-tier replicas.

The advantages of using this topology include the following:

- The model is easy to implement and maintain.
- The model is architected to discourage the possibility of multiple deliveries of the same replication directive.
- The model does not need not any conflict detection and resolution mechanism.
- No data schema alterations are required to implement the integration of replication alternatives.

The major disadvantage of using the integration strategy is that it is a somewhat inflexible infrastructure, a trait that could encourage unnecessary data redundancy at hubs.

Integration of synchronous and asynchronous replication across the same data structures

When mixing both synchronous and asynchronous replication across the same data structures, issues arise because of the potential for a target replica to receive the replication directive to update n times where n is a number greater than 1. If only one method of replication is used, the potential for this occurring is zero because the replication service *should* guarantee that each target replica receives the notification to replicate only once. However, when two or more replication alternatives are integrated, only a well-designed integration strategy can prevent redundant updating. Because none of the replication alternatives communicate with each other, the responsibility for this integration falls on the firm's architects and implementers.

Synchronous replication and a messaging type of asynchronous replication integrate more easily than do synchronous replication and a database-to-database communication type of asynchronous replication. When the application is coded to perform a distributed unit of work—synchronous replication—messaging alternatives that include calls to APIs can also be part of the application design initiative. With the database-to-database communication type of asynchronous replication, integration is more complex because application code is not generally part of the equation. Therefore, either the asynchronous replication software must filter out the synchronous replication, or the subscribing replica(s) must be able to identify what update activity was part of the synchronous replication effort. The following case study illustrates the point.

For this case study a distributed primary fragments model is used for the application data design (see Chapter 2). With this model each replica owns a portion of each of the tables and, as such, is the primary source for that portion. However, for this example there is an additional requirement that a few transactions must update across multiple owners within the defined ownership scheme. In financial trading institutions, this would occur where each branch "owns" its deals but certain traders are allowed to trade across the ownership lines—that is, these deals affect more than one fragment. If all data updating for these deals took place at the local branch replica, data conflicts could occur between the designated owner branch for that fragment of data and the trader using the locally owned and non-owned fragments of that replica. To avoid the complexity and possible loss of data integrity associated with conflict detection and resolution schemes, one alternative is to allow multiple fragment trades to be implemented as distributed units of work—that is, synchronous replication. For these trades, the transaction would update synchronously all the primary fragments required to complete the transaction. Asynchronous replication could then be used to keep all non-primary fragments at all other replicas consistent. Note that this is a more complex version of the asynchronous replication example discussed in Chapter 6, where a remote unit of work was used to solve the business problem and ensure that all update activity occurred at the designated primary replicas. A remote unit of work was used because only one primary was affected by the transaction. In the Chapter 6 example, the complication was that the originating transaction was not local to the updatable primary source. With this example, the update transaction must update more than one primary source within its commit scope. Figure 7.5 illustrates this replication infrastructure.

It is possible to implement a distributed unit of work across all the necessary primary fragments and let asynchronous replication be used to bring all non-primary fragments of each replica to a consistent state. However, the flaw with this implementation affects transactional query integrity at all the replicas involved in the distributed unit of work and those receiving all update activity asynchronously. For those replicas that are part of the distributed unit of work where only the primary fragments are updated synchronously, any user querying the local replica will view only part of the complete transaction until the asynchronous replication technique brings the non-primary fragments to a consistent state. This may or may not be acceptable from a business perspective. Similarly, because all replicas are receiving asynchronous updates from a distributed unit of

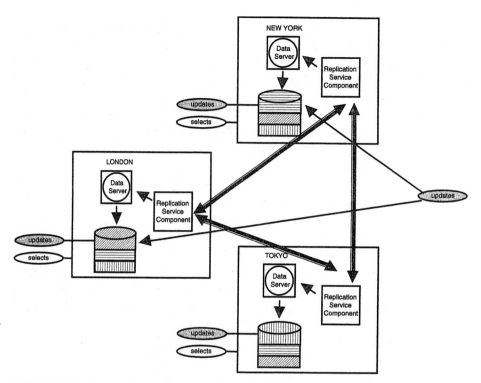

FIGURE 7.5 Case study on the integration of synchronous and asynchronous replication.

work, each portion of the update that occurred at a different location arrives as a separate asynchronous update. Remember that distributed units of work are not reunited at target replicas.

To allow all users to view a transactionally consistent database, the distributed unit of work should update all replicas' primary and non-primary fragments within its commit scope. Every replica is now transactionally consistent; however, each non-primary fragment will receive the synchronous update through the asynchronous mechanism as well. In other words, for this case study the goal is to prevent the synchronous update from being re-replicated asynchronously.

Solution with messaging type of asynchronous replication

When integrating synchronous replication and the messaging type of asynchronous replication, the solution is incorporated into the application design and coding effort. When the application is coded to perform the distributed unit of work (synchronous replication), the messaging alternatives are also incorporated into the code. For this case study, options include the following:

- *No calls to the message publish API.* This would occur if no processes other than the existing application are interested in the synchronous replication event and all primary fragment replicas were included in the distributed unit of work.
- *A single call to the message publish API.* This would occur either if some of the primary fragment replicas were not part of the distributed unit of work and their replicas must be updated asynchronously, or if other processes external to the application being coded were interested in the event. In both cases, the message would contain the necessary data so that the event subscriber could perform the required update activity on its replica.
- *Two calls to the message publish API.* Two different messages could be sent: one uniquely tailored for internal application use (for those distributed primary fragment replicas not part of the originating distributed unit of work) and a second uniquely tailored for external processes that were interested in the event.

Solution with database-to-database type of asynchronous replication

With database-to-database communication type of asynchronous replication either the capture portion must be instructed to ignore specific types of transactions or the database subscriber must be able to filter out all distributed units of work. With these alternatives designers and implementers are not working with the application code, thereby making these solutions more complex.

Two approaches for this replication integration case study will be addressed. Both involve compromises, so the trade-offs should be weighed carefully. The first alternative is product-specific and involves assigning specific user account IDs for designated transactions. The second alternative is generic and involves altering primary data source schemata so that subscribing target replicas can filter out the duplicate replication directives.

The product-specific solution uses the Sybase Replication Server product, which is architected with a log pull type of data capture facility. The apply portion uses a designated account ID to perform all database updating at any given target replica. To avoid the potential for infinite replication loops, the log pull mechanism does not pull transaction data from the log for updates performed by the Replication Server apply account ID called the rs_maint_id. The combination of these facts allows the synchronous replication transactions to be kept out of the asynchronous replication environment. The user account ID that is used to perform the distributed unit of work is the Replication Server apply account ID. The log pull mechanism is instructed to ignore the transactions that performed this specific distributed unit of work; however, the solution is not ideal. The compromise involves the audibility of specific transactions. This solution is based on the internal architecture of the Replication Server product.

WARNING

Care and common sense must be exercised with non-mainstream solutions so that the solution does not become a maintenance nightmare that infringes on future flexibility and scalability.

The second solution that can be used with the database-to-database type of event propagation is to modify the existing data structures. A column is added to the relational tables involved within the distributed primary fragment model. The column is used to identify the type of transaction that was executed to update that row. Subscribing target request can now have the option of subscribing to all update activity or to only the asynchronous updates. In other words, subscribers can use the new column to filter out any synchronous replication update activity. The compromise with this alternative is that the data structures are altered to add integration capabilities to the replication infrastructure. Once data structures are altered, application code must be implemented to maintain these new columns.

Solution with the refresh type of asynchronous replication

Generally there is little demand for integrating synchronous replication and the refresh type of replication technology, largely because synchronous replication is typically not required on data stores that use the refresh type of replication. If, however, integrating synchronous replication with refresh technology is required, then one of the following approaches can be used:

- *Adding a data column to the primary source(s) that can be used as a filter for the extract process.* This is the same process that is outlined above for filtering within synchronous and database-to-database type of asynchronous replication. A column is added to primary sources to identify the updating agent for that row. Then the extract process is coded to ignore the data modified via synchronous replication.
- *Modifying the load utility or transformation services to handle auto-correction.* With this approach, the load utility is modified to handle cases where the data already exists at the target replica. When auto-correction is in effect, inserts are converted to a delete followed by an insert; updates are converted to a delete followed by an insert, and delete "row-not-found" conditions are ignored. If it is not possible to modify the load operation, then this conversion effort can occur as part of the data transformation service.

Integration of various types of asynchronous replication

The approaches identified here can also be used to integrate multiple types of asynchronous replication. However, the major concern with integrating various modes of asynchronous replication involve recovery processing, especially recovering to a specific point in time. When integrating synchronous replication with an asynchronous approach, all synchronous updates are already part of the resource manager log and will, therefore, be part of the restore from log activity. The asynchronous delta event type of propagation queue can then be replayed to catch the events that now need to be reapplied. The complexity arises when trying to resynchronize across two or more separate queuing replication services because each queuing service operates totally independently to the others. To get to the exact same point in time, each queue should have available data fields that can be used to reposition within the queue at the appropriate location to begin the replaying of events with respect to a point in time. Because multiple vendors' asynchronous replication solutions might be used within the firm, there is no guarantee that the same data structures are available or that they can be used for the same purpose. If data integrity is paramount to the business, the recovery process might need to be a complete re-initialization of the damaged target replica.

Implementing the Replication Infrastructure

When implementing replication within a firm, a robust infrastructure is a critical component. The infrastructure includes not only the actual physical and technological environment but also all the best practices (policies, templates, and procedures) needed to support an efficient and effective replication environment. This chapter provides a template for building this required infrastructure.

OVERVIEW OF A WORKPLAN

To establish the infrastructure that will support a replication service, a plan is required. The workplan should include the following tasks:

1. *Define the approach to be used.* Either use a top-down approach by obtaining an organizational commitment or use a bottom-up approach by forming an internal consortium of initial replication users.
2. *Make sure individuals receive appropriate training.*
3. *Establish firmwide standards and procedures across all environments:*

- For roles and responsibilities
- For replication objects and users
- For security
- For data server environments
- For monitoring the replication process
- For administering the replication environment

4. *Define tactical replication infrastructure.*
5. *Define strategic replication infrastructure.*

The following sections expand on this task list. Because all products are unique, the standards identified here should be considered only templates. They should be modified and expanded as appropriate to create a good fit within your firm.

APPROACHES USED TO INSTITUTE A REPLICATION SERVICE

Earlier we defined a replication service as a robust, multitiered environment that provides a complete copy management facility for a distributed, heterogeneous resource manager environment. Meeting this requirement demands an architectural effort and a strong support infrastructure. Establishing the infrastructure can be part of either a top-down or a bottom-up approach; in either case, it does require strategic planning. It is the end product of this planning effort—that is, the replication best practices—that will ensure that replication remains open and scalable, maximizes the efficient use of all resources (network, hardware, software, and people skills), and provides for ease and consistency in administration.

Top-down approach

A top-down approach is initiated with a commitment from upper management. Upper management has been "sold" on the importance of using replication to maintain data consistency across their distributed environment. They have been made aware of the complexities associated with establishing a global replication service and have made a commitment to assigning resources to the tasks necessary to implement a robust infrastructure. This is an ideal situation because it does the following:

- *It provides the necessary commitment.* Tapping the appropriate resources needed to establish critical policy decisions becomes relatively straightforward because all resources are aware of the firm's commitment to this global effort.
- *It creates a culture more willing to modify existing policies.* As replication becomes part of the existing infrastructure, roles and responsibilities will be altered. In addition, replication standards and guidelines will have to be integrated with existing policies. The replication service cannot behave as an entity unto itself; it must exist and interface with the present support infrastructure.
- *It creates a forum for addressing existing infrastructure shortcomings.* Adding replication to the existing infrastructure might serve to point out already overused resources. The sooner these capacity issues are identified, the more lead time is available for correcting the shortcomings.

To get initial management commitment for instituting replication, define business drivers that stress the risk to the business of making bad business decisions due to data inconsistencies. Citing instances where differing values are reflected on what are believed to be creditable data sources and reports illustrates the potential risk. Cite examples within the firm where data is currently being rekeyed into systems. For every reentry process entry errors may occur. Do a cost-benefit analysis of eliminating these parallel efforts. Finally, show how replication can be used to correct these situations.

Bottom-up approach

A bottom-up approach is initiated with a commitment from pockets of potential application architects, developers, and business users. They have repeatedly dealt with users who complain about data inconsistencies and demand that these situations be corrected. These architects and developers are already aware of the role that replication can play, and they know of the complexities involved with making it work correctly at all locations and with, potentially, any and all applications. They appreciate the requirement for an overall strategy that will govern all development efforts, and they are willing to participate in an endeavor to establish the initial guidelines to get replication "off the ground" within the firm. They generally do not have many available resources that can be committed to this formidable task, but they are willing to work with other development teams to establish the initial guidelines and infrastructure. They are fully aware that these initial efforts will be modified and enhanced as other application teams gather under the replication umbrella.

For firms that use this approach, I have found that establishing a Replication Consortium works well. For approximately six months, representatives from each interested area within the firm participate in weekly meetings. At these meetings, the workplan addressed above is executed. At designated times, internal experts are recruited to aid in the resolution of conflicts and help with integrating the new standards with existing guidelines. The final deliverable for the consortium is a Replication Best-Practice Guide that then becomes the framework for future implementation efforts.

A bottom-up approach can be more difficult to implement than one initiated by upper management. The pitfalls to avoid include the following:

- *Lack of common goals across implementation groups.* The goal of this best-practice effort should be to ensure an infrastructure that guarantees efficient replication anywhere. If the guidelines do not resolve this issue, multiple inconsistent replication domains may be established. When it becomes necessary to replicate across these isolated domains one or more applications will have to be reinstalled instead of just migrated.
- *Getting the commitment of time and resources to make the consortium effort a success.* This truly is a case of "pay me now or pay me later." If the initial infrastructure is not strategically architected, much time and effort will be required to correct the interoperability and scalability issues that crop up later.
- *Adding undue complexities to an already complex process.* It is

important for the consortium to leverage existing knowledge within the firm to ensure that the replication service integrates well into the existing support infrastructure. The existing structure includes not only accepted policies but also currently used support tools. If appropriate expertise is not available when specific standards are established, the new replication guidelines could conflict with these acknowledged practices.

The consortium approach does work. However, it does need the commitment of a few core individuals who will keep the "replication ball rolling" in a timely and professional manner, especially when conflicts arise. This is as much a people task as it is a technical one.

Getting the appropriate training and expertise in-house

Vendor-supplied replication software packages are complex products. I have found that using these products is not intuitively obvious. Therefore, appropriate training on both the use of the vendor software as well as the general concepts underlying replication is imperative. The vendor training should help to establish a thorough understanding of the internal architecture of the replication software being used and foster a familiarity with the techniques used to implement the functionality. Those individuals who receive training should either represent a cross-functional team whose members represent the following organizational roles or be responsible for transferring knowledge to appropriate individuals within the following organizational roles:

- System administrators, whose role is to support all system software
- Database administrators, whose role is to support database objects and structures (It is especially important to involve those administrators who support the databases participating in the replication process)
- Data administrators, whose role is to work with business users to define the data and rules used to support the business of the firm

- Security officers, whose role is to define and support the security requirements of the firm
- Network administrators, whose role is to implement and support the communications infrastructure of the firm
- Tactical infrastructure architects, whose role is to perform capacity planning in preparation for the replication infrastructure
- Strategic infrastructure architects, whose role is to integrate and align replication with other strategic initiatives within the firm

In addition to receiving vendor-specific technical training, individuals who will establish replication best practices must also be thoroughly familiar with the firm's other in-house best practices. They should also be conversant with any other industry-compliant standards and policies to which the firm subscribes.

DEFINING FIRMWIDE STANDARDS

To establish a strong support infrastructure for replication, firmwide standards and procedures should be in place. The key to building this infrastructure is getting the correct mix of organizational units involved. This serves two purposes: It serves as a cross-organizational replication training forum and it gets the buy-in of the appropriate organizational groups. The buy-in factor should not be underestimated. When people have an investment in establishing standards and procedures, they understand the reasons for these policies and have a sense of ownership for their enforcement, thereby helping to ensure success. Groups to involve include those identified in the training effort described above.

Applying standards across all environments

As standards are defined for an organization, they should form a basis for all the technical environments supported within the firm. This includes development, quality assurance, production, and any other technical environments that might exist within the firm. Generally, standards and guidelines are created for the production environment first. These same standards are usually applicable to the quality assurance environment because that environment should mirror that of the production arena. For the development environment, *some* standards can be relaxed to some extent. For example, in production, all applications might function within the same replication domain—they are supported by the same physical replication infrastructure. However, in development, each application area might compose its own replication domain. This allows more freedom within the development arena, and it isolates well-behaved development efforts from those that perform poorly. In other words, no development team can negatively affect another team's efforts.

 TIP

All naming standards should be applicable across all environments so that there is no requirement to alter replication object names as an application migrates from development, to quality assurance, and finally to production.

Defining roles and responsibilities—the administrative infrastructure

The various participants who support the replication service have specific responsibilities based on their maintenance role within specific environments. These roles and responsibilities are critical to the firm; any erroneous replication can have serious implications on all subscribing applications. Correcting error conditions in a replicated environment can be much more complex than in a non-replicated environment.

Data Administrators

From a data perspective, it is the role of data administrators to establish the framework by which data enters into the replication service and the rules by which it is applied at subscribing replicas. In essence, it is their job to do the following:

- *Ensure that only the data that a firm allows to be replicated enters into the replication service*

- *Work with security officers to enforce appropriate data security levels*
- *Provide the rules for data transformation and for the apply process at target replicas.* The definition of these rules is a joint effort of individuals who represent the business, application developers and analysts, and data administrators.
- *Ensure good quality data through coordination with business data stewards*
- *Oversee the integration and quality assurance of external data*—that is, data entering the firm from external sources
- Assist with making the meta-data publicly available

Database Administrators

From a database perspective, it is the role of database administrators to support the database objects (stored procedures and triggers) and structures (relational tables and indexes) involved in the replication process. In essence, it is their job to do the following:

- Ensure that database configuration parameters are monitored and tuned to support replication efficiently
- Work with security officers to enforce appropriate database security levels
- Provide full administrative support for all database objects and structures
- Manage database design

System Administrators

From a systems perspective, it is the role of systems administrators to support all systems software, which includes vendor replication software, operating system software, and any other extraneous software used to support the replication process. In essence, it is their job to do the following:

- Ensure that all system software is configured to support replication efficiently
- Maintain secure file structures, and enforce all security guidelines
- Provide full administrative support for all system software, including monitoring and resolving all system errors, and inspecting all log files regularly

- Manage the upgrading of system software and educate others with respect to new system functionalities

Security Officers

It is the role of security officers to define all security requirements for the firm. The replication environment must be fully compliant with the firm's established security policies and procedures. It is the role of the security officers to do the following:

- Establish guidelines for maintaining a secure global infrastructure, which includes file structures, password selection, and encryption recommendations
- Ensure well-selected passwords that change frequently
- Monitor access to and use of sensitive data

Network Administrators

From a network perspective, it is the role of network administrators to support the communications infrastructure of the firm. With respect to replication, it is their job to do the following:

- *Ensure that the network infrastructure is sufficiently robust to support the traffic generated by the replication service.* Capacity planning for replication is critical. If the network infrastructure is not robust, data latency at target replicas increases.
- *Provide full administrative support for all network software, which includes the monitoring and resolving of all network system errors.* The replication service should use networks with approved firewalls.

Defining roles and responsibilities—the implementation infrastructure

The application development team generally defines the requirements for replication and executes the initial implementation effort. In addition to the analysts and coders, the development team also has representatives from the data, database, and systems administration groups. A workplan for this implementation effort is presented in Chapter 9.

Defining standards for replication objects and users

The importance of understanding the internal architecture of the replication software being used cannot be emphasized enough. It is this architecture that can impose restrictions on the replication environment as a whole. These restrictions, if not handled correctly on initial implementation, can limit future flexibility and scalability. One example of this appears in the case where the replication software expects that all published definitions are unique throughout each domain. A domain is a group of replication components and their associated data servers that function as an isolated whole. If early replication initiatives are implemented as separate domains with no established standards, there is a very strong possibility that some duplication in naming has occurred. If this has happened, then either the established domains cannot roll under the same domain (that is, they cannot replicate to each other or replicate to the same target replicas), or one or both must be completely reinstalled with new naming conventions.

Although all vendor solutions are relatively unique given that few industry standards exist with respect to replication, the next sections can be used as templates that help ensure a flexible and scalable environment.

Replication object naming

All vendor replication software has objects created explicitly to support the process of replication. These objects range in scope from technical servers and permanent relational storage tables to published definitions and subscription requests. Appropriate modifications to the templates that follow will be required to merge these recommendations successfully into your firm's established naming standards.

For permanent technical servers, keep in mind the following points:

- *Size and character usage restrictions imposed by the operating environment.* In some situations, naming size might be restricted in length. Also keep in mind that some operating systems are case-sensitive and some software prefers underbars to hyphens.
- *Distributed nature of the organization.* Always try to preserve a naming convention that supports location transparency.

Table 8.1 presents a recommended template for naming server objects, composed of the following components: {ENV} {BU} {APPL}{OBJECT ID} {SEQ NUM}. This combination, with or without slight modifications, should provide a unique identifier.

For publish/subscribe components, keep in mind the following:

- *Names of published objects generally must be unique.*
- *Subscribers need alternatives on which to filter out unwanted data or messages.*

TABLE 8.1 Recommended Template for Naming Server Objects

Template component	Component description and valid values	Additional comments
ENV	Environment identifier: P = production D = development Q = quality assurance	This component is important if multiple environments are supported on the same physical server.
BU	Business unit identifier: Banking examples include: CS = corporate systems TA = trading applications CC = credit card applications	The business identifier represents the business organizational unit owns the application.
APPL	Application identifier: Banking examples include: RM = risk management EB = employee benefits GL = general ledger	The application identifier is an acronym that represents the application name.
OBJECT ID	Object identifier: Sybase Replication Server Example: RS = replication server RA = replicating agent SD = system database (RSSD)	The replication object identifier is specific for each vendor's architecture.
SEQ NUM	Sequence number	A sequentially assigned number that maintains uniqueness across the same type of replication objects that support the same business unit and application.

- *Do not include an environmental identifier.* By omitting the environment identifier, migrating replication publish and subscribe components across environments—moving a published definition from the development environment into the quality assurance and production environments—is very easy.

Table 8.2 illustrates a recommended template for naming publish components, composed of the following components: {OBJECT ID} {APPL}{TBL/MSG ID} {SEQ NUM}. This combination, with or without slight modifications, should provide a unique identifier.

TABLE 8.2 Recommended Template for Naming Publish Components

Template component	Component description and valid values	Additional comments
OBJECT ID	Object identifier: Sybase Replication Server Example: TD = replication definition for a table FD = replication definition for a stored procedure SB = replication subscription	The replication object identifier is specific for each vendor's architecture.
APPL	Application identifier: Banking examples include: RM = risk management EB = employee benefits GL = general ledger	The application identifier is an acronym that represents the application name. If the application identifier is not unique within the firm, preface the application identifier with a business unit identifier.
TBL/MSG ID	Table or message identifier	Character string that represents the table name of the primary source or the message identifier.
SEQ NUM	Sequence number	A sequentially assigned number that maintains uniqueness across the same type of replication object that is primary sourced in multiple locations.

Replication user accounts

All vendor replication software has specific roles that must be assigned to designated account IDs. In addition, some products require that special IDs be created to perform these roles. Security officers should work with system administrators to ensure that these account IDs have only the privileges necessary to perform their specific role. Granting privileges above those specifically needed, or granting additional privileges to already existing account IDs, can lead to the blurring of roles and responsibilities, potential security violations, and complexities for auditors monitoring account ID activity.

TEMPLATES FOR FIRMWIDE PROCEDURES

The following recommendations can serve as templates for integrating replication into a firm's already existing procedures. The goal is simply to point out the importance of having established policies in these areas. It is less important what the policy is than that it exists.

Recommendations for data administration

From a data perspective, procedures should be established for the three participants within the replication environment:

- Providers of primary sourced data, stored procedures, messages or other forms of business rule enforcement
- Subscribers to primary sourced data, stored procedures, messages or business rules
- The replication service itself

Data providers

A framework for data providers should govern the replication by either database-to-database communication or process-to-process communication. To be a provider—a publisher of data—certain required information should be made available to those who have a business requirement to subscribe to that data, stored procedure, message or business rule. Table 8.3 provides a starting point for defining the required meta-data for table replication. Although

TABLE 8.3 Meta-data Requirements for Table Replication

Required information	Example and/or comments
Business name of physical relational table	Customer
Alias names that may exist for this table (optional)	Client
Business description	This structure holds pertinent data about the individual with which the firm does business.
DBMS used for the primary source	IBM's DB2
Table name within the primary sourced DBMS	customer_detail
Business guardian	Name of business unit responsible for: • Maintaining business accuracy of the information • Giving permission for replication • Defining security requirement both internally and externally to the firm
System owner	Name of business unit responsible for administrating the table from a systems perspective. It may or may not be identical to the business guardian.
Business usage indicator	Indicator that reflects the global nature of the information. Options include: • Global • Regional—specific region only • Multiregional but not globally • Local
Typical cardinality and as of date (defines the typical number of rows within the table)	Table typically contains 10,000 rows. At year close, all customers with which the firm has not done business over the last three years are purged.
Typical daily delta change amount: • Via OLTP activity • Via batch processing	Typical daily activity is an insert of 10 rows and updates of 50 rows. Generally delete activity only occurs during the year close processing. At that time typically 2,500 rows are deleted.
Business constraints enforced via indexes	Customer identifiers are unique.
Referential integrity rules supported	If a customer has any open orders or unpaid receivables he or she cannot be purged.
Business constraints enforced via triggers or other mechanisms	On insert new customers become part of a workflow process that performs extensive credit checking. Another more complex business constraint would be that the total dollar amount for a customer order cannot exceed the customer's credit limit.

a relational DBMS table is used for illustration, the concepts can be adapted for other file structures.

Table 8.4 continues defining requirements with respect to meta-data. It addresses the column requirements within the tables identified in Table 8.3. One matrix as represented by Table 8.4 should be filled out for every column involved in data replication.

All of the data requirements that apply to table replication are equally applicable, and in some ways amplified, for the process-to-process type of replication, largely because the process-to-process type of replication is less application transparent than the database-to-database type of replication. Rigorous application quality testing procedures should be in place to ensure that the

TABLE 8.4 Meta-data Requirements for Columns Being Replicated

Required information	Example and/or comments
DBMS and table name as identified in previous matrix	IBM's DB2, customer_detail
Business name of data column	Customer number
Alias names that may exist for this column (optional)	Client number
Business description	Unique identifier that distinguishes each customer.
Business data type	Character
Business data length	7
Business requirements for security	Encrypt for network usage. Requires secure receiving location.
Physical DBMS data name	id_cust
Physical data type	Integer
Physical data length	Byte count is 4.
Nulls allowed	No
Default value	N/A
Allowable values	Stored as integer but only 7 digits are allowed on input.
Integrity constraints: • Intrarow dependencies	Define how constraint is physically implemented.
Integrity constraints: • Interrow dependencies	Define how constraint is physically implemented. For example, for foreign key columns supply the kernel entity and the column name within that entity.

level of data consistency required by the business is supported by the application's apply processes.

For stored procedure replication, all the parameters passed to the stored procedure should have the same attribute-level information as identified in Table 8.4. For messaging, Table 8.5 addresses typical meta-data requirements.

Data subscribers

Subscribers to data and/or processes have various levels of responsibilities, based on their business requirement for maintaining data consistency. Three levels of subscriber responsibility exist. For the database-to-database type of replication, these levels include the following:

- Subscribers who mirror exactly with no alterations to schema or data content
- Subscribers who alter schema and/or data content with no further propagation
- Subscribers who alter schema and/or data content with further propagation to new subscribers

The same three levels of responsibility exist for the process-to-process type of replication. They include the following:

- Subscribers who mirror exactly with no alterations to process functionality and/or parameter content
- Subscribers who alter process functionality and/or parameter content with no further propagation
- Subscribers who alter process functionality and/or parameter content with further propagation to new subscribers

Subscribers whose business requirement dictates an exact mirroring with no alterations to schema, data or parameter content, or process functionality, have minimum responsibility within the replication environment. Their responsibilities include the following:

- Maintaining Database Definition Language (DDL) that mirrors that which resides at the primary source
- Participating in recovery procedures across replicas

TABLE 8.5 Meta-data Requirements for Message Replication

	Information required	*Additional comments*
Header • Contains technical and business details regarding the delivery of the message • Describes the sender of the message • All attributes are public		
	Technical variables required by the message delivery mechanism	Specific to the product being used
	Name of business unit publishing the message.	
	Sender identifier (identifier of individual sending the message)	Used for auditing and administration
	Location of sender	
	Time (Greenwich mean time of when message was sent)	
	Subject identifier (identifier of the message)	
	Name of business event that originated the message	
	Message purpose	
	Expected message response	Options could include: • Process with no response required • Process with an asynchronous response requested • Process with a synchronous response
Content • Contains the actual message data • All attributes are private		
	Self-describing set of one or more data structures or a predefined content structure	

- Performing periodic reconciliation procedures for validation of data consistency

Subscribers whose business requirement dictates altering schemata, data or parameter content or process functionality have greater responsibility. Their responsibility increases based on the amount of alterations implemented. If no further propagation exists, their responsibility includes the following:

- *Maintaining DDL for altered schema that permits replication.*
- *Supporting all cross-mappings to local schema.* With the database-to-database communication type of asynchronous replication, this includes altering and maintaining internal replication objects. With the process-to-process type of asynchronous replication, this includes maintaining application code for the apply process.
- *Participating in recovery procedures across replicas.*
- *Performing periodic reconciliation procedures for validation of data consistency.*

Subscribers whose business requirement dictates an altering of schemata, data or parameter content or process functionality, with the addition of further propagation, have all the responsibilities of the subscribers identified above. In addition, they inherit all the responsibilities identified for data providers, as defined in Tables 8.3, 8.4, and 8.5. In essence, the subscriber has become a provider and, as such, must assume all of the associated responsibilities.

Within this model, it is important to note that the replication service has only the following responsibilities:

- Guaranteeing delivery between providers and subscribers
- Providing tools for managing and monitoring the replication process
- Handling replication distribution errors and recovery

The replication service does *not* modify data content. All changes to data should occur at primary sources where the appropriate code exists for data entry validation.

TIP

Best practices should be in effect to prohibit the changing of data content from within the replication service.

Recommendations for security

Replication software, queuing devices, and user accounts must totally adhere to all the security polices defined for the firm. With respect to replication, the following security issues should be addressed:

- *All stored and/or displayed passwords must be encrypted.* Passwords must be stored securely so that they cannot be obtained by unauthorized individuals or processes.
- *All "pseudo-user" accounts must comply with the firm's security policies.* Pseudo-user accounts are account IDs required by replication software. These accounts perform such functions as database updating at target replicas. Knowledge of these passwords should be limited.
- *All file systems, raw devices, and/or database structures used to store queued data and/or messages must be secure.* The file protection system must ensure against unauthorized access by users and/or processes.
- *Encryption techniques must be able to be integrated within the replication service.* This is especially important when replication occurs outside the firm's firewalls.

Recommendations for change management

Procedures should be established for change management of all components within the replication environment. These components include vendor replication software and primary and target replica structures and their associated replicate objects.

Vendor replication software

Change management procedures for vendor-supplied replication software should address migration procedures from one release of vendor-supplied software to the next upgraded release. Replication software should be able to function with more than one release level within the same environment. If this is not the case—the software requires that all replication participants upgrade to the new release level in order to use the new release functionality—then procedures may have to be established to swap applications not prepared for an upgrade into a staging replication environment until they are ready for the upgrade. They will then be swapped back to the upgraded environment when they are ready. This swapping allows more rapid use of the functionality of new releases.

The release upgrade issue can get quite involved. For example, a new release of a vendor-supplied replication software package might require an upgrade to the operating system used to support that software. Let's suppose a firm uses a replication package that currently runs on a version of Sun's UNIX operating system. A new release of the replication software is obtained that runs only on the Solaris version of the Sun operating system. This involves the initial upgrading of the operating systems of all the servers where the replication components are currently executing. Only after this operating system upgrade is completed can the replication software be upgraded. This requires coordination across the firm. Change management for replication software must integrate into the firm's already established change management procedures.

Primary and target replica structures and their associated replicate objects

Change management procedures should also exist for all objects involved in the replication process itself. These procedures will be both product- and firm-specific, and they will affect both resource manager objects and replication service objects. These procedures should address how to handle any of the following situations:

* *Changes in the number of data elements currently involved in the replication process.* For example, procedures should outline the required task to perform when a parameter for a replicated stored procedure is added, altered, or deleted, or when a heretofore non-replicated column is added to an existing published table definition.
* *Changes in the characteristics of the data elements currently involved in the replication process.* For example, a parameter

passed to a replicated object is currently defined as data type of character with a length of 30 is expanded to a length of 40.

- *Changes in the underlying database object that is to be replicated.* For example, procedures should outline the required tasks to perform when the DDL for a primary source database is altered. If a replicated table is altered so that a new column is added to the existing relational table, a rippling change management effect takes place. The published definition of that replicated table must also be altered. Likewise, at target replicas, the receiving table may also have to be altered. If the receiving table is altered, then the apply portion or the replication process must also be modified to handle the new column.

- *Changes in the underlying structure of a message.* For example, procedures should outline what to do when a parameter within the message content is added, altered, or deleted. A more complex situation occurs when the message header portion must be altered. This type of change can affect the delivery portion of the messaging infrastructure.

Recommendations for quality assurance

The existing quality assurance best practices should easily incorporate the addition of replication testing. Generally, there are two areas of concern. The first is that the replication software is well behaved, and the second is that the applications that use replication services are designed for efficient use of replication technology.

WAN certification of replication system software

When a firm first commits to replication technology, it is a nicety to WAN certify the replication system software within the network infrastructure currently supported by the firm. This establishes a baseline for the network traffic generated by the introduction of replication software. The certification process involves installing the replication software in a controlled environment (a technology lab) and monitoring network traffic with and without replication. Any replication or messaging software will generate some background traffic as components communicate with each other. The firm will want to measure the extent of this background traffic. With replication in place, the firm will also want to establish how well behaved the replication process is. For example, are network packets appropriately filled, and are there ways to send only changed column data, not complete rows? This type of testing is critical if home-grown replication solutions are being used.

While WAN certification is being performed, other resource components can be monitored. For example, how efficient is the subscription resolution engine? This will help with capacity planning for the machines where the resolution engines will reside permanently. It will also help with architecting the final infrastructure with respect to component placement. For example, if background traffic is high for communications between a log pull mechanism and its queuing device, then it is probably not a good idea to have the database log pull mechanism and the stable queuing device at different nodes on the WAN.

The critical aspect of this testing is to get to know the "personality" of the replication software being used. Because no software is ideal, understanding its strengths and weakness allows the firm to maximize its infrastructure and work with any idiosyncrasies within the software. The published outcome of this testing also serves to alleviate any fears within the firm, voiced or not, about the effects of replication on existing resources. An important aspect of introducing new technology is managing people's expectations.

WAN certification of applications using replication software

Once the replication software has been WAN certified, each and every application using replication across the firm's WAN resources should also be certified regarding its behavior as a "good WAN citizen." Because WAN resources are expensive and shared by all users, applications should be designed and coded to use the WAN efficiently.

If an application performs poorly in the WAN lab, consider that a definitive statement about how it will perform within the production environment, where it can also have a negative impact on all other users of WAN resources. Consider the trade-offs associated with allowing this application to move onto production WAN resources. Methods of correcting this situation can vary from having the application designers and coders alter the application so that it makes better use of sharable resources, to increasing the capacity of the sharable resources so that production rollout can occur as scheduled.

Recommendations for recovery

Depending on the type of failure and the types of replication being used, recovery procedures can be either relatively straightforward or very complex. If the replication environment uses only synchronous replication (distributed unit of work) to maintain data consistency, recovery procedures are identical to what would currently exist in any OLTP transactional system. Because synchronous replication uses real-time transactional updating, recovering from database logs is the accepted procedure. Similarly, if only a refresh type of asynchronous replication is used, recovery procedures are identical to what would currently exist in any batch-processing environment. Because the refresh type of asynchronous replication uses full or incremental updating from within a batch window, the recovery procedure would entail restoring the resource managers from a pre-job backup and rerunning the update job. Depending on the refresh load utility being used, in all likelihood a restart mechanism may already be part of the utility.

Recovery complexity for replication is primarily in the realm of the asynchronous event type of replication and in the mixing of multiple replication alternatives. With asynchronous event type of replication, the challenge is that a middle layer between the replica resource managers has been introduced with its own persistent storage mechanism. In some respects, the middle layer for recovery purposes can be thought of as transactions in flight. The updates have been committed at the primary source but have not yet been applied at receiving replicas.

Knowing that recovery within this type of environment can be complex, the following three principles help make the recovery process more manageable:

• *An ounce of prevention is worth a pound of cure.* The more safeguards that can be built into the replication infrastructure to catch a problem before it occurs, the less frequent recovery scenarios must be invoked.

- *Follow the "keep it simple" approach to architecting the replication environment.* The more the replication environment is the result of a well-thought-out design effort, the simpler the recovery scenarios become. If all replicated objects have only one primary source, recovery is simplified because there is no requirement for a conflict detection and resolution mechanism.
- *Be prepared.* Before an application that uses replication is migrated into the production arena, a replication operations and recovery manual should be available to all personnel whose job description includes production support for the replication service. This manual should be replication product-specific, should thoroughly outline all steps to perform for each type of potential failure, should have been thoroughly tested, and should contain the names and beeper numbers of a replication SWAT team who can be called for expert assistance. The manual could be vendor-supplied, but more likely it is vendor-supplied with a good deal of in-house modifications and enhancements.

It is beyond the scope of this book to supply recovery procedures for all vendor replication alternatives, but I will address areas of concern and offer hints and tips for recovering within an event-based type of asynchronous replication environment.

Preventive measures

Table 8.6 presents a list of preventive measures that should help circumvent a large percentage of potential problems. These recommendations should be expanded to incorporate other product-specific measures.

Operations and recovery manual

The operations and recovery manual is generally divided into three sections. The first addresses normal monitoring procedures, the second addresses recovery procedures, and the third addresses trouble-shooting. The recovery procedures should thoroughly outline the recommended tasks for recovering from the following types of failures:

TABLE 8.6   Preventative Measures for Replication Recovery

Replication component	Preventative measure	Additional comments
Primary database in database-to-database type of asynchronous replication	Log size: If a log pull mechanism is used the size of the log should be sufficient to hold the transaction volume equivalent to the anticipated disconnect period.	If a primary database log is full and the truncation points established for the log pull mechanism must be ignored in order to dump the log, recovery becomes complex. Old logs must be restored and replayed for the log pull mechanism, or all target replica(s) must again be reconciled with the primary database.
	Warnings for non-typical transaction volumes: Publishers should be aware of the consequences of producing massively larger volumes of replicated data than they have defined as typical.	Good publishers should alert the replication service support team and/or subscribers when they anticipate producing significantly larger than normal transaction volumes. If this alert is not given, there is a good possibility that the replication service queues could run out of space and/or target replicas will not have enough space in their database log files.
Replication service queuing mechanism	Queue size: The size of the queue should be such that it can continue to receive from publishing sites even during long outages from any and all target replicas.	
	Queue thresholds: Warning levels should be established for queues that alert monitors when certain percentage full conditions are reached.	The lower the percentage values, the greater the amount of time for support personnel to correct the condition.

TABLE 8.6 *(cont.)*

Replication component	Preventative measure	Additional comments
Replication service queuing mechanism (*cont.*)	Queue save intervals: Using only logical deletes for deleting from queues after an event has been received by all target replicas is a method that allows either an individual queue to be rebuilt from its immediate providers or receiving events to be replayed at any target.	
	Queue mirroring: Mirroring queue devices enables continued operation in cases of a device failures.	Generally replication queues should be raw devices or database tables.
Target database with any type of asynchronous replication	Log size: The size of the log should be sufficient to hold the transaction volume equivalent to at least two times the anticipated replication volume. Where volume fluctuation is severe, some firms have established procedures that scan queues and either trigger an alert or stop replication if a defined threshold is reached.	If more transactions than are anticipated are executed at any primary database, there is the potential that the log at any target replica could be flooded.

- *Replication software component failure.* These components include log pull mechanisms, or triggers, subscription resolution engines, and apply mechanisms.
- *Hardware failure.* Hardware failure can occur on the hardware supporting a primary source, a target replica, or a replication software component. Most data servers support some sort of disk mirroring, which will aid with resolving some of these types of failures.

- *Network failure.*
- *Out-of-space conditions;* for example, database log full conditions at either primary or target replicas, or out-of-space conditions on internal replication service queuing devices.
- *Resource manager component failure.*

Recommendations for data reconciliation alternatives

In addition to the aforementioned recovery procedures, it is also imperative to have data reconciliation procedures in place. These procedures are used either to validate data consistency across replicas or to resynchronize data after a replica has become inconsistent. Data can become inconsistent due to any sort of component failure, coding errors within the apply portion of asynchronous replication, or unscheduled dynamic updating performed by support personnel (a database or system administrator).

When replication is first introduced into a firm, these types of procedures are important because they can be used to validate that replication is working correctly. This assures both end users and any doubters within the systems area that replication technology performs as described and is a sound investment. It also validates that the published definitions and subscription requests have been executed correctly and that the apply code is bug-free. Alleviating any doubts and fears about using replication is an important aspect of instituting the replication service. Users must have faith in the technology.

Reconciliation procedures usually consist of running some sort of data compare utility. Many vendor-supplied replication packages come with this type of utility. It can be run in a report mode or a data correct mode. The utility compares the data in a target replica with what is defined as the primary source. It either reports on the differences or updates the replica to match the designated primary source.

After certain kinds of failure this type of utility is invaluable for resynchronizing inconsistent replicas. It is generally faster than reloading a replica, and it can be initialized to validate and/or correct only designated portions of the data. For example, some firms run reconciliation procedures on a weekly basis. They have incorporated within their data a time stamp that is updated every time any data within that relational row has changed. Restricting reconciliation to just that week's designated slice ensures that minimal resources are used in the reconciliation process.

If this type of utility is not supplied with your vendor software or if your firm uses replication software developed in-house, I highly recommend that a home-grown version of this compare utility be developed. It is an extremely handy tool not only for replication validation, but also for debugging apply code.

Recommendations for error resolution

Procedures should also be in place to handle error-resolution alternatives. The goal here is to ensure that after an error has occurred a thorough resolution will be forthcoming. For example, in database-to-database asynchronous replication, an error such as different index structures at a target replica can cause a transaction to fail. Generally, this type of replication software can be configured to send the transaction that caused this specific type of error to an error log file and then allow further replication to continue. However, the software or individuals who monitor the replication process must be alerted to this skipped transaction—the situation warrants attention. Maybe the skipped transaction should be ignored because the differences in index structures between the primary source and the target replica were deliberately created to filter out specific types of transactions. However, the more likely situation is that a new index was added at the target replica to enhance performance and that the target replica does need the transactional update to preserve data consistency. In this situation, the index incompatibilities must be resolved and the skipped transaction reapplied.

Establishing strong error-resolution procedures serves multiple purposes. It helps to catch design and coding errors that slipped through the pre-production testing, and it validates post-production changes that were not thoroughly tested in an integrated environment. Replication spans applications and integrates data from multiple sources. Thorough testing across a heterogeneous environment is not easy. Therefore, strong error-capture and -resolution procedures are critical if the goal of globally consistent data is to be achieved.

Recommendations for administrative tools

Once the software package to be used for replication has been selected, the administrative support staff may want to develop in-house tools and support scripts to aid with the replication's administrative and monitoring tasks. Some suggestions in this area are as follows:

- *Use a spreadsheet to aid with capacity planning.* Spreadsheets can be used to determine queue sizes based on anticipated replication volume.
- *Implement replication hooks for firmwide monitoring integration.* The monitoring and alert procedures currently used within the firm should be integrated into the replication monitoring process. This allows replication monitoring to be integrated into the existing global monitoring tool set.
- *Use a tool to aid with automating replication object creation and modification.* Vendor tools for replication object creation and/or modification may not be as automated or sophisticated as desired. Therefore, in-house scripts and tools can be created to automate the process of creating and modifying published definitions and subscription requests. The scripts for creating published definitions generally read the database catalog of the primary data source(s) and create control statements for definitions with naming standards that conform to those identified within the firm's best practices
- *Develop a tool to reverse-engineer control statements from the replication catalog.* Once the replication objects have been created it saves time to be able to reengineer the control statements from the source where they permanently reside. The

replication catalog represents this definitive source of control statements. Even though developers create a file structure to store all the control statements, sometimes objects are changed dynamically and no control statements are saved. Therefore, executing statements from a saved file structure might not represent the most current version of the replication object.

DEFINE THE TACTICAL REPLICATION INFRASTRUCTURE

Defining the tactical infrastructure is the process of integrating each application that uses replication software into the firmwide replication framework. It addresses such issues as replication component placement and all forms of capacity planning. Chapter 9 defines these tasks in detail.

DEFINE A STRATEGIC REPLICATION INFRASTRUCTURE

Defining the strategic infrastructure is the process of integrating the replication framework with all other firmwide strategic initiatives. Areas of concern include the following:

- *Integration with the firm's commitment to be compliant with designated industry standards.* For example, replication should be integrated with the firm's commitment to use DCE for security and naming services.
- *Integration within the firm's architectural objectives.* For example, the replication solution(s) should be integrated into a three-tier architecture or should ensure reuse of apply code at target replicas.
- *Integration with the firm's existing and future network topology.* The network topology reflects the distributed nature of the organization. Because replication supports distributed applications, its use should mirror data and process distribution strategies.

- *Creation of a replication repository.* A replication repository is a software dictionary that documents all data placement decisions and records the complete picture of primary sources and target replicas. It incorporates replication meta-data from all replication solutions. It is an invaluable tool for disaster recovery because it creates a total portrait of data flow throughout the firm.
- *Interoperating with other strategic replication and messaging services.* For example, templates should be created that help in the selection process for choosing between distributed units of work, database-to-database asynchronous replication, or messaging (See Figure 8.1).

These templates should reflect the strategic direction of the firm and stress the use of preferred technologies. Figure 8-1 illustrates such a template. This template is a decision tree for the selection between various replication alternatives.

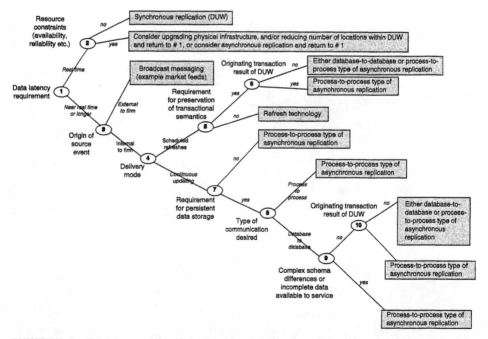

FIGURE 8.1 Decision tree for the selection of replication alternatives.

Reading the Decision Tree for Selecting Replication Alternatives

This decision tree (Figure 8.1) is read from left to right. Each circled number represents a decision point. The question to ask at that decision point is to the left of the circle, and the possible answers—that is decisions—are listed on the paths to the right. At the end of any branch is the most appropriate architectural pattern for the decisions selected along the path. For example, if real time data consistency is required and there are no resource constraints then the architectural pattern to use is synchronous replication.

The ten decision points within this tree are listed below with their appropriate alternatives. The user of the decision tree needs only to follow the path at each decision point that represents the answer selected for that question. At the end of the path is the most appropriate replication alternative for the selected answers.

1. What is the data latency required at the target replica? The possible alternatives are either real time or near-real-time and longer.
2. Are there any resource constraints such as availability limitations, reliability concerns, or network restrictions that could cause the distributed unit of work (DUW) used to implement synchronous replication to fail? The possible answers are either yes or no.
3. What is the origin of the primary source event? The alternatives are that it originated either from within the firm or external to it.
4. What is the user's choice for delivery mode? The possible alternatives are to have continuous replication that occurs throughout the day, or to have scheduled refreshes. Typically scheduled refreshes occur after end-of-day processing.
5. Is there a requirement to preserve the transactional semantics of the originating event throughout the replication process? This would include the capture, the distribution, and the apply components of the asynchronous replication processes. See Chapter 1 for a discussion of this topic. The alternatives are either yes or no.

6. Was the originating event the result of a distributed unit of work (DUW)? The possible alternatives are either yes or no. If a DUW was used for the originating event and a log pull mechanism is used for asynchronous replication capture, the distributed portions of the originating transaction will be delivered as separate transactions to each target replica.

7. Is there a requirement for persistent storage at the target replica? In other words, is the requirement to replicate to the cache of a workstation, or to an actual database? The alternatives are either yes or no. If no database is required for a target replica, process-to-process replication is the better choice.

8. What is the type of communication desired? The options are either process-to-process or database-to-database.

9. What are the complexities of the required data transformation and mapping? Is all the required data that is needed for transformation and mapping decisions available to the replication service? The possible alternatives are either yes or no.

10. Was the originating event the result of a distributed unit of work (DUW)? The possible alternatives are either yes or no. See decision point six above.

This decision tree should be used as a tool to aid with the decision process. None of the variables used within the decision tree were weighted to reflect a firm's preferences, nor was it possible to include all possible variables. Therefore firms should adapt this tool to better suit their particular environment. It should serve as a starting point for the selection process.

Implementing Applications Using a Replication Service

9

The previous chapter addressed the tasks required to implement the replication infrastructure; it took a strategic view of replication. This chapter takes a more tactical look at a replication service. It first explains how to select the initial applications that will use the replication service. It then presents a workplan that outlines the tasks to be performed by the application teams using replication technology. In other words, it provides a template for using the replication infrastructure defined and created in the previous chapter.

SELECTING THE FIRST APPLICATIONS THAT USE THE REPLICATION INFRASTRUCTURE

The first few applications that a firm implements using replication technology should also serve to validate the replication infrastructure. Consider the following guidelines when selecting these initial application candidates:

- *Choose an application with high visibility and low risk.* To qualify as low risk, the application should be well defined and not overly complex. It should *not* have high replication volume with strict performance and latency requirements, nor should it have complex security stipulations. If an overly complex application is selected, any non-scheduled delays could be blamed on the use of replication, which is an unfair assumption.

- *Ensure that the application has the backing of business users.*
- *Guarantee that the application has legitimate business drivers for the use of replication technology.*
- *Choose an application that has an anticipated development time of three to six months with four to six people.* These deadlines should be realistic in terms of number of people, skills available, and functionality desired. Incorporate a slightly longer development time due to the learning curve for replication technology.
- *Select an application that can be delivered successfully.* Set and manage expectation levels of all individuals associated with the implementation.

The initial applications will be a learning experience for all individuals involved in the process. As technical expertise grows, replication volumes and application complexity can increase because performance tuning and configuration skills have been acquired. Therefore, choose initial applications that will allow for a margin of error and time to reevaluate and modify initial implementation decisions.

An application that I have often used as the initial replication application is reference data distribution. Remember that reference data is that relatively stable data that all applications need in a read-only mode. In all likelihood, it is primarily sourced from a central location and is currently distributed via some sort of home-grown nightly extract, file transfer, and load. Applications using this distributed reference data generally have requirements for receiving this data in a more near-real-time manner—that is, with reduced latency. Reference data replication is a good initial application choice because it can be implemented for just one or two locations, it already has a backup application, it has strong business drivers, it has low replication data volumes, and it uses a simple, one-way replication model. Once the replication infrastructure has been validated, rolling other target replicas under the reference data replication umbrella is relatively easy. An additional plus of this selection is that it establishes a global infrastructure for replication by placing required replication components throughout the firm's network.

IMPLEMENTATION TASKS FOR THE SYSTEMS SUPPORT STAFF

To implement the replication environment described in the previous chapter and to install the appropriate software, the firm's systems support group must be intimately involved. Because each vendor's replication software is unique, a detailed workplan for the systems staff is not possible; however, Table 9.1 presents a generalized workplan. The workplan should be adapted to fit each firm's organizational structure and the software being used.

IMPLEMENTATION TASKS FOR THE APPLICATION DEVELOPER

To implement an application that efficiently and effectively uses replication, a workplan is required. The workplan should include the following tasks:

1. Obtain appropriate training.
2. Review the distributed nature of the application design.
3. Validate the selection of the application model.
4. Define specifications for all mapping and transformational service requirements.
5. Define configuration parameters for resource managers.
6. Assist with configuring the replication infrastructure and software.
7. Address any application-specific issues related to the model being implemented.
8. Create the required replication objects.
9. Code and test the application.

10. Test recovery scenarios with replication in place.
11. Certify the application for WAN use with replication in place.
12. Tune for performance.
13. Create thorough documentation.
14. Migrate to the production environment.

TABLE 9.1 Workplan for Building the Replication Environment

Task/Dates completed	Development environment	Test and quality assurance environments	Production environment	Additional comments
Define and create tactical replication infrastructure— systems perspective				
• Preparing for software installation				
validate correct release levels of all system software (Operating System, Database, Network connectivity)				
perform capacity planning (follow the guidelines presented by the software vendor)				
alter the required database objects if a log pull mechanism of capture is being used				
validate log sizes for all primary sources if a log pull mechanism of capture is being used				
if need be, modify database utilities that might currently not write to the log if a log pull mechanism of capture is being used				
validate appropriate network connectivity				
create necessary user accounts				

Task/Dates completed	Development environment	Test and quality assurance environments	Production environment	Additional comments
grant required privileges to replication software user accounts				
have appropriate user accounts create the database objects necessary for the replication software being used				
• Install replication software				
identify appropriate number of domains if required by the replication software				
download tape and follow directions in replication software manual				
• Configure all replication components				
• Create any additional replication objects needed to support the replication software				
• Create data reconciliation procedures for system software components				
• Create procedures for error resolution of system software components				
• Integrate replication monitoring with the monitoring tools currently being used within the firm				
Define strategic replication infrastructure				
• For integration with other strategic initiatives				

NOTE: Abide by all firmwide standards and best-practice recommendations across all environments.

The following sections expand on this fourteen-step task list. Because applications are unique, the tasks should be considered templates. They should be modified and expanded as appropriate to create a good fit within the firm.

Obtain appropriate training

As stated in Chapter 8, vendor-supplied replication software packages are complex products, and their use is not intuitively obvious. Appropriate training on the use of the selected software is imperative. This training should establish a thorough understanding of the internal architecture of the replication software and a familiarity with the techniques used to implement its various functionalities. In addition to this product-specific training, both implementers and support staff need to be thoroughly familiar with all of the firm's best practices. These include the replication best practices, as identified in previous chapters, and all other pertinent policies and procedures. Product proficiency and conformance to the firm's best practices will enable an efficient, scalable, and maintainable replication implementation.

Review the distributed nature of the application design

Review the selected data placement scheme, which is the final deliverable from the distribution methodology presented in Chapter 5. This review confirms that all primary sources for data and processes have been identified and that distribution was judiciously performed. The distribution choices for primary and target replicas is the most important part of the application design effort with respect to replication. Remember that data should be redundantly stored only if the performance and availability gains outweigh the cost associated with maintaining its consistency. In particular, pay close attention to all the constraints that were identified. If not tactically corrected or accommodated by design workarounds, these constraints will impede performance and maintenance.

Validate the selection of the application model

Chapter 2 addresses various application models for replication. Task 6 of the distributed methodology in Chapter 5 asks that one solidify the selection of an application model. This current task reviews that selection. It is closely aligned with the previous task. This review effort should involve not only application team members but also participants from other technical support areas within the firm. Their involvement will ensure that the final design reflects a tactical solution for the application and is fully compliant with the strategic direction of the firm.

The objectives of this review are to ensure that the application model legitimately solves the business problem and can be easily migrated into the production environment. The following checklist should aid with this validation process:

- *Ensure that the data latency requirements of business users at each distributed location are met.*
- *Validate that the rough estimates used to predict replication volumes are correct.*
- *Validate network capacity for all WAN traffic to and from the distributed locations.* Initially consider the traffic generated by the application under development. Include both synchronous and asynchronous replication traffic, plus all traffic associated with any type of remote access. Then readdress this traffic analysis from a firmwide perspective. Consider the current WAN capacity of the involved locations and the current and anticipated use of these bandwidths from all sources.
- *Ensure that the appropriate replication technique is used.* This involves validating that the most appropriate replication alternative is selected. In Chapter 8, Figure 8.1 presents a decision tree that helps resolve this issue. The replication alternative selected must satisfy the business requirements without adding unnecessary support and maintenance overhead. Choosing an alternative that is too sophisticated adds implementation and support costs, while choosing one that requires many enhancements and modifications to meet the requirements is also expensive. The goal is to match the business requirements with the appropriate product functionality. Pay close attention to the

requirements for transactional integrity within the capture, distribution, and apply portions of asynchronous replication. See Chapter 1 for details concerning this topic.

- *Revisit resource-sharing opportunities.* Consider sharing opportunities for hardware, software, data, and processes from within the application and from outside sources.
- *Revisit ownership issues with respect to data, stored procedures, and other reusable processes.*
- *Ensure that all data security requirements, as dictated by the designated owners and/or guardians, are met.*
- *Ensure that all production support issues have been resolved.* This includes the availability of trained support staff for all of the distributed locations.
- *Ensure that recovery specifications have been defined.*

Analyze location requirements carefully because it is not a requirement that the same model be implemented at all locations. For example, a distributed primary fragment model where each source stores a complete replica could be used for large locations that have a high number of users and a strong technical support staff. Smaller locations requiring access to the application could use remote access to one of the larger sites. When and if a smaller location reaches a certain critical mass, a distributed primary fragment could be rolled out to that location. Factors that influence whether a location has its own primary fragment or uses remote access to a more robust location include the following:

- Number of users at the location
- Transaction volume generated from the location
- Volume of data required by query users
- Availability of technical support staff for that location

Define specifications for all data mapping and transformational service requirements

Whenever data is stored redundantly, there is no guarantee that the data schemata are identical. In fact, the schemata used at each replica should reflect the data usage for that replica. Query patterns should be analyzed and used as input into the physical database design. If schemata differences exist between primary sources and target replicas, then some sort of data mapping and possibly transformational services are required.

Mapping and transformational services provide various levels of service complexities across replicas. Replicas can be identical or semantically equivalent. Identical replicas have the same platform, same informational content, and same data types, whereas semantically equivalent replicas have the same informational content but reside on different platforms and possibly have different data type.

Mapping services handle the charting of a primary data element to its replicate counterpart. Transformational services provide for the "repairing" of data content. As explained in Chapter 2, these transformations can include the following:

- Correction for data type mismatches
- Correction for data value mismatches
- Correction for denormalized data structures

 TIP

Transformational services should never change the informational content of the data. If data content is changed, it should always be accomplished through the application processes that maintain the primary data source.

All requirements with respect to data mapping and transformation should be well defined. Depending on the replication mechanism being used, the replication service can provide some of these services. Once the mapping and transformation requirements are complete, the development team must also address differences in index structures between primary sources and target replicas. These differences in indexes can cause some replication efforts to fail. The potential for failure should be identified as early as possible within the application life cycle. Once identified, the business rules across the replicas should be examined to pinpoint any conflicts. Conflicts should be resolved among the appropriate business users.

Define configuration parameters for resource managers

The configuration parameters for all resources managers (databases) should be defined. This includes resources managers that store primary sourced data and those that store target replicas. Chapter 6 supplies reference material concerning these topics. Parameters and issues to consider include the following:

- *Release and "fix" levels.* Resource managers that act as primary sources may have to be at more current release levels than those that act only as target replicas. This is particularly true if a log pull mechanism is used for the capture process.
- *Sort order.*
- *Character set.*
- *Time services to be used across all resource managers.* Possibilities include the use of DCE or NSP.
- *Data server mirroring requirements.*
- *Data types to involve in replication.* This is important because some replication products do not support the replication of all data types.
- *Data server log size.* This is important for primary source resource managers if a log pull capture mechanism is used as well as for all target replicas.

Assist with configuring the replication infrastructure and software

Every application team planning to use replication should abide by all the best practices defined in Chapter 8. In addition, they must also supply critical application information with respect to replication volumes and recovery requirements to those individuals whose job it is to install the replication software and configure the replication environment. In that sense, every replication software installation is unique, and it must be tailored to meet the requirements of the application being developed.

Topics that should be addressed jointly by the systems and

network support staff and the application developers include the
following:

- *Capacity planning with respect to replication software.* Areas of
  concern include anticipated replication traffic from each primary source and the length of time queuing devices might need
  to store data in transit due to the unavailability of any target
  replica. Another area to address is the length of time that data is
  allowed to stay on the queuing device(s) after it has been applied
  to all targets. This additional save time is sometimes referred to
  as the *save interval.* Having a long save interval makes recovery
  from certain types of failures quite simple and straightforward:
  One can just replay the appropriate apply queues. The anticipated traffic from each primary source is used to size the capture mechanism and the stable queuing device(s) used in the
  distribution process. The save interval is critical with respect to
  sizing the stable queuing device(s) and ensuring that additional
  storage segments are available when and if the need arises.
  These capacity planning figures should also be forwarded to the
  support staff for the production environment. Remember that a
  lead time is required for attaining additional storage devices.
- *Placement alternatives for replication software components.*
  Replication volumes, types of capture and apply mechanisms,
  and network capacities help to determine where the components of the replication software should be placed within the
  firm's physical infrastructure. Placement has an impact on
  the quality of service provided.
- *Recoverability alternatives for replication software components.*
  Depending on the recovery requirements of the application,
  various recovery alternatives can be implemented for replication software components. If queues are used as part of the
  store-and-forward mechanism, decisions must be made with
  respect to what mirroring techniques should be implemented.
  Options include RAID (redundant arrays of inexpensive
  disks) devices (see glossary) and software approaches. All
  replication software recovery requirements should be clearly
  defined at this time. The implementation and testing of recovery scenarios occur within a later task.

Address any application-specific issues related to the model being implemented

Some replication models are relatively simple to implement and administer while others are more complex. Whichever model is selected, in all likelihood it will not only be adopted but also adapted. Some examples of the areas where adaptation may be necessary include the following:

- *Implementing logical deletes versus physical deletes.*
- *Adding a "date/time" field to aid with data reconciliation efforts.* This can be used to narrow the scope of the reconciliation process.
- *Integrating enhanced security for sensitive data.* For example, data encryption for WAN traffic or non-repudiation scheme can be integrated.
- *Altering database objects that may be affected by replication.* Chapter 6 thoroughly addresses these database issues. An example would be reviewing database triggers to avoid duplicate updates at target replica(s).

These issues generally are not specific to a particular model, but some models do have specific issues. For example, when using flavors of the distributed primary fragment model, it is important to validate that fragment ownership has been defined and that a technique for ownership transfer has been outlined, if applicable. Other modeling concerns include the assignment of globally unique keys across multiple primary sources and the use of database partitioning at either primary and target replicas. Chapter 6 addresses these topics in detail and can therefore be used as a checklist for model modifications and enhancements.

If the application under consideration involves the replication of data between OLTP and OLAP environments, then specific application issues must be addressed. These issues include the following:

- *Identification of the means that will be used to distinguish the changed records within the OLTP environment.* If a complete refresh approach is used, this is not an issue; however, if an incremental refresh is used then some mechanism must be incorporated into the primary data sources to identify what data should be extracted and used for the incremental load. Possible approaches include the adding of a "date/time" column to all database tables so that this column is updated whenever any data within that row is modified, or the altering of the application code that supports the OLTP databases to write changed data to an additional output file. Either of these approaches requires some modification to existing systems. Keep in mind that some vendor products will aid with this effort by providing both data extraction and transformational services for the refresh type of asynchronous replication. If a database-to-database type of event propagation is selected as the asynchronous replication approach, then the replication middleware collects the changed data in an application transparent manner. The only issue is the question of whether the replication middleware can handle the complexity of the mapping and transformation services that may be required. If a process-to-process type of event propagation is used, the message apply portion should be able to handle any complexities with respect to mapping and transformation services, but the application code that supports the OLTP databases must be modified in order to build and "put" the message on a message queue.

- *Identification and building of any additional aggregates that should be persistently stored within the database.* Once the OLAP query tool(s) and query patterns have been identified, it might be necessary to incorporate additional data aggregates within the database to meet the service-level requirements of the query users. These new data elements must be supported by both the transformational and replication services.

- *Identification and implementation of a system that will be used to assure quality in the OLAP data environment.* This task entails ensuring that all primary sources have sent their relevant data to the OLAP environment, that all transformational and apply components have worked correctly, and that all users have been notified regarding the degree of quality of the data. Because a warehousing environment represents a specified picture of consistent data, users of the warehouse must know the status of their environment. For example, they should know if all of the data suppliers have reported in, if a large amount of data posed exceptions to the transformational service, or if built-in validation totals have registered significant mismatches. They may still elect to use the OLAP environment for querying, but they are using the environment with full knowledge of the quality of the data. They should be sophisticated enough to interpret and possibly adjust their query results as they deem appropriate.

Create the necessary replication objects

In Chapter 8, one of the suggestions in "Recommendations for Administrative Tools" was to develop tools or scripts that would help automate the process of creating and modifying replication objects. Here is one of the important places where these tools and scripts are used. Because vendor-supplied tools for this creation effort usually fall short of the sophistication desired, use of home-grown alternatives can truly shorten this tedious task. In general, these scripts read the database catalog of the primary data source(s) and create published definitions with naming standards that conform to those identified within the firm's best practices.

Additional hints and tips for creating replication objects include the following:

- *Abide by all naming standards for replication objects, hardware, and software components.* This will simplify the migration to production effort because no recoding or component renaming will be required. See Chapter 8 for suggestions.
- *Create a well-organized file structure to store scripts, input templates, and output control statements.* The more organized the implementation, the easier it will be to find specific objects when anything needs to be recreated.
- *Take regularly scheduled backups of the directories that store the object create scripts and control statements.*
- *Execute replication object control statements only from saved files.* If objects are created or changed dynamically then there is no recorded history of what was executed. This makes it difficult to recreate objects. If a reverse-engineering tool has

been developed that can recreate objects from the replication catalog, then this recommendation can be relaxed.

- *Develop procedures that handle the tasks associated with modifying the existing primary sources and target replicas.* During the course of application development, database and replication objects will be recreated multiple times. Procedures to help with this recreation process are valuable. For example, in a relational environment, these procedures would handle adding a new table, altering an existing table, and dropping and recreating either a source or a target table.

Code and test the application

When replication is being used, additional tasks must be incorporated into the application coding and testing effort. Some of these tasks are replication product-specific, but most are required for all development efforts. A typical listing of these additional tasks follows:

- *Define, code, and test the mechanisms to be used for initializing target replicas.* The approach could be a complete refresh from the primary source or a complete refresh from a backup with subsequent replay of the current day's activity. Some replication products provide tools to help with this initialization effort. However, remember that when the application migrates into the production arena there might not be the luxury of a batch window in which to generate a complete snapshot of the primary sources. In addition, primary data sources and application teams do not want to be negatively impacted during the initialization effort. It is generally best to limit WAN usage during all initialization efforts. For example, do not execute a slow build process across the WAN; instead do a complete extract of the primary source, compress the file, and use FTP (file transfer protocol) to send it to the target location where an uncompress and a load are executed. If the primary source is in constant use, reconcile only for the missing transactions across the WAN.
- *Define, code, and test data reconciliation procedures.* Reconciliation procedures will initially serve to validate that the replica-

tion infrastructure and procedures are performing correctly. This is important because some bugs will be discovered. These reconciliation procedures can also be used for other purposes. As specified in Chapter 8, they can be used to alleviate the fears of any doubters regarding the maturity of replication technology. They can also be used in the production environment to resynchronize a target replica with its primary source(s) after certain types of failures.

- *Define, code, and test scripts to add and/or alter authorities on target replicas.*
- *Define, code, and test scripts to handle any of the database conditions identified in Chapter 6.* Examples include scripts to remove or alter triggers at target replicas and scripts for modifying nested transactions.

Test recovery scenarios with replication in place

The development and testing of application-specific recovery scenarios is a critical part of preparing the application for production rollout. With respect to replication, the following types of failures should be incorporated into the application's recovery plan:

- Failure of any replication software component
- Failure of the store-and-forward queuing devices
- Out-of-space conditions of the store-and-forward queuing devices
- Long outages at publishing and/or subscribing locations
- Unrecoverable resource manager error at publishing and/or subscribing locations
- Capacity shortages of hardware and software supporting the replication processes
- Out-of-space conditions at a primary or target database, such as log full conditions at a primary or target database

Because replication products differ in their architectures, there are no standard procedures that can be used for recovery. Every product, though, does have an Administration Guide. Within that manual, one should find recommendations and template procedures to handle all of the failures just described. With replication, the support issues are much more complex than the application implementation challenges. Having all recovery scenarios thoroughly tested and documented before the application migrates into the production environment is extremely prudent.

Certify the application for WAN use with replication in place

All applications that use a firm's WAN resources should be tested in a controlled environment before they are allowed access to these sharable production resources. This certification effort ensures that each application behaves as a "good WAN citizen." If the tenets defined in Chapters 5 through 8 are followed, then the application should have a good data distribution strategy, have databases designed for efficient use of replication, and be architected with a good physical replication infrastructure. In essence, the application should easily pass WAN certification.

A certification committee should review the results of the lab testing effort. The goal of the committee is to be the guardian of the network resources. If the application and the replication processes are not well behaved, then some redesigning or tuning should be explored to correct the poor resource utilization.

Tune for performance

Once the results of the certification testing are complete, the next task is to review those results for areas where tuning can improve performance. Areas to consider include all hardware, software, and network components, as well as replication component placement decisions. Hardware tuning addresses capacity issues for memory and for devices. It also includes upgrading hardware to incorporate more CPUs. Newer software is designed to exploit hardware functionalities.

Software tuning addresses all configuration parameters used for installation. This is a complex area, but it offers many opportunities to increase performance. If software expertise is not available in-house, then contact either the vendor or a specialty consulting firm. Software tuning is generally not accomplished through exploring vendor manuals. It requires extensive use of the software in question. If outside resources are used for tuning, have in-house personnel involved in all aspects of this effort. The goal should be to tune the software and achieve a complete knowledge transfer during the tuning effort. This allows in-house expertise to grow and gives the firm the biggest bang for its consulting dollar.

WAN certification will also expose areas where network capacity could be increased. Even though this type of infrastructure enhancement is costly, the gains in performance it yields can be significant. An inexpensive modification that can also improve performance is the altering of the placement of replication components.

Create thorough documentation

In addition to the traditional documentation produced during any development life cycle, some replication issues should be addressed:

- *An expansion of the Administration Support Manual to include replication-specific topics.* These topics include application-specific procedures for replication monitoring, error handling, and recovery.
- *A comprehensive where-used listing.* The listing represents the actual physical implementation of the application model selected in Chapter 5. It should show all the hardware, software, data, and process components used within the application. As mentioned earlier, this production repository is an invaluable tool for any sort of change management issue. Most replication software products include within their components a replication catalog. This catalog can be considered a poor man's replication repository because it generally lists the publish definitions and the subscription requests controlled by that instance of the software. At a minimum, the where-used listing should incorporate a listing of all published objects created by this application and a listing of subscribers to these objects. This listing should be used as input into the cor-

porate replication repository identified in Chapter 8, which lists replication objects across all the replication alternatives used within the firm.

Migrate to the production environment

With all of these tasks completed, the application can now be rolled out to the production environment with complete assurance that it will fit well into the global replication architecture and physical infrastructure. Decisions regarding replication component placement and opportunities for physical sharing of replication components have already been identified. All that is required is to implement those decisions.

THE "GOLDEN RULES" FOR APPLICATION DEVELOPERS

If the following basic rules are obeyed, then most pitfalls associated with implementing replication can be avoided:

- *Do not make the implementation more complex than necessary.* Replication is an interesting and challenging technology, but do not use technology for technology's sake. Replication should not be viewed as a solution looking for a problem.
- *Make sure that the application model solves the entire business problem.*
- *Abide by all standards defined in the firm's replication best-practice guide.*
- *Use phasing-in strategies for complex replication implementations to help lower the risk.*

Section  **III**

Case Studies

Case Study 1—Using Replication within an OLTP Environment

This case study illustrates the effective use of data distribution and replication in an OLTP environment. The requirement is for the distribution of processes and data to multiple investment trading locations. The results of these trades will later be merged and consolidated for use within an OLAP environment. The OLAP portion of this problem is developed in Case Study 2 in Chapter 11. In other words, this chapter builds the operational trading environment, which is further expanded into a decision-support system in Chapter 11.

Due to the necessity for a high level of data integrity, the application model to be used for asynchronous replication must be based on the master/slave model. Government regulations would not allow an update-anywhere model where compensating transactions were allowed to alter the trading event after the fact.

OVERVIEW OF BUSINESS PROBLEM

A global investment banking institution needs to implement a trading application that traders who operate out of 12 global locations can use. Because of the nature of the trading business, the online transactions must be short and the infrastructure must provide a high degree of availability and reliability. Traders want to make deals—for them, time is money.

Assumptions and requirements regarding the environment include the following:

- All reference data needed to validate and complete trades is maintained by legacy systems on a mainframe in New York. This reference data should be replicated asynchronously to all locations where trade information is stored locally.
- At present, there are 12 trading branches. The service-level requirements for applications that perform trade entry are traditionally very strict; they demand very fast response times for all users of the application, regardless of the location of trade entry.
- All back-office trade processing occurs in one of two international hubs. One hub in New York services North America, South America, the Far East, and Australia; and a second hub in London services Europe and the Middle East.
- Results of all trades are forwarded to the appropriate regional center for back-office processing and subsequently forwarded to the headquarters in New York. This occurs as part of the nightly batch processing. In addition, all global positions and risk are maintained in near-real time in New York and appropriately adjusted after back-office processing at each regional center.
- The trading environment should be available to all traders as per the requirements identified in the physical infrastructure profile, which is defined in "Prepare a Physical Infrastructure Profile" later in this chapter. Global risk management, which is performed out of New York and Frankfurt, is beyond the scope of this application. What is in its scope is the requirement to forward the results of each trade to the global risk management system in New York.
- Normally each trader is assigned to a specific trading book, and all trades executed by that trader are against that book. There are, however, a few exceptions to this rule. Certain types of financial instruments are traded across books. For these deals, all global data sources affected by that trade must be updated as part of a single unit of work. In addition, the trader who

would normally support that book must be notified that a trade was executed against a book that he or she supports. The notification must take place in near-real time so that the normally assigned trader can modify the trading activity accordingly.
- Data distribution and replication services for this OLTP environment must be scalable and flexible so as to support future expansion initiatives. The firm anticipates opening new trading branches in emerging markets.

APPLYING DATA DISTRIBUTION METHODOLOGY

The distribution methodology presented in Chapter 5 is used as the workplan for the following section. All data distribution decision points associated with this case study will be thoroughly identified and explained.

Prepare an application distribution profile

As identified in the distribution workplan, the objectives of this task are to describe the distributed nature of the application and to start solidifying network requirements. The suggested deliverable is an application distribution profile. To complete this profile, it is necessary to know the potential deployment locations and understand the processing requirements of the trading application. Table 10.1 illustrates a completed profile for this case study.

Note that traders not only perform trade entry but also do some analysis and reporting, which supports the trade entry process. These are quick querying reports in that the average number of report rows returned to the trader is less than 20 rows 90 percent of the time. It is anticipated that these reports will be executed against the production OLTP databases.

Prepare a physical infrastructure profile

The objectives of this task are to document the physical resources available at each potential deployment location and to identify any potential distribution constraints. The suggested

TABLE 10.1 Application Distribution Profile

Application Name: Case Study 1—Replicating Within a Global Trading Environment

Location types	Locations	User types anticipated numbers	Business transactions with anticipated execution rates
Headquarters	New York	Global risk manager (1)	Global risk analysis (40/daily)
			Consolidated reporting (90/daily)
Regional processing centers	New York		Back-office trade processing (nightly)
	London		Back-office trade processing (nightly)
Trading centers	New York	Local traders (50)	Trade entry (5,000/daily)
			Local reporting (2,100/daily)
	Chicago	Local traders (30)	Trade entry (2,200/daily)
			Local reporting (1,200/daily)
	Los Angeles	Local traders (20)	Trade entry (1,600/daily)
			Local reporting (900/daily)
	Mexico City	Local traders (7)	Trade entry (280/daily)
			Local reporting (300/daily)
	Buenos Aires	Local traders (8)	Trade entry (320/daily)
			Local reporting (160/daily)
	Tokyo	Local traders (9)	Trade entry (680/daily)
			Local reporting (400/daily)
	Singapore	Local traders (10)	Trade entry (700/daily)
			Local reporting (400/daily)
	Sydney	Local traders (7)	Trade entry (380/daily)
			Local reporting (290/daily)
	London	Local traders (40)	Trade entry (3,700/daily)
			Local reporting (1,700/daily)
	Paris	Local traders (25)	Trade entry (1,800/daily)
			Local reporting (1,000/daily)
	Milan	Local traders (7)	Trade entry (500/daily)
			Local reporting (300/daily)
	Frankfurt	Global risk manager (1)	Global risk analysis (40/daily)
		Local traders (9)	Trade entry (900/daily)
			Local reporting (400/daily)

deliverable is a physical infrastructure profile. To complete this profile, it is necessary to know the existing physical infrastructure at each potential deployment location and to be aware of any possible constraints that exist within the environment. After conducting the appropriate interviews and examining the existing documentation, the application developers completed the profile. The results of their efforts are illustrated in Table 10.2.

Note that there is a requirement that local trade data be stored at Frankfurt due to governmental regulations. Compliance with this regulation is essential.

Figure 10.1 graphically represents some of the data accumulated thus far. Depicting the details within an illustration is often very useful. Figure 10.1 illustrates the existing global network topology.

Create referentially tied data recovery groups

The objectives of this task are to identify data recovery groups and to identify potential opportunities for implementing data partitioning by physical location.

The approach used to complete this task includes all the steps outlined in Chapter 5. After thorough analysis of the entity relationship diagram prepared for this application by the data administration team, the following data recovery groups were identified:

- *Tightly tied trade transaction data.* This transactional data must be recovered as a set.
- *Weakly tied reference data.* This data is primary sourced by applications that reside on the mainframe and is persistently stored in DB2/MVS. It is required by the trade entry processes for validation purposes. It is always used in a read-only mode and can have a near-real-time consistency with the updatable trade data.

It was decided that reference data should be replicated to all processing locations where trade data will be persistently stored. Because its updatability is orthogonal to the trade data,

TABLE 10.2 Physical Infrastructure Profile

Application Name: Case Study 1—Replicating Within a Global Trading Environment

Location/ Location type	Network connectivity (WAN and LAN)	Hardware resources (e.g., servers)	Software resources (e.g., OS, DBMS)	Security level code	Availability level code	Administrative support and constraints	Additional constraints and concerns
New York /Headquarters, Regional processing center, Trading center	T1 line—London, 256 kB—Chicago, 256 kB—Los Angeles, 64 kB—Mexico City, 64 kB—Buenos Aires, 128 kB—Tokyo Token Ring and Ethernet	1 IBM mainframe host, 1 Sun SPARC 2000	• IBM MVS • Sun Solaris • IBM DB2/MVS • Sybase SQL Server • Sybase Replication Server	High	7 × 24	Full support	
London /Regional processing center, Trading center	T1 line—New York, 128 kB—Frankfurt, 128 kB—Paris, 64 kB—Milan Token Ring and Ethernet	1 Sun SPARC 1000	• Sun Solaris • Sybase SQL Server • Sybase Replication Server	High	7 × 24	Full support	
Chicago /Trading center	256 kB— New York Token Ring			High High	14 hours/day 7 AM–9 PM local time	Full support during operational hours. Remote support provided by New York.	
Los Angeles /Trading center	256 kB—New York Token Ring			High	14 hours/day 7 AM–9 PM local time	Full support during operational hours. Remote support provided by New York.	

Location	Network	Hardware/Software	Priority	Hours	Support	Notes
Mexico City /Trading center	64 kB—New York Token Ring		High	12 hours/day 8 AM–8 PM local time	Limited local support. Remote support provided by New York.	
Buenos Aires /Trading center	64 kB—New York Token Ring		High	14 hours/day 7 AM–9 PM local time	Limited local support. Remote support provided by New York.	
Tokyo/Trading center	128 kB—Tokyo 64 kB—Singapore 64 kB—Sydney Token Ring	1 Sun SPARC 51 • Sun Solaris • Sybase SQL Server • Sybase Replication Server	High	7 × 24	Full support	
Singapore /Trading center	64 kB—Tokyo Token Ring		High	14 hours/day 7 AM–9 PM local time	Full support	
Sydney/Trading center	64 kB—Tokyo Ethernet		High	14 hours/day 7 AM–9 PM local time	Full support	
Paris/Trading center	128 kB—London Token Ring		High	12 hours/day 7 AM–7 PM local time	Full support	
Milan/Trading center	64 kB—London Token Ring		High	12 hours/day 7 AM–7 PM local time	Limited local support. Remote support provided by London.	
Frankfurt /Trading center	128 kB—London Token Ring		High	18 hours/day 5 AM–11 PM local time	Full support locally. Remote support provided by London.	Local regulations require trade data to reside within the country.

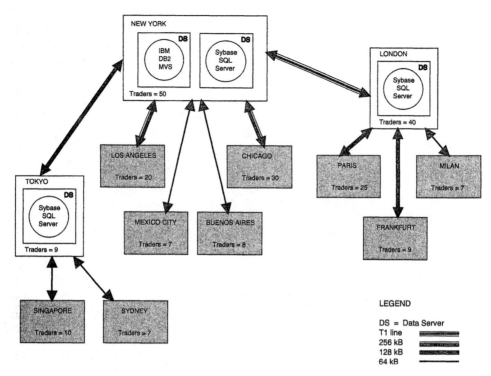

FIGURE 10.1 Case Study 1—OLTP environment network topology.

using near-real-time replication will meet the data latency requirements and still preserve data integrity. In the past, this reference data was delivered to trading application by means of a nightly batch update process; however, the firm experienced a significant trade rejection rate. Within the last six months the firm has implemented a reference data replication service that uses a database-to-database type of asynchronous replication to deliver the necessary reference data in a manner that is totally transparent to both the existing supplier applications on the mainframe and the subscribing distributed targets. The transactional integrity of the originating event is preserved throughout the capture, distribution, and apply portions of this asynchronous replication service. The developers of this trading application have decided to take advantage of the reference data replication service. Details on how they subscribe to this service are explained as the case study unfolds.

With respect to data partitioning, each trade entry location must incorporate a branch code as part of the trade entry process. This is required because all trades are forwarded to their designated regional hub for back-office processing where trader commissions, risk assessments, and the like are appropriated by values that vary across branches. This branch code column is a perfect candidate for use as a data partitioning key because the firm already divides itself organizationally along the values used within this column. Because partitioning by branches will be used, it was further decided that each branch's trading system will represent its own recovery group. Backups will be scheduled as part of each branch's end-of-day processing.

Prepare a process-to-data use profile

The objectives of this task are to identify data use across application processes and to highlight "heavy-hitter" processes. A CRUD matrix was produced that illustrates this use. This matrix will validate the partitioning scheme and data schemata created in previous tasks. A very simplified illustration of this matrix is depicted in Table 10.3.

Integrate global data usage with process-to-data use profile

The objectives of this task are to integrate global data usage with the application's process-to-data use profile and to negotiate service-level agreements. For the trading application under consideration, this entails identifying source databases that supply read-only reference data to the trade entry process (that is, external inputs) and notifying the global risk management system (external output). This identification process names the data guardian of each data source and describes the current business use of each piece of data that will be used as input to the trade validation process. This task also identifies the data that must be included as part of the global risk management notification process. In essence, the data flows into and out of this trading application are identified.

In addition, service-level agreements are negotiated. For

TABLE 10.3 Process-to-Data Use Profile (CRUD Matrix)

Application Name: Case Study 1—Replicating Within a Global Trading Environment

Entity => Process:	Customer	Customer Acct	Finc Acct	Position	Instru- ments	Trade Details	Confirm	Settle	Currency	Branch	City	Cntry	Empl	Trader Risk
Get customer info	R	R												
Add trade*	R	RU	R		R	C			R	R	R	R	R	RU
Update financials*		R	RU			R								R
Update risk*			R	RU		R								
Create confirmation	R	RU	RU			R	C							
Create settlement	R	RU	RU	R		R		C						

*Identifies "heavy-hitter" processes

this trading application, the following service-level agreements are required:

- *Roles and responsibilities for the receiving of read-only reference data from mainframe systems.* As stated earlier in this case study, the firm has already implemented a reference data replication service. Multiple applications currently receive their read-only reference data by means of this service. The replication service is well defined and cost-effective for the firm. To receive reference data, application developers need to negotiate a service-level agreement with the owners of the reference data replication service. Owners of this service have a repository that lists available reference data, full descriptions of data content, security requirements for persistent storage and for distribution across a network, and all algorithms that might be necessary to transform the data for trading use as per predefined business rules. Data change rates are also identified. For the application developers of this trading system, this part of the process is like "going shopping." They read data "nutritional labels" and choose the required items. What has to be spelled out within the service agreement is the latency requirement for each target replica, an assurance that all security requirements will be met, and a decision as to whether there should be a warning system to alert the trading applications if the volume of reference data should ever fluctuate greatly. Because the reference data replication service is a well-established service, they guarantee reference data delivery to targets by means of an asynchronous database-to-database communication process within four minutes 90 percent of the time as long as sufficient network capacity exists for that target. It is the responsibility of the application development team to perform the necessary network evaluations. In addition, the service provider offers two levels of alerts; one is a manual process that notifies targets when designated data volumes exceed specified rates, and the other is an automated implementation of the same functionality. Because the reference data needed by this trading application has very low change volumes, it was decided that a manual alert process was sufficient and definitely the cheaper of the two options. Part of the service provided by the replication service support team is that it creates a reference data database at each designated target and provides a recovery service and error notification when any replication failures occur. It was agreed that the application developers would perform network evaluations and be responsible for ensuring that the appropriate bandwidths are available. A preliminary agreement was negotiated.

- *Identification of the mechanism that will be used to notify the global risk management system.* The mechanism used for notification must support the data latency requirements for risk management users. For this OLTP application, it will definitely be an asynchronous replication mechanism because the trade entry process must be completed quickly. It is unacceptable for the trade entry process to fail because the risk management system could not be notified as part of the same unit of work, that is, synchronously. This explains the application requirement that all global positions and risk are maintained in near-real time, not in real time. Therefore, an event propagation type of asynchronous replication will be used. Because multiple trading applications are required to notify the risk management system, the firm has implemented a risk management message queuing service. This message queuing service uses a process-to-process communication type of asynchronous replication. It is technically based on a store-and-forward paradigm. The application development team decided to make use of this messaging service, based on the fact that a message specification template and the risk management apply code already exist. Reusing these components will shorten the development life cycle for this trading application, will ensure apply-code consistency, and is cost-effective. After thorough analysis, it was verified that all the data needed to fill the message envelope was available during trade entry and that the apply process could be reused with no modifications. A service-level agreement between the risk management messaging service providers and the OLTP application team was negotiated. It states that asynchronous replication to the risk management system in New York will occur with a maximum latency of four minutes 90 percent of the time and that messages will be archived for a duration of 48 hours for recovery and replay purposes.

Create data placement scheme

The objective of this task is to integrate all of the knowledge assembled thus far and to formulate a first-pass data placement scheme. After analysis of all of the deliverables created thus far, the following data placement scheme was drafted.

Because the requirement is for real-time trade entry with subsequent notification to the global risk management system, multiple databases will be created. In essence, this case study uses two models. The first is a master/slave model with non-fragmented primaries and one-to-many target replicas. This is used for the simple one-way replication of reference data to all locations where trade entry data will be persistently stored. The second is a consolidation model (master/slave model with distributed primary fragments and a single consolidated replica). This is used to notify the global risk management system of all trade activity. See Chapter 2 for details regarding each model.

The task at hand is to decide where trading data should be persistently stored. There are 12 trading locations, each with a varying number of traders and different constraints. After thorough analysis, the following data distribution decisions were made:

- *Trade data should be persistently stored in New York and London.* This decision is based on the number of traders and the lack of any constraints at these two locations.
- *Trade data should be persistently stored in Tokyo.* This decision is based partly on the number of traders in Tokyo, but primarily on the desire of the firm to have a Far East hub. The combined trading volume across all of the Far East trading locations dictates this decision. At an earlier time, the firm chose Tokyo rather than Singapore to function as this hub.
- *Trade data should also be persistently stored in Frankfurt.* This decision is solely based on local governmental regulation.

- *Trade data should* not *be persistently stored at any other locations at the present time.* This decision is based on the fact that the other trade locations have a small number of traders and that some of these smaller locations also have administrative support constraints. However, the principle deciding factor is the desire to practice judicious distribution. This is not only a goal of the firm but is especially critical for this trading application. It was stated in the requirements for this case study that even though each trader is assigned to a specific trading book and all trades executed by that trader are against that book, certain financial instruments are traded across books. For these deals, all global data sources affected by that trade must be updated as part of a single unit of work. Due to this business requirement and the limitations of this technology, it is best to keep the scope of a distributed unit of work to a minimum number of locations. (See Chapter 1 for more details.) With respect to the trader notification requirement for these cross-book deals, it was decided that this will be met by means of phone calls to the appropriate traders. At present the number of these deals is extremely small, so placing phone calls is a very inexpensive solution. Phone calls will also permit the traders to exchange any other additional information relating to the multibook deal that has just been committed. At a later time, if the volume of these deals increases, this notification process will be automated. An added plus to using a manual process initially is that during this manual effort additional requirements regarding what information should be included within an automated message system can be identified.

Processes will be distributed within a three-tier architecture. Presentation logic will reside on each trader's workstation. Business logic will reside on application servers distributed to all trade entry locations. The distribution of processes will be configurable and scalable to meet the requirements of each trading location. Performance will be enhanced either by increasing the number of CPUs available on a single box or by replacing a single machine with several. Application processes will be assigned among these platforms as needed to meet performance and reliability requirements.

Validate placement scheme against existing constraints, capacities, and technologies

The objective of this task is to ensure that the existing physical infrastructure can support the proposed data distribution scheme. It entails a methodical review of each deployment location with respect to any and all constraints, possible capacity limitations, and any lack of support for specific technological requirements. The outcome of this analysis for this case study follows.

The proposed data distribution scheme dictates that data will be persistently stored in Frankfurt. This will entail not only the purchase of the necessary hardware and software licenses for Frankfurt, but also the addition of an administrative support person. Because this is a non-negotiable requirement, one dictated by the German government, the expenses associated with adding the necessary physical and support infrastructure are simply the costs of doing business within this jurisdiction. The firm has only two options: electing not to trade within Germany or, if electing to trade within that country, complying with existing regulations. Because the firm believes that strong trading possibilities exist within Germany, they will build the necessary infrastructure.

Validate placement scheme against service-level requirements

The objective of this task is to ensure that the proposed data distribution scheme and the existing physical infrastructure can meet the performance requirements specified within the service-level agreements. Thorough paper analysis confirmed that the proposed distribution scheme should initially allow for compliance with all service-level agreements.

It should be noted that the number of traders in Paris is high and might be great enough to require a network upgrade in

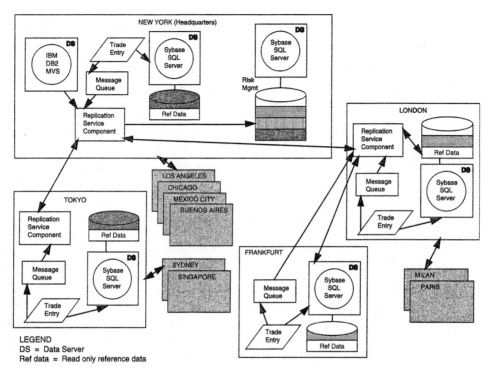

FIGURE 10.2 Case Study 1—Final OLTP environment.

the not-so-distant future. It was decided to monitor the network traffic across this bandwidth closely and perform an upgrade when and if it becomes necessary.

Implement distribution scheme

The proposed distribution scheme can now be implemented. Figure 10.2 illustrates the final OLTP environment.

IMPLEMENTING APPLICATION WORKPLAN

The application workplan presented in Chapter 9 is used as the workplan for the following section. All decision points associated with this case study will be thoroughly identified and explained.

Obtain appropriate training

Because the firm has already built some data replication and messaging services, the application developers for this case study need only understand the required interfaces to these two services. This does not mean that they should not invest in replication training for the appropriate individuals. It only means that they do not have to master every intimate detail. In general, the more information regarding the use of a technology that can be disseminated to all users of the technology, the better the implementations of that technology will be. Knowledge is a wonderful thing; if an individual understands the trade-offs associated with technology alternatives, he or she has a better chance of selecting and growing with a particular alternative.

With respect to this case study, the reference data replication service will build, initially populate, and continually replicate to a reference database at each of the four locations where data will be persistently stored. The application developers have already identified their reference data requirements, and they have negotiated a service agreement so their responsibility for this task is completed. They should, however, perform monitoring to ensure that all requirements within the agreement are being met.

With respect to the risk management notification interface, the developers need to have a thorough understanding of the message "put" call that will be incorporated into their code. The coders must build the message content and place a call to the messaging service's API, which will put the message on a store-and-forward queue for delivery. Transactional integrity must be preserved between the database update and the "put" call to the queuing mechanism. See Chapter 1 for more details on the importance of preserving transactional integrity within a messaging service.

Because this application requires transactional integrity between the database update and the insert into a message queue and the use of distributed units of work for trade entry across books, it was decided that a distributed TP monitor/transaction manager would be used to provide this functionality. This is not as straightforward as it may appear, so appropriate training for all coders using this technology is required.

Review the distributed nature of the application design

This task validates the decisions made within the data distribution model. It confirms that all primary sources for data and processes have been identified and that distribution was judiciously performed. Because requirements change during an application's life cycle, this review effort is necessary. With respect to this case study, the reevaluation effort found no discrepancies.

Validate the selection of the application model

As stated in Chapter 9, this review effort should involve not only application team members but also participants from other technical support areas within the firm. The objectives of this effort are to ensure that the final design for this trading application not only reflects a tactical solution but also ensures that the design decisions are fully compliant with the strategic direction of the firm.

For this case study, the models identified during the create data placement scheme task were deemed correct. In addition, network capacity appears to be adequate, with the possible exception of Paris. All were in agreement with the recommendation set forth within the validate placement scheme against service-level requirements task. The connection between Paris and London will be monitored closely. When and if an upgrade becomes necessary, it will be performed at that time.

It was decided that a member of the support staff in London would be sent for a three- to six-month temporary assignment in Frankfurt. During this time in Frankfurt, the individual will hire and train a database and replication support person. It is important that the newly hired person be well versed in both the required technologies and the firm's implementation and support best practices. Therefore, an in-depth training session with an in-house support person was deemed the best approach.

The application developers were given high marks and a promise of a financial bonus for deciding to use the data replication and messaging services available within the firm. This type of reward system offers incentives for application development teams complying with the strategic direction of the firm. It is also cost-effective for the firm in that the benefits of service-based architecture can be achieved.

Define specifications for all data mapping and transformational service requirements

Because existing firmwide services are being used by the application development effort for this case study, very little labor is required for this task. The reference data replication service provides for a reference data database, both its creation and its continued maintenance. The application coders need only refer to this database within their stored procedures or DML calls.

The same minimal effort is required for the risk management interface. The application coders need only know the API and the required data content for the message envelope. The apply code for the message is already used by other trading applications in New York. In addition, the store-and-forward message queuing mechanism is provided by the messaging service.

Define configuration parameters for resource managers

Because the same application processes will be run in all 12 trading locations, the database design that will be used for the four persistent storage locations will be identical. The only concerns that must be addressed are configuration issues across the reference data database and the trading database. In anticipation of building a service-based architecture, the firm has already addressed the majority of these issues when it created a best-practice guide for data server installations. The firm uses the same sort order and compatible character sets for all data server installations. In addition, it has implemented DCE time services so all data servers display synchronized time. For this case study, there are no further issues to address with respect to configuring resource managers.

Assist with configuring the replication infrastructure and software

The application development team supplied all critical replication volumes and recovery requirements to the replication architecture team. The replication architecture team has the responsibility of installing the replication software and configuring the replication environment. A number of infrastructure planning sessions were held and the following recommendations were made:

- *No new replication service components will be added for asynchronous reference data replication.* Replication service components already reside on hardware in New York, London, and Tokyo. They are now being used to replicate reference data from the mainframe in New York to other globally distributed trading applications. These replication components are underutilized. These components definitely have enough existing capacity to meet the replication demands of this new trading application, so a replication infrastructure sharing approach will be used. No replication service software components will be placed in Frankfurt at the present time. The replication service component in London will use remote access to the data servers residing in Frankfurt. Multiple factors influence this decision, including the facts that only a small amount of reference data will be replicated to Frankfurt and that the reference data is used in read-only mode. No log pull mechanism will be required for Frankfurt because the risk management system receives notification by means of the messaging service—an API puts the message on a store-and-forward queue. An additional factor is the current lack of administrative support in Frankfurt. After a support person has been hired and trained, this decision can be readdressed.
- *Message queuing components will reside in all locations where data is being persistently stored.* A messaging queue currently resides in New York, London, and Tokyo. These queues are used by existing trading systems to forward risk management information to the New York risk management system. A message outbound queue will be created in Frankfurt. This local

store-and-forward queue is essential for the completion of local trades. The network in not reliable enough to support a distributed unit of work between Frankfurt and London for each trade entered in Frankfurt. The distributed unit of work (two-phase commit protocol) is necessary to ensure transactional integrity between the database update in Frankfurt and the insert into the existing message queue in London. Therefore, a message queue will be created in Frankfurt. The distributed unit of work is now processed across only LAN resources, not WAN resources. The Frankfurt trades should not have any network issues with just local updating. Once on the outbound queue in Frankfurt, a messaging component asynchronously forwards each message to London and then New York.

Address any application-specific issues related to the model being implemented

For the case study under consideration, the following model-related issues were identified:

- *Requirement to add a "date/time" field to data rows within the reference data database.* This field will be used to aid with data reconciliation efforts between the mainframe and the target replicas. It will be used to narrow the scope of the reconciliation process since reconciliation will occur over WAN resources.
- *Requirement to integrate enhanced security for sensitive data.* The data being forwarded to New York for global risk management is extremely sensitive. Therefore, encryption software will be used for all messages within the global risk management environment.
- *Requirement to have a sufficient message queue size at each persistent data storage location.* This queue size is important in that messages will continue to build up within the queue if there are any failures within the message pull and distribution mechanisms for that location. If the queue cannot receive any messages, the trade entry process for that location cannot be used. Remember that there is a two-phase commit process

across the database update and the message queue. If either one of these is unavailable, the whole transaction fails.

Create the required replication objects

Because the application development team is making use of both the reference data replication service and the global risk management messaging queuing service, they have no responsibility for creating the necessary replication objects. The replication infrastructure is being supported by the service providers. The development team should, however, do a thorough job of testing to ensure that all aspects of the contract are adhered to by each service provider.

Code and test the application

Because this application will be distributed to multiple locations, a strong design effort is necessary. The application must be scalable to small and large branches, and it must be efficient when performing local as well as remote data access. Depending on the architecture chosen (two or three tiers), the resulting design will be different. The firm under consideration has a strong commitment to a multitier architecture, as can be seen by the technical services already available to the application developers (a replication and messaging infrastructure). By choosing a multitier approach within a distributed environment, the following benefits can be achieved:

- *Increased availability and performance.*
- *Increased scalability.* System performance can be increased in proportion to the hardware resources added.
- *Decreased scope of failures.*
- *Increased configuration flexibility.* This approach makes distribution a tuning issue.
- *Increased opportunities for parallelism.* System performance can be enhanced by replacing a single machine with several.

The testing effort should include data reconciliation procedures for reference data. The reference data replication service provider probably already has some procedures in place, but they should be retested and validated for this application.

Test recovery scenarios with replication in place

Because two methods of asynchronous replication are being used, a thorough job of recovery testing is required. Both replication techniques are orthogonal to each other. The reference data replication service provides read-only data as input to this application, and the risk management messaging queuing service provides notification to the risk management system (an output). In addition to testing the normal application recovery scenarios, the following scenarios should be included: the recovery from any failures with replication components supplying reference data to this application and the recovery from any message queuing failures that provide input into the risk management system. Possible component failures are detailed in Chapter 9. Depending on the vendor products and home-grown solutions being used, the recovery solutions will differ. The important aspect is that recovery procedures are in place to handle these failures.

Certify the application for WAN use with replication in place

In addition to certifying remote data access from a number of branches, this certification effort should also verify efficient WAN usage for the reference data replication service and the risk management message queuing service. A critical aspect is the certification of the reference data reconciliation procedures. Reference data reconciliation will occur across WAN resources. To make this process more efficient, the date/time field was incorporated into the reference data rows. Depending on the size of the tables being reconciled, this procedure could use a lot of network resources. It is important to know the WAN usage for this procedure before going into production. All reconciliation procedures should be scheduled during times of non-peak WAN traffic.

Tune for performance

As stated previously, a multitier architectural approach is being used. All of the tuning options identified within that section are available. During this tuning effort, those options should be explored.

Create thorough documentation

In addition to providing the documentation that is normally supplied at completion of an application's development life cycle, the following should also be supplied:

- Operating procedures with recovery scenarios for the reference data replication service
- Operating procedures with recovery scenarios for the risk management message queuing service

Migrate to the production environment

Now that all of these tasks have been completed, this trading application can be migrated into the production environment with complete assurance that it will fit well into the global replication architecture and physical infrastructure. Decisions regarding replication component placement and opportunities for physical sharing of replication components have already been identified. All that is required is to implement those decisions.

Case Study 2—Using Replication with an OLAP Operational Data Store

This case study illustrates the use of judicious distribution and asynchronous replication in a decision-support environment. The requirement is for the data used within the decision-support system to have only a very small degree of data latency with the OLTP databases. In other words, the requirement is for an OLAP operational data store. It uses a master/slave model with the OLTP systems acting as the master and the operational data store acting as the slave.

OVERVIEW OF BUSINESS PROBLEM

A global investment banking institution needs to implement a decision-support system that can be used by trade managers and analysts to query the results of the international trading environment on a near-real-time basis. The requirement also involves the desire to support leading-edge technologies such as data mining and data visualization.

Assumptions and requirements regarding the environment include the following:

- *Reference data needed to validate and complete trades is maintained by legacy systems on a mainframe in New York.* This reference data is currently replicated asynchronously to all locations where trade information is stored locally. Some of this reference data will need to be forwarded transactionally with the trade data to the reporting environment.

- *Decisions on which branches should store trade data locally have already been made as part of the OLTP trading application design effort.* See Case Study 1 in Chapter 10. Factors that influenced the decision were regulatory issues specific to the country of that branch, number of traders and trade volume generated from that branch, technology constraints, and administrative support level and skill set available for that branch. As other branches are added to the organization or as trade volumes grow, the data distribution issue is readdressed. At present, there are 12 trading branches, and 4 of them store trading information locally. Figure 11.1 illustrates the global topology for the OLTP trading applications of the firm.

- *All back-office trade processing occurs in one of two international hubs.* One hub in New York services North America, South America, the Far East, and Australia; the other hub in London services all of Europe and the Middle East.

- *Results of all trades are forwarded to the appropriate regional center for back-office processing and subsequently forwarded to the headquarters in New York.* All global positions and risk are maintained in near-real time in New York by means of the risk management message queuing service. These values are adjusted after back-office processing at each regional center and then reset for the next business day. The start of the firm's global business day equates to 1:00 a.m. in New York. The existing risk management system stores only very limited risk data for the current business day. This information is used to comply with domestic and international trading regulations. The OLAP application under consideration will store expanded risk and trade data as well as trader details. The historical duration for this consolidated database will be a rolling five years. In addition to the consolidated databases, each trading location needs a local reporting database for its local analysts, who need trade details for a rolling three years.

- *The OLAP environment should store all details and sufficient summary information to meet the performance requirements of each type of query user (local analysts and global risk managers).* These requirements are specified in the service-level requirements. The firm has two global risk managers who travel among the branches, so global access to the consolidated databases is required. Even though they do a lot of traveling, the global risk managers are permanently assigned as follows: one resides in New York, and the other has permanent residence in Frankfurt.

- *The firm wants to use the OLAP environment not only for traditional analysis but also for data mining, data visualization, and other leading-edge technologies.*
- *Data distribution and replication services for OLTP and OLAP must be scalable and flexible so as to support future directions for trading in emerging markets.*

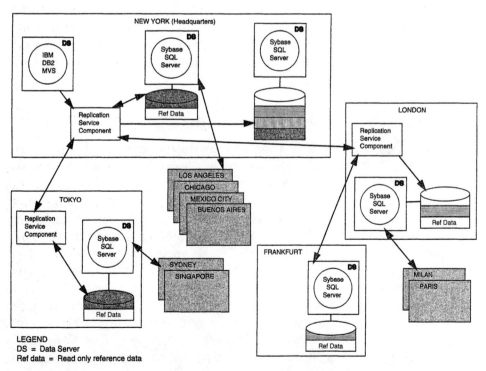

FIGURE 11.1 Case Study 2—OLTP environment requiring OLAP support.

APPLYING DATA DISTRIBUTION METHODOLOGY

The distribution methodology presented in Chapter 5 is used as the workplan for the following section. All data distribution decision points associated with this case study will be thoroughly identified and explained.

Prepare an application distribution profile

The objectives of this task are to describe the distributed nature of the application and to start solidifying network requirements. The suggested deliverable is an application distribution profile. To complete this profile, it is necessary to have knowledge regarding the potential deployment locations and to be aware of the reporting and querying requirements. Table 11.1 illustrates a completed profile for this case study.

Note that the role of global risk management is shared across two locations. It is anticipated that some of the reports will be scheduled to run every 15 minutes during the global trading day. The results of these reports will be linked to data visualization tools that will send warnings and alerts when designated thresholds are reached.

Prepare a physical infrastructure profile

The objectives of this task are to document the physical resources available at each potential deployment location and to identify any potential distribution constraints. The suggested deliverable is a physical infrastructure profile. To complete this profile, it is necessary to have knowledge regarding the existing physical infrastructure at each potential deployment location and to be aware of any possible constraints that exist within the environment. Table 11.2 illustrates a completed profile for this case study.

Note that local trade data is stored at Frankfurt to comply with governmental regulations. In addition, it might be necessary to install a network connection between New York and Frankfurt. This connection would provide more network capacity to Frankfurt, thereby allowing it to be used more effectively

TABLE 11.1   Application Distribution Profile

Application Name: Case Study 2—Replicating to an Operational Data Store

Location types	Locations	User types and anticipated Numbers	Business transactions with anticipated execution rates
Headquarters	New York	Global risk manager (1) Global analysts (5)	Global risk analysis (40/daily) Consolidated reporting (90/daily)
Regional processing centers:	New York London	Regional analysts (6) Regional analysts (4)	Regional reporting (30/daily) Regional reporting (20/daily)
Trading centers	New York	Local analysts (6)	Local risk analysis (40/daily) Local reporting (120/daily)
	Chicago	Local analysts (4)	Local risk analysis (40/daily) Local reporting (80/daily)
	Los Angeles	Local analysts (3)	Local risk analysis (40/daily) Local reporting (60/daily)
	Mexico City	Local analysts (2)	Local risk analysis (40/daily) Local reporting (40/daily)
	Buenos Aires	Local analysts (3)	Local risk analysis (40/daily) Local reporting (60/daily)
	Tokyo	Local analysts (2)	Local risk analysis (40/daily) Local reporting (40/daily)
	Singapore	Local analysts (2)	Local risk analysis (40/daily) Local reporting (40/daily)
	Sydney	Local analysts (2)	Local risk analysis (40/daily) Local reporting (40/daily)
	London	Local analysts (5)	Local risk analysis (40/daily) Local reporting (100/daily)
	Paris	Local analysts (3)	Local risk analysis (40/daily) Local reporting (60/daily)
	Milan	Local analysts (2)	Local risk analysis (40/daily) Local reporting (40/daily)
	Frankfurt	Global risk manager (1) Local analysts (2)	Global risk analysis (40/daily) Consolidated reporting (50/daily) Local risk analysis (40/daily) Local reporting (40/daily)

TABLE 11.2 Physical Infrastructure Profile

Application Name: Case Study 2—Replicating to an Operational Data Store

Location/ Location type	Network connectivity (WAN and LAN)	Hardware resources (e.g., servers)	Software resources (e.g., OS, DBMS)	Security level code	Availability level code	Administrative support and constraints	Additional constraints and concerns
New York /Headquarters Regional processing center Trading center	T1 line—London 256 kB—Chicago 256 kB—Los Angeles 64 kB—Mexico City 64 kB—Buenos Aires 128 kB—Tokyo Token Ring and Ethernet Possibly might want to install a 64 kB to Frankfurt	• 1 IBM mainframe host • 2 Sun SPARC 2000	• IBM MVS • Sun Solaris • IBM DB2/MVS • Sybase SQL Server • Sybase Replication Server • Sun Solaris	High	7 × 24	Full support	
London /Regional processing center, Trading center	T1 line—New York 128 kB— Frankfurt 128 kB—Paris 64 kB—Milan Token Ring and Ethernet	• 2 Sun SPARC 1000 Server	• Sun Solaris • Sybase SQL Server • Sybase Replication Server	High	7 × 24	Full support	
Chicago /Trading center	256 kB—New York Token Ring			High	14 hours/day 7 AM–9 PM local time	Full support during operational hours. Remote support provided by New York.	

Location	Bandwidth	Hardware	Software	Priority	Hours	Support
Los Angeles /Trading center	256 kB—New York Token Ring			High	14 hours/day 7 AM–9 PM local time	Full support during operational hours. Remote support provided by New York.
Mexico City /Trading	64 kB—New York Token Ring		8 AM–8 PM local time	High	12 hours/day	Limited local support. Remote support provided by New York.
Buenos Aires /Trading center	64 kB—New York Token Ring			High	14 hours/day 7 AM–9 PM local time	Limited local support. Remote support provided by New York.
Tokyo /Trading center	128 kB—New York, 64 kB—Singapore, 64 kB—Sydney Token Ring	1 Sun SPARC 51	• Sun Solaris • Sybase SQL Server • Sybase Replication Server	High	7 × 24	Full support
Singapore /Trading center	64 kB—Tokyo Token Ring			High	14 hours/day 7 AM–9 PM local time	Full support
Sydney /Trading center	64 kB—Tokyo Ethernet			High	14 hours/day 7 AM–9 PM local time	Full support
Paris /Trading center	128 kB—London Token Ring			High	12 hours/day 7 AM–7 PM local time	Full support
Milan /Trading center	64 kB—London Token Ring			High	12 hours/day 7 AM–7 PM local time	Limited local support. Remote support provided by London.
Frankfurt /Trading center	128 kB—London Token Ring Possibly install a 64 kb line to New York	1 sun SPARC 51	• Unix OS • Sybase SQL Server	High	18 hours/day 5 AM–11 PM	Full support locally. Remote support provided by London. Local regulations require trade data to reside within the country.

for global risk management. It will also provide a meshed network for Frankfurt—an alternate route in cases of network failure or overload between Frankfurt and London.

Some upgrades to hardware and software already have been purchased and installed. These upgrades have been allocated specifically for support of this decision-support system. If after further analysis more upgrades are warranted, money has been set aside to cover these costs.

Create referentially tied data recovery groups

The objectives of this task are to describe data recovery groups and to identify potential opportunities for implementing data partitioning by physical location. Because this is a local and consolidated reporting application that will draw its data from existing OLTP trading databases, this task is relatively straightforward. It should include the following subtasks:

- *Analysis of the data schemata used at each OLTP persistent data store.* This analysis identifies the data that is to be forwarded to the reporting databases. It also identifies the grain of the facts, the meaning of the lowest level of stored information, and ensures the additive nature of the facts that are to be consolidated.
- *Creation of reporting database schemata that will meet the performance requirements of the query users.* After considerable analysis, it was decided that the consolidated schema would be a star join schema that represents a central fact table and its associated dimension tables. The central fact table has a composite key comprised of all of the single primary keys of the dimension tables. The fact table is joined to a number of the single-level dimension tables to resolve queries. Any relational DBMS will support a star join schema. The major deciding factor for electing to use a star join schema was that technical representatives from the OLAP tool vendor of choice stated several times that the best performance with their OLAP product could be achieved only with a star join schema. Even with the star join schema storing ag-

gregate data will be necessary to meet query performance requirements.

With respect to data partitioning, each entry location already incorporates a branch code as part of the trade entry process. This is required because each entry location forwards all trade data to its regional hubs for back-office processing. This branch code will be used to partition data for querying and administrative purposes.

It was decided that each reporting database should represent its own recovery group. For the local databases, backups will be scheduled as part of their end-of-day processing. For the consolidated databases where asynchronous replication will occur continually, it was decided to suspend replication during scheduled backups. In addition, the consolidated locations will incorporate sophisticated mechanisms to improve availability and fault tolerance.

Prepare a process-to-data use profile

The objectives of this task are to identify data use across application processes and to highlight "heavy-hitter" processes. Because the case study under consideration is a reporting application, it entails identifying the queries with high usage and the associated data that they access. The application development team produced a CRUD matrix that illustrates this usage. This CRUD matrix will also serve to validate the partitioning scheme and the data schemata created in previous tasks. If the data is distributed in a fashion that mirrors the existing OLTP environment, invariably every query will either access a local reporting database or a consolidated one.

The complexity of this task is not in identifying the "heavy-hitter" queries but in trying to get a good understanding of the ad hoc queries that will be used. In reality, this is an almost impossible task because the more sophisticated the analysts become, the more complex their queries. In addition, the business itself changes over time in ways that cannot be predicted. These changes alter query patterns. At best, one can only affirm the appropriateness of the partitioning scheme at the local and consolidated levels.

Integrate global data use with process-to-data use profile

The objectives of this task are to integrate global data use with the application's process-to-data use profile and to negotiate service-level agreements. Because the case study under consideration is a reporting application, it entails identifying source databases that are to be used as primary sources for the querying databases. This identification process names the data guardian of each data source and describes the current business usage of each piece of data that will be used as input into the decision-support databases. In addition, it starts defining the data transformational requirements. With respect to global use, this task merges the query use patterns identified for this application in the previous task with any other potential query use by other global users. In other words, data flows into and out of this OLAP application are identified.

In addition, service-level agreements are negotiated. For this decision-support system, the following service-level agreements are required:

- *Roles and responsibilities for an automatic warning system.* During the process of identifying the typical change rate for each piece of data, it was discovered that the data change rate for many of the data elements within the OLTP trading environment fluctuate to a very great extent. Therefore, it was decided that an automatic warning system that alerts the OLAP environment when an extraordinary amount of data will be replicated was necessary. The roles and responsibilities for implementing this warning system are part of the service-level agreement between the OLAP application developers and the owners and support personnel for the primary data sources that will feed the OLAP databases.
- *Identification of the replication mechanism that will be used to support the decision-support databases and the service levels it*

can support. The mechanism used for replication must support the data latency requirements for query users. For this OLAP application, it will definitely be an asynchronous replication mechanism. Because the requirements for this application state that all global positions and risk are maintained in near-real time, an event propagation type of asynchronous replication will be used. The decision on whether to use a database-to-database communication or a process-to-process communication type of replication will be based solely on the complexities of the data transformations required. After the analysis of all primary data sources is completed, this decision can be made. This analysis must be extremely detailed. The analysts must identify the mapping for each element within the reporting databases and confirm the correctness of each transformation algorithm with business users. This ensures the data integrity of the reporting databases. For this case study, after thorough analysis, it was discovered that only moderate data transformation was required. Therefore, the replication mechanism to be used is a database-to-database type of asynchronous replication. A service-level agreement between the replication service support group and the OLAP application team was reached; it states that replication will occur with a maximum latency of five minutes 90 percent of the time.

• *Roles and responsibilities for data transformational services.* Because the transformational requirements for this OLAP case study are moderate, the apply portion of the database-to-database asynchronous replication mechanism will be modified to perform this service. The responsibility for this development effort resides with the OLAP application developers; however, some assistance will be provided by the supporters of the replication software. This was decided as part of the service-level agreement between the replication service support group and the OLAP application development team.

The application development team explored multiple approaches for getting the required OLTP data into the OLAP environment. The first was to use the risk management message queuing service, as identified in Chapter 10. This service is used by all trading applications to forward critical risk information to New York in near-real time for global risk management. At first it seemed a viable alternative; however, after thorough analysis a number of flaws with this approach were discovered. The message content for the risk management message queuing service contained only about one-third the required data for the consolidated reporting database. The data within the existing message was applicable across all trading applications and financial instruments; however, for the reporting database each trade must also include data that is specific for that instrument. The options were either to expand the message envelope to include all possible data for each instrument or to have each application send two messages. One message would contain the data relevant to all instruments, and the other would contain the data specific for that instrument. With either of these options, existing trading applications would have to be opened up and the code modified either to add more data to the existing content envelope or to build and send another message. This task would affect many applications and take months to accomplish.

The second alternative was to implement a database-to-database asynchronous replication alternative. This approach is totally transparent to existing application code. It pulls transactional data from a database log and forwards it to the appropriate reporting databases. The major negative for this approach was that some of the trade data would be sent across the network twice—once within the message envelope of the risk management message queuing service and a second time to the reporting databases by means of the database replication mechanism. This approach definitely does not make the most efficient use of network resources. After a cost-benefit analysis, the decision was made to use the second approach. The cost and risks associated with opening up so many modules of trading application code far outweighed the cost of sending a small amount of trade data across the network twice.

Reusing existing replication processes and data is definitely worth exploring. For example, if one assumes that the message content of the risk management message queuing service contained all the data content needed by the consolidated database reporting environment, then it would be very efficient either to receive the same message and use it to populate the five-year consolidated reporting database or to use database-to-database asynchronous replication from the current day risk management database to populate the five-year consolidated reporting database. In either case, the message is sent across the WAN only once.

Create data placement scheme

The objective of this task is to integrate all of the knowledge assembled thus far and to formulate a first-pass data placement scheme. After analysis of all of the deliverables, the following data placement scheme was drafted.

Because near-real-time local and consolidated reporting is required, multiple databases will be created. In essence, this case study uses a flavor of the consolidation model (master/slave model with distributed primary fragments and a single consolidated replica), as defined in Chapter 2; however, it incorporates the additional requirement for local reporting and the possibility that the single consolidated replica might itself need to be replicated in full or part to other locations. The initial assumption regarding the distribution of these reporting databases is that the topology should reflect the existing OLTP environment. In other words, the four existing branches that store trade data will also support a *local* reporting database, optimized for local query use. In addition, all reporting data will be forwarded to a consolidated database located in New York. This decision was based on the fact that all trade data is already forwarded to either New York or London for back-office trade processing. There is a potential flaw with this design in that one of the two global risk managers is not located in New York. Each risk manager must receive very fast query response time from the consolidated database, with a very high degree of availability and reliability, so this decision might need to be modified.

Validate placement scheme against existing constraints, capacities, and technologies

The objective of this task is to ensure that the existing physical infrastructure can support the proposed data distribution scheme. It entails a methodical review of each deployment location with respect to any and all constraints, possible capacity limitations, and any lack of support for specific technological requirements. The outcome of the analysis for this case study follows.

Because one of the Sun SPARC 2000 machines in New York was purchased for use with this decision-support application, there appear to be no hardware constraints. In addition, there seem to be no availability, security, or administrative support issues. However, performance and capacity problems might arise for the global risk manager residing in Frankfurt. It was noted on the physical infrastructure profile that installing a network connection between New York and Frankfurt may be necessary. This network upgrade will provide faster query response time between Frankfurt and New York, and it will also mesh Frankfurt's access by providing an alternative route in cases of network failure or overload between Frankfurt and London.

A cost-benefit analysis was performed between two alternatives. One alternative was to upgrade the network by creating a link between Frankfurt and New York, as identified above. The other was to have a replica of the consolidated New York database in either London or Frankfurt and upgrade the network connection between London and Frankfurt to a 256 kB line. After thorough analysis, it was decided to implement a phased-in approach of the second choice. The New York to Frankfurt line will be very expensive, considering it has only one primary user and that the role of that user may very likely change as the firm experiences growth and potential reorganizations. The storing of a second consolidated database in London made good business sense. It offers a contingent database for consolidated reporting and global risk management. Therefore, this replica of the consolidated New York reporting database will be implemented as phase one of the solution. Once implemented, traffic between Frankfurt and London will be monitored. If it appears that the quantity of traffic is sufficient to justify an upgrade to the bandwidth of that line, it will be implemented as phase two of the solution.

Validate placement scheme against service-level requirements

The objective of this task is to ensure that the proposed data distribution scheme and the existing physical infrastructure can meet the performance requirements agreed to within the service-level agreements. Thorough paper analysis confirmed that the proposed distribution scheme should allow for compliance with all service-level agreements initially. As reporting traffic increases, network upgrades as identified above may be required as a second phase. By implementing network upgrades as a second phase and only after quantifying the actual traffic, the firm is controlling cost expenditures and limiting the risks taken at any one time.

Implement distribution scheme

The proposed distribution scheme can now be implemented. Figure 11.2 illustrates the final OLAP environment.

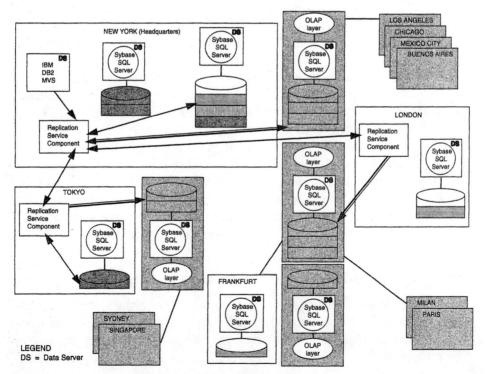

FIGURE 11.2 Case Study 2—Final OLAP environment.

IMPLEMENTING APPLICATION WORKPLAN

The application workplan presented in Chapter 9 is used as the workplan for the following section. As with the previous case study, all decision points will be thoroughly identified and explained.

Obtain appropriate training

For this OLAP application the firm has no reusable services that can be employed; however, a knowledge base for replication and messaging technologies already exists. These resources should be tapped as heavily as possible. If templates and scripts have been produced that will assist with the creation of replication objects, these aids should be used. In addition, any and all best-practice documents that exist within the firm should be studied and applied.

There are two areas where training for the application developers will be essential. The first concerns the database-to-database asynchronous replication product, and the second concerns use and support of the OLAP query tool. For the replication product, specific team members will have to master the details involved with implementing the replication solution and extending the apply code to perform data mapping and transformation. These individuals should have strong system administration, database administration, and coding skills. These abilities will shorten the learning curve considerably.

For the OLAP tool, the team members will have to understand the architectural approach used by the vendor, be able to implement a database schema that has been optimized for the designated tool, and be able to tune the database and possibly the query tool itself. These individuals should have strong data administration and database administration skills.

Review the distributed nature of the application design

This task validates the decisions made within the data distribution model. It confirms that all primary sources for data and processes have been identified and that distribution was performed effectively. This task is critical for an OLAP application.

Whenever data is merged or transformed from multiple primary sources, there is a strong possibility that a data element may be called by the same name across multiple application systems but, in reality, may represent something slightly different from a business perspective. All of these anomalies must be detected and resolved. In this case study, a number of anomalies existed across the trading systems that will be used as primary sources for the reporting database. Joint sessions were held across business units, and all discrepancies were resolved.

Validate the selection of the application model

This review effort should involve not only application team members but also participants from other technical support areas within the firm. The objectives of this effort are to ensure that the final design for this decision-support application not only reflects a tactical solution but also integrates well into the data warehousing strategy of the firm.

For this case study, the models identified during the create data placement scheme task were deemed correct. Because a second consolidated reporting database will reside in London, the necessary hardware and software licenses must be acquired and installed. In spite of the additional expense, all reviewers agreed with the contingency plan decision. The firm would definitely be at risk if the consolidated database were not available for a long period of time.

Define specifications for all data mapping and transformational service requirements

Because the consolidated database merges input from multiple OLTP trading databases, this task is very labor-intensive. Each primary source must be examined separately, and all mapping and transformation requirements must be defined. These requirements will eventually be the specification used to enhance the apply code of the asynchronous replication product. To the greatest extent possible, scripts, tools, and repositories should be used to help automate the apply code modifications. A good percentage of this effort should have been completed as part of the data distribution methodology task entitled Integrate Global Data Usage with Process-to-data Use Profile as described in Chapter 5.

Define configuration parameters for resource managers

This case study involves the creation of local reporting databases and the creation of the consolidated reporting databases. The local reporting databases will reside at the four persistent storage locations and will have identical schemata, which means the same apply code modifications for asynchronous replication can be used at all locations. This will shorten the development effort considerably. The size of the local reporting databases are all under 2 gigabytes. These local databases will use a star join schema, have a fact table grain of the trade transaction, and use the same OLAP reporting tool to enable the sharing of predefined reports across all locations.

For the consolidated database, a star join schema will also be used; however, the grain of the fact table will be at a higher level—the trade group level. At this level, all transactions associated with the individual settlements of the trade are merged. Because of this higher level, the apply code modifications for the consolidated database are more complex than those used with the local reporting databases.

As identified in Chapter 10, this firm has created a best-practice guide for data server installations. Therefore, the same sort order and compatible character sets are used for all data server installations. In addition, they have implemented DCE time services so all data servers display synchronized time. For this case study, there are only two configuration issues left to address. The first relates to the parameters associated with the size of the consolidated database, which are specific to the RDBMS being used.

The second relates to the log sizes of the primary source databases. Because a log pull mechanism will be used, the size of all of the primary sourced database logs must be reevaluated to ensure that trading at all primary sources can continue even though a log pull mechanism failure or a network outage might occur. See Chapter 6 for a detailed discussion of this issue.

Assist with configuring the replication infrastructure and software

In addition to supplying all critical replication volumes and recovery requirements to the replication architecture team, the application development team should also be involved in defining the replication infrastructure that will support its application. Even though the replication architecture team is responsible for installing the replication software and configuring the replication production environment, the application development team should be part of the infrastructure planning sessions. A number of these planning sessions were held and the following recommendations were made.

New replication service components will be added for asynchronous replication to the decision-support databases. Replication service components already reside on hardware in New York, London, and Tokyo. They are used within the OLTP environment to replicate reference data from the mainframe in New York to globally distributed trading applications and to replicate trade data back to the consolidated risk management database in New York. These replication components have sufficient capacity to handle the replication requirements of this reporting system. Therefore, the replication infrastructure sharing approach discussed in Chapter 10 will be used. In New York, London, and Tokyo, the existing replication components will be enhanced to replicate data from the local OLTP trading databases to their designated local OLAP database and to the consolidated reporting databases in New York and London. A new replication service component will be added in Frankfurt to support the same functionality. Multiple factors weighed into this decision, including the fact that log pull mechanisms will now be required for the OLTP trading databases residing in Frankfurt. Up to this time, Frankfurt only had to store an outbound message queue. The consensus of the architects was that with sufficient trade activity in Frankfurt, placing the log pull mechanisms in London would cause excessive network traffic. In addition, the six-month training session for the Frankfurt database and replication support person was now complete. It was felt that there were no constraints that would limit the placing of these data replication components in Frankfurt.

Address any application-specific issues related to the model being implemented

For the OLAP case study under consideration, the following model-related issues were identified:

- *Requirement to add reconciliation procedures to ensure that the reporting databases are in agreement with their primary sourced OLTP databases.* For the consolidated databases, these procedures will be executed as part of the nightly back-office processing that occurs in the New York and London international hubs. For the four local reporting databases, these procedures will be part of their nightly batch processing.
- *Requirement to integrate enhanced security for sensitive data.* The data being replicated to the consolidated databases in New York and London across WAN resources is extremely sensitive. Therefore, encryption software will be used for this data replication.
- *Requirement to have sufficient database log sizes at each OLTP primary source database.* This requirement was addressed as part of the discussion in "Define Configuration Parameters for Resource Managers," above.

Create the required replication objects

For this case study, there is a shared responsibility between the replication service support group and the OLAP application development team for creating the necessary replication objects. The roles and responsibilities were explicitly defined within the service-level agreements. (See "Integrate Global Data Usage with Process-to-data Use Profile," above.) The OLAP application developers are to create the replication objects within the development environment with the assistance of a mentor from the replication service support group. The mentor will advise, provide training for the existing scripts and tools that help to automate the object create process, and ensure that the development effort is in compliance with all best-practice guidelines. In addition, the mentor will provide the necessary consulting services to enable a smooth migration into the production environment.

With respect to the apply code modifications that will be used for data mapping and transformation, the service-level agreement was very specific. It stated that the responsibility for this development effort predominantly resides with the OLAP application developers and that limited assistance will be provided by the replication service support group. The specifications for this coding effort have been defined as part of the define specifications for all data mapping and transformational service requirements task. To the greatest extent possible, scripts, tools, and repositories should be used to automate the creation of the apply code modifications. As stated earlier, only two sets of apply code are required. One is for the local reporting databases and the other is for the consolidated databases. Opportunities for code reuse should be explored and exploited.

Code and test the application

Because this application will merge data from multiple trading applications, a strong analysis and design effort are necessary. The replication portion of this OLAP application must be scalable to receive both small and large amounts of replicated data. Replication volumes reflect the amount of trade activity at any given branch. In addition, the automated warning system that alerts the OLAP environment when an extraordinary amount of trade data is about to be replicated must be incorporated into the replication infrastructure. The roles and responsibilities for implementing this warning system were defined as part of the service-level agreement between the OLAP application developers and the owners and support personnel of the primary data sources that will feed the OLAP databases. For this case study, the warning system was developed and integrated into the replication infrastructure with just a minimal set of challenges.

Other important coding issues concern the databases which must be designed to perform efficiently with the OLAP query tool of choice. For this case study, this involves a star join schema, appropriate aggregation levels, and robust index structures. In addition, decisions must be made with respect to what portions of the OLAP tool are rolled out to various types of users. Generally, OLAP tools support two flavors of users. The executive type of user needs a very friendly front end that enables simple report selection and execution, which are usually based on a point-and-click mechanism or simple icon selection. The second type of user is much more sophisticated. This user is well versed in the tool, the technology, and the business reporting requirements. This user can create the "canned" reports for the executive type of user and can also perform complex analysis independently. For this case study, the user community is composed of both types of users. The OLAP application developers will be creating the standard reports required for the executive users. The sophisticated query users will be trained on OLAP tool usage. Once trained, these users will create and execute all their own reports.

At a later time, World Wide Web access to the reporting databases will be implemented. At present, decision makers within the firm believe that security challenges have not been sufficiently resolved to make this feasible; however, the OLAP tool of choice has an integrated Web front end. This portion of the tool will be implemented when security issues have been resolved and users are more familiar with the OLAP tool's reporting capabilities.

Another coding and testing effort for the developers is the creation of an exception processing and notification system. This system is used to notify query users when one or more branches are not forwarding data to the reporting environment due to some sort of failure. It also incorporates quality control functionality—processes that validate that the whole environment is working correctly. Users must be alerted to all types of exception conditions because an incomplete set of data can have an impact on how they interpret the results of their queries. This exception processing and notification system is a critical aspect of performing quality assurance for the decision-support system.

The testing effort for this OLAP application should include the testing of all canned reports, the automated warning system, and the exception and notification system. The components are first tested individually and then tested as an integrated whole.

Test recovery scenarios with replication in place

Recovery for the local reporting database is relatively straightforward. Each local database has only a single primary source. However, for the consolidated databases, data is being replicated and merged from multiple primary sources. This makes recovery more complex. The database administrator restores data at a table level during a recovery process, but the data must be reconciled at the row level based on values in the branch code column. This involves multiple data reconciliation procedures.

Recovery procedures are dictated by the vendor tool and the utilities provided. The critical aspect for this testing effort is that all types of recovery scenarios are identified, appropriate procedures defined, and all possibilities thoroughly tested. See Chapter 9 for a detailed listing of possible failures. It is extremely frustrating for both users and support staff to be in a recovery situation with no plan in place.

Certify the application for WAN use with replication in place

Three areas of WAN certification are required for this case study. The first is the data replication functionality for the consolidated databases—the input to the decision-support system. The replication tool of choice should behave as a good WAN citizen. (See Chapter 9 for details.) The second area to evaluate is the WAN behavior of the OLAP tool of choice. It too should behave efficiently over WAN resources. If the tool supports an architecture of three tiers or more, make sure that the components are placed appropriately. If the middle tier of the OLAP tool brings back large amounts of data and performs the data filtering and sorting functions, then place the middle tier on the LAN of the data server being queried. Try to maximize the firm's sharable WAN resources. The third area for certification is the data reconciliation procedures for the consolidated databases. It may be necessary to incorporate a data/time field, as in the case study in Chapter 10. This will make the reconciliation process more efficient because only smaller portions of the databases are reconciled at any given time. It is important to know WAN usage for these procedures before going into production. As with the previous case study, the scheduling of these reconciliation procedures should also be addressed.

Tune for performance

Because multiple tools are being used as part of this decision-support system, many areas for tuning are available, including the following:

- *Replication software.* As stated earlier, in a multitier architecture, replication can be considered a technical service within the middle tier and is configurable. Placement of replication components and modification of the configurable parameters can be used to increase replication throughput; however, effective tuning requires thorough knowledge of the software and an understanding of the available options.
- *Database design and index structures.* The database design and index structures should be tuned to provide optimal performance from the query tool.
- *OLAP tool configuration.* As with the replication software, a thorough knowledge of the internals of the OLAP tool are required for effective tuning.

Because multiple vendor software is involved, investing in a few days of consulting services from each vendor might be beneficial. Request a performance design review from their technical support staff. Design reviews represent excellent opportunities for knowledge transfer.

Create thorough documentation

In addition to providing the documentation that is normally supplied at the completion of a decision-support application, the following should also be supplied:

- *Operating procedures with recovery scenarios for asynchronous replication to both the local and consolidated databases.*

- *Operating procedures with recovery scenarios for the automated warning system and the exception and notification system.*
- *Executive users' handbook that explains in business terms the use of the executive reporting system.* This system represents the canned reports that were generated by the application develop team.

Migrate to the production environment

Now that all of these tasks have been completed, this decision-support system can be migrated into the production environment. It should fit well into the global replication architecture, the physical infrastructure, and the data warehousing strategy of the firm.

Case Study 3—Using Replication within a Mobile Computing Environment

This case study illustrates the use of asynchronous replication in an OLTP environment that supports mobile users. The requirement is for the distribution of processes and data to many mobile workers that are part of a domestic insurance claims system. Because this design paradigm is very different from the typical client/server model being used within the firm, it presents many technical and cultural challenges.

In addition to asynchronously replicating local database changes back to a consolidated OLTP database, each mobile user also needs his or her read-only reference data refreshed to a snapshot consistent with that of the rest of the firm. This read-only data refresh uses the incremental refresh type of asynchronous replication. This same type of replication is also currently being used to support the firm's data warehouse environment. Therefore, the products, expertise, best-practice guides, and administrative skills already exist within the firm.

CHALLENGES ASSOCIATED WITH MOBILE COMPUTING

Managing data and processes in a distributed environment where all devices and administrative support staff are usually available to all users is not easy; however, adding the complication of many points of distribution that are connected to the core systems only intermittently adds many complexities.

The tenets associated with client/server computing break down when using a model where the client is connected to the network only intermittently. Most client/server applications assume an online high-bandwidth connection and low latency between the client and server. They fail to accommodate the multiple devices and connection methods typically used by mobile workers. Mobile workers generally have high latency and limited bandwidth for communications. Mobile workers need to do as much work as possible without being connected to back-end resources. When mobile users are connected to firm resources, they need to use that connection time to transfer and resynchronize their data. In essence, the architectural requirement for mobile computing dictates a relatively "fat" client.

Mobile applications must be designed for use by disconnected users who require both online and deferred access. The application designer must decide which processes are conducted online and which should use deferred access (a store-and-forward paradigm). The factors that influence these decisions are as follows:

- *Business requirements of the application being developed.*
- *Transactional design.* This involves the demarcation of a business transaction into one or more software transactions. These transaction boundaries must preserve the integrity of the data and reflect the business requirements with respect to recoverable units (logical units of work).
- *Data consistency requirements.* For example, when should the consolidated database reflect a consistent whole?
- *Cost of one approach over others for that particular process.*
- *Time that the mobile user needs to spend on the network to accomplish the task.* The actual connect time should be kept to a minimum to maximize the mobile user's time.
- *Security issues.*

Mobile users take on additional responsibilities relative to their client/server counterparts. When mobile workers are not connected to their local or wide area networks, they can rely on minimal assistance from the firm's technical support staff. As a result, mobile users must be responsible for local administration of their hardware and software, and for scheduling the synchronization of information across devices. This is a major responsibility, one that is critical to the firm's data integrity. The administrative training of mobile users should not be overlooked.

OVERVIEW OF BUSINESS PROBLEM

An insurance company needs to implement a mobile claims entry system that can be used by its domestic claims agents who operate in 12 Northeastern states. Headquarters for this insurance company is in Princeton, New Jersey. A mobile solution was chosen for this claims entry system because the firm wants its claim agents to deal face-to-face with potential claimants. This approach helps to reduce fraudulent claims because the agent works directly with the claimant and can immediately view the alleged damages. In addition, the firm wants to support its marketing image as the caring insurance company that provides fast service in times of disaster. The firm also felt that other objectives could be met by using this paradigm, including the following:

- *Increase claim agent productivity*. It offers the freedom of anytime and anywhere computing.
- *Decrease time spent commuting into branch offices to perform claim entry*. Claim entry can occur immediately from the location of the disaster or accident. Agents no longer have to commute into a branch office to perform claim entry and client querying, thereby allowing agents to recapture the time spent commuting. The managers of the claims department have stated that this recaptured time should be used to handle additional customers. The firm anticipates restrictions on hiring any new claims agents for the next year and having the existing staff handle an increased workload.
- *Decrease facility costs*. Claim agents no longer need office space to perform claim entry and client query. In essence, they can use their home, motel room, or commuter train as an of-

fice. Their local database will store all the data needed to enter and validate claims.

Assumptions and requirements regarding the environment include the following:

- *All reference data needed to validate and complete a claim entry transaction is maintained by legacy systems on a host in Princeton, New Jersey.* A narrow set of this reference data will be replicated asynchronously to all mobile users. The requirement for only a subset of reference data is based on the desire to keep the size of the mobile reference database small and to not replicate data of a sensitive nature outside the firm's firewalls.
- *Each claims agent will be equipped with a laptop computer and the required applications for claims entry and simple decision support.* Each laptop computer will also have the software needed to handle data transfer between the mobile unit and the central computer system at Princeton. Training for all mobile users will be essential.
- *In addition to corporate headquarters in Princeton, there are four branch offices.* These local branch offices serve as meeting points and conference centers, but none of these local offices has sophisticated computing resources. They all have small LANs that provide personnel productivity tools for all sales force members and claim agents working within that vicinity. These productivity tools include word processing, spreadsheet, and presentation software. The local offices have network connectivity to corporate headquarters in Princeton for data entry and query purposes; however, none of these locations persistently stores sales or claims data. All sales and claims data entered remotely from a branch office becomes part of that night's batch processing.
- *Every claims agent is assigned to one of the five offices.* Local branch offices and the corporate office perform the same claims entry function.
- *The service-level requirements for applications that perform claims entry are quite strict.* Customers are demanding; therefore, the goal is to provide them with fast claims entry and

processing. For the firm, this is a component of marketing strategy.

- *All back-office claims processing occurs at the corporate headquarters in Princeton.* Results of all mobile claim entries are forwarded daily to Princeton for that night's batch-processing cycle.

- *The firm supports a large reporting database that is refreshed at the end of the nightly batch-processing cycle.* All users have access to this database, which is used heavily by managers, sales force members, and claims agents. This reporting environment is expected to become part of an OLAP Web service that will be used by the new mobile claims agents.

- *Each claims agent represents a primary source for data and, as such, is assigned a specific set of customers and policies to support.* Even with diligent data partitioning, conflicting updates may occur across the many primary sources. In essence, this is a hybrid of a master/slave model and an update-anywhere model. By partitioning and assigning ownership, the number of conflicts can be kept to a minimum, but they still will occur. For example, when a physical disaster occurs, different agents might end up dealing with different members of the same family or policy, or a claimant could deal with an agent and then immediately seek additional services from corporate headquarters. Therefore, a pure master/slave model does not exist. The new claims processing system should be able to detect these conflicts. Once detected, their resolution will involve both automated and manual procedures.

- *Mobile users will need to send and receive information through a single communications session.* The synchronization process must be able to handle data transformations and mapping for schemata differences. In addition, it must know what data to synchronize and the authorizations of each mobile user. Each mobile user is expected to connect to the host system at least once during every business day. Generally each mobile user will connect to the host system twice, once at the beginning of the business day to receive the results of the previous night's processing, and once at the end of the business day to transfer his or her claim entry data for batch processing. Data received from each mobile user becomes part of that night's batch processing. The window for data transfer is between 6:00 AM and 10:00 PM Eastern standard time. Between 10:00 PM and 6:00 AM the nightly batch cycle is executed.

- *Data distribution and replication services for this mobile OLTP environment must be scalable and flexible.* They must support future developments as the sales force is added to the cast of mobile users.

The goal of the firm is to reduce costs and increase productivity by means of introducing a mobile worker paradigm. As the paradigm shift is accepted, the firm plans to reduce the size of all local branch offices. Figure 12.1 illustrates this new topology for the firm.

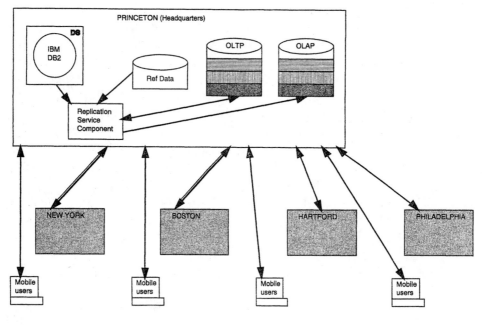

LEGEND
DS = Data Server
Ref data = Read only reference data
256 kB = ═══════
64 kB = ──────

FIGURE 12.1 Case Study 3—Replicating within a mobile computing environment.

APPLYING DATA DISTRIBUTION METHODOLOGY

As with the previous case studies, the distribution methodology presented in Chapter 5 is used as the workplan for the following section. All data distribution decision points will be thoroughly identified and explained.

Prepare an application distribution profile

The objectives of this task are to describe the distributed nature of the application and to start solidifying network requirements. The suggested deliverable is an application distribution profile. Table 12.1 presents a completed profile for this case study. Note

TABLE 12.1 Application Distribution Profile

Application Name: Case Study 3—Replicating Within a Mobile Computing Environment

Location types	Locations	User types anticipated numbers	Business transactions with anticipated execution rates
Headquarters	Princeton	Claims department managers (3) Claims analysts (2) Sales agents (40) Claims agents (21)	Agent performance reporting (daily) Claims analysis (40/daily) Claims entry (640/daily) Local reporting (100/daily)
Local branch offices	New York	Office manager (1) Sales agents (50) Claims agents (31)	Claims entry (930/daily) Local reporting (160/daily)
	Boston	Office manager (1) Sales agents (40) Claims agents (18)	Claims entry (600/daily) Local reporting (100/daily)
	Hartford	Office manager (1) Sales agents (27) Claims agents (16)	Claims entry (400/daily) Local reporting (80/daily)
	Philadelphia	Office manager (1) Sales agents (24) Claims agents (15)	Claims entry (390/daily) Local reporting (90/daily)

that with a mobile computing environment the logical location types and user types are few, but the number of member types can be large.

Prepare a physical infrastructure profile

The objectives of this task are to document the physical resources available at each potential deployment location and to identify any potential distribution constraints. The suggested deliverable is a physical infrastructure profile. Table 12.2 presents a completed profile for this case study. Note that the deployment locations for this case study represent two logical types: the host environment in Princeton and the mobile worker's laptop computer.

Create referentially tied data recovery groups

The objectives of this task are to identify both data recovery groups and potential opportunities for implementing data partitioning by physical location. Because this application represents a mobile computing environment where the mobile users will be receiving updated versions of read-only reference data and will be forwarding completed claim entry transactions back to the host environment, this task is relatively straightforward. It includes the analysis of the data schema used for the existing claims database on the host system in Princeton. This analysis identifies the data that will be required for claim entry at each mobile unit.

After thorough analysis of the entity relationship diagram of the claims database, the following data recovery groups were identified:

- *Tightly tied claim entry transaction data.* This transactional data must be recovered as a set.
- *Weakly tied reference data.* This data is primary sourced by other applications that reside on the host computer. It is required by the claims entry processes for validation purposes. It is always used in a read-only mode and does not require real-time consistency with the updatable claims data.

TABLE 12.2   Physical Infrastructure Profile

Application Name: Case Study 3—Replicating Within a Mobile Computing Environment

Location/ Location type	Network connectivity (WAN and LAN)	Hardware resources (e.g., servers)	Software resources (e.g., OS, DBMS)	Security level code	Availability level code	Administrative support and constraints	Additional constraints and concerns
Princeton /Headquarters	256 kB—New York 256 kB—Boston 64 kB—Hartford 64 kB— Philadelphia Ethernet	• 2 IBM host • 50 Intel-based workstations • 25 Intel-based notebooks • IBM DPROPR/2 • IBM DataHub/2	• IBM AS/400 • IBM DB2/400 • IBM OS/2 • IBM DB2/2 • IBM DPROPR	High	7 × 24	Full support	Full technical support provided to all local branches
New York /Local branch office	256 kB—Princeton Ethernet	• 75 Intel-based workstations • 40 Intel-based notebooks	• IBM OS/2 • IBM DB2/2	Medium	10 hours/day 8 AM–6 PM local time	Minimum local support during office hours	
Boston /Local branch office	256 kB—Princeton Ethernet	• 45 Intel-based workstations • 20 Intel-based notebooks	• IBM OS/2 • IBM DB2/2	Medium	10 hours/day 8 AM–6 PM local time	Minimum local support during office hours	
Hartford /Local branch office	64 kB—Princeton Ethernet	• 40 Intel-based workstations • 20 Intel-based notebooks	• IBM OS/2 • IBM DB2/2	Medium	10 hours/day 8 AM–6 PM local time	Minimum local support during office hours	
Philadelphia /Local branch office	64 kB—Princeton Ethernet	• 40 Intel-based workstations • 20 Intel-based notebooks	• IBM OS/2 • IBM DB2/2	Medium	10 hours/day 8 AM–6 PM local time	Minimum local support during office hours	

The partitioning aspects of this task are very critical because this is a hybrid of a master/slave model and an update-anywhere model. By partitioning and assigning ownership, the number of conflicts can be kept to a minimum. The keys to conflict resolution are ownership and notification. Data element ownership is important because it will be used to determine which updater "wins" when conflicts are detected. Notification will be used to alert a claims administrator, who will verify the correct resolution of each conflict.

For this case study, a customer/policy ownership table is incorporated into the database. For each customer/policy, this table identifies the primary data owner. In addition, a last updater column and a last update time stamp column are incorporated into every table that will reside within the laptop databases. This additional data will aid in the conflict resolution process. The laptop application does a lookup into the ownership table and alerts the user if he or she is updating outside of the scope of ownership. The application, however, allows the transaction to complete. As part of that transaction, the entry is flagged as a potential conflict. Conflict detection and resolution will take place on the host system as part of the apply process.

Each laptop database represents its own recovery group. Therefore, each claims agent is expected to perform local backups and to synchronize local data with the host databases at the close of the business day. A host monitoring system records who has and has not executed the daily data synchronization process.

Prepare a process-to-data use profile

The objectives of this task are to identify data usage across application processes and to highlight "heavy-hitter" processes. Because this application represents the migration of the claims entry processes from a wholly host environment to a combination of host and mobile user environment, the existing CRUD matrix for the current claims entry process is used as the deliverable for this task.

Integrate global data usage with process-to-data use profile

The objectives of this task are to integrate global data usage with the application's process-to-data use profile and to negotiate service-level agreements. Because the case study under consideration is a migration of the existing claims entry system to a more distributed environment, the challenge of this task is the detection and resolution of any and all conflicting updates within this multiple primary source environment. The apply portion in the host environment is where these conflicts are detected and ultimately resolved. These challenges will be addressed as this task unfolds.

This application interfaces with other systems in two areas. One is the receiving of read-only reference data to each mobile unit; this data is used to validate all claims entered via the mobile laptops. The other is the integration of all of the claims transactions entered from the mobile units into the existing claims database on the host in Princeton. This is where the conflict and resolution processing must occur. Each of these interfaces will be addressed in detail.

The reference data analysis is the same analysis that occurred as part of Case Study 1. This entails the identification of the required data, the definition of a schema that will perform efficiently for mobile users, and a clarification of any mapping or transformation services that will be required. The schema that will be used is a subset of the one currently being used for the claims database within the host system. In addition, the firm will reuse the current asynchronous replication infrastructure that is being used to build their data warehouse environment. This infrastructure uses a refresh type of asynchronous replication. It is a vendor-supplied solution that pulls data from the host databases and stores this data in staging tables. At the time the data is written into the staging tables, the transactional nature of each software transaction is discarded—the BEGIN and COMMIT portions are no longer available for target replicas. (See Chapter 1 for a detailed discussion of the loss of transactional semantics during the replication process.) For the reference data under consideration this is a very appropriate technology. The mobile users are disconnected from the host system for the majority of their working day. The requirement is to have this data synchronized once a day. The users need either an incremental or complete refresh at the start of each business day. This data snapshot represents a picture of the reference data at the end of the nightly batch-processing cycle. This point-in-time consistency is exactly what is needed. All mobile users, whether they perform their reference data synchronization at 6:00 AM or at 10:00 AM, will receive the same picture of that business day's reference data.

For this case study, no new service-level agreement is required with reference data suppliers because the developers are responsible for the existing claims entry system and the new mobile version of the same application. The application developers create the necessary staging tables for the reference data and use the vendor capture software to populate them. An advantage to this type of refresh technology is that it supports "condensed" data. This means that if a reference data row changes 40 times during the course of the day, the apply process for the mobile users receives just the final image of that row. It does not receive 40 individual, transactionally consistent update events. This is important for the mobile user because it shortens the time required for the reference data synchronization process.

The integration of all the claims transactions that are entered from the mobile units into the existing claims database on the host in Princeton presents interesting challenges. This is where conflict detection and resolution processing come into play. To simplify this processing, it is important to limit the number of conflicts and to provide sufficient information for correct resolution; this is why the database schema was modified in the create referentially tied data recovery groups task. Remember that a customer/policy ownership table was created and two columns were added to each table. These columns were the last updater column and a last update time stamp column. The vendor replication solution being used forwards all claims entry data changes to the host environment during a communication session.

The claims department managers in Princeton monitor claims activity and agent performance; the time of each communication session is recorded. This information is used to evaluate the completeness of that day's claim activity. For example, what percentage of the agents have reported in and what is the expected dollar value of the entered claims? At the start of the nightly batch processing, around 10:00 PM, a process is invoked that scans the staging tables received from the mobile users and searches for data update conflicts. The process looks for updaters who have updated outside their designated data ownership range and for duplicate rows regarding the same customer/policy. Once the potential conflicts are detected, business rules are applied to attempt resolution. The business users have been diligent, and approximately 80 percent of the potential conflicts have business rules that aid with the resolution. The 20 percent that cannot be immediately resolved are written to an exceptions file that is resolved manually the next business day. For the 80 percent that potentially have been resolved, notification messages are written to each losing agent's electronic mail queue. These messages alert the claims agent that the data he or she submitted was the "loser" in a conflict detection and resolution scheme. It also lists one of the three claims department managers who is responsible for further resolution if the agent chooses to pursue the conflict further. Once the conflict detection and resolution processing are complete for the staging tables, these tables enter the nightly batch processing of claims. As part of the update process to the claims database on the host system, the same conflict detection and resolution processing occur again. This is necessary because the claims database on the host also serves as a primary data source.

Create data placement scheme

The objective of this task is to integrate all the knowledge assembled thus far and to formulate a first-pass data placement scheme. For this case study, the task is very simple. A claims database residing on a host system stores a consolidated view of all OLTP claims transactions. Each mobile user has a subset of this database. This subset reflects a local view in that it stores all open claims assigned to agents within their local branch. If the agent needs to view data beyond this scope he or she needs only remotely connect to the host system in Princeton. After passing designated security checks, the agent is able to query and view the complete claims database.

Slicing the data in this fashion permits the amount of data stored on any mobile unit to be relatively small. In addition, it limits the number of slices that must be defined. Because each agent is assigned to one of the five branches, only five views of the consolidated database are required. A further advantage of partitioning the transaction database in this manner is that it shortens the time involved in data synchronization.

Two replication models are used to implement this case study. The first is a master/slave model with non-fragmented primaries and one-to-many target replicas. This is used for the simple one-way replication of read-only reference data to all mobile units. The second is a consolidation model (master/slave model with distributed primary fragments and a single consolidated replica). This is used to collect all claims data entered from mobile units into a consolidated whole within the host environment. Each model is orthogonal to the other in that each supports different data elements. See Chapter 2 for details regarding each model.

Validate placement scheme against existing constraints, capacities, and technologies

The objective of this task is to ensure that the existing physical infrastructure can support the proposed data distribution scheme. It entails a methodical review of each deployment location with respect to any and all constraints, possible capacity limitations, and any lack of support for specific technological requirements. For this case study, there are really only two deployment locations to consider: the host environment and the mobile user environment.

With respect to the host, no restrictions were identified. With respect to the mobile units, the only constraint is the amount of data that should be persistently stored within the database. The size of the reference data subset required to validate a claim during the claims entry process is small. In addition, by having only open claims for a designated branch reside on a mobile unit, the size of the database is kept reasonable. After additional analysis, it was agreed that the required database sizes were within the range that a laptop computer can support.

Validate placement scheme against service-level requirements

The objective of this task is to ensure that the proposed data distribution scheme and the existing physical infrastructure can meet the performance requirements specified in the service-level agreements. The only restriction identified is the amount of time required to perform data synchronization. The claims agents have said that they feel this task should take no more than 15 minutes. Because the firm is new to this technology, preliminary analysis affirmed that the 15-minute limit could be met with the existing physical infrastructure; however, to ensure future scalability, the firm explored using clusters of host machines. As more mobile users are added, the firm will be able to disperse the users across multiple host machines. This should help to ensure that the required data synchronization time restrictions can continue to be met.

Implement distribution scheme

The proposed distribution scheme can now be implemented. A phased-in approach will be used. Only one branch at a time will shift its claims agents to the mobile environment. The Princeton office will be first. After successful integration, each of the other four branches will be added over the span of four months.

IMPLEMENTING APPLICATION WORKPLAN

The application workplan presented in Chapter 9 is used as the workplan for the following section. As with the previous case studies, all decision points will be thoroughly identified and explained.

Obtain appropriate training

For this application, the firm has no reusable technical services that can be employed; however, it does have a knowledge base and infrastructure for using the refresh type of asynchronous replication. It is currently being used to maintain data consistency between the host OLTP systems and the OLAP environment. These resources will be used to assist in establishing the mobile computing infrastructure. In addition, the existing best-practice documents will be studied, applied, and modified to meet the needs of the new mobile paradigm.

Training will be essential in two areas for the success of this system. The first area involves training the application developers. They must understand the design trade-offs associated with developing a mobile application. They must be able to make intelligent decisions regarding which processes are to be conducted online and which are to use deferred access.

The second area of training involves the mobile users. Each claims agent must use the claims entry and decision support systems efficiently and effectively perform the administration functions necessary to support his or her laptop computer. To meet this goal, claims agents will receive two types of training. They will attend classes that cover the firm's claim entry and processing procedures and that present computer hardware and software fundamentals and procedures. They will also receive copies of in-house-developed troubleshooting guides. As a further aid, a hot line will be established to answer questions from the field.

Review the distributed nature of the application design

This task validates the decisions made within the data distribution model. It confirms that all primary sources for data and processes have been identified. By simply stating that this application supports a mobile computing environment, the distributed nature of the application becomes apparent. For this case study, this task should ensure the accuracy of the reference data subset with respect to claims entry and processing. It should also validate the data partitioning scheme being used and the accuracy of ownership assignments.

Validate the selection of the application model

This review effort should involve not only application team members but also participants from other technical support areas within the firm. The objectives of this effort are to ensure that the final design for this mobile application not only reflects a tactical solution but also integrates well into the existing physical infrastructure of the firm.

For this case study, the models identified during the create data placement scheme task were deemed correct. In essence, a mobile environment represents two replication models. Each model is used against a different set of data (orthogonal data). One model is the one-to-many replication of reference data out to the mobile users; the other is the many-to-one replication of claims' transactional data back to a consolidated whole. If need be, both of these asynchronous replication processes can occur during the same communication session.

Define specifications for all data mapping and transformational service requirements

Data mapping and transformational services may be required in two areas for this case study. The first is the replication of reference data from the host to the mobile units. The vendor solution being used supports staging tables and the ability to subscribe to a relational view of these staging tables. Because the mobile units require only a subset of the reference data currently being used in the host system, the view of the staging tables contains only the columns necessary to populate the subset tables. No data transformation is required.

For the propagation of claims data from each mobile unit, staging tables are again used. Each mobile user transfers his or her claims data to the staging tables during the communication session. The advantage on the agent side is that no additional processing is required prior to the communication session.

Define configuration parameters for resource managers

Because identical application processes will be executed on each mobile unit, the same database design will also be used on each laptop database. The only concern that must be addressed is the configuration parameters to use for this environment. In anticipation of building a mobile environment, the firm has already addressed the majority of these issues. It modified its existing best-practice guide for data server installations to incorporate the use of laptop computers. The firm has elected to use the same sort order and compatible character sets for consistency across the host and mobile environments. In addition, it has implemented time services that synchronize the time on each mobile unit during the initialization of each connection to the host. The training sessions for the claims agents cover these topics in detail. Agents are warned not to modify any of the configuration parameters. For this case study, there are no further issues to address with respect to configuring resource managers.

Assist with configuring the replication infrastructure and software

For this case study, the application development team will define and support certain portions of the replication infrastructure. They must determine replication volumes and recovery requirements. Once capacity planning is complete, they will work with the systems support staff who install the replication software to configure the replication environment and create all the necessary staging objects. A number of these planning sessions were held, and the following recommendations were made:

- The staging tables should have sufficient capacity to support fluctuations in data volumes from the mobile users.
- The number of concurrent users should be monitored so that host capacity limits are not reached.
- The security functionality should be robust, yet user friendly so that legitimate users are not denied access erroneously.

Address any application-specific issues related to the model being implemented

For the case study under consideration, the following model-related issues were identified:

- *Lack of strong backup procedures for the mobile units.* Even with the computer training offered to the agents in the field, countless variables could trigger the complete loss of an agent's data. For example, the laptop could be stolen or dropped; the agent could inadvertently delete data; or, through poor administration, the database could become corrupted. Therefore, a fallback position must be in place. In the insurance industry, data becomes more valuable with time. It is used to provide legal proof of recorded events. Data loss is not an acceptable situation. Therefore, it was decided that during the end-of-data communication session, the host will receive a complete backup of each mobile unit. This nightly backup can be used to restore a mobile unit to a consistent point in time should a disaster occur. The agents will also be directed to preserve a paper trail for the current day's business.
- *Requirement to integrate enhanced security for distributed data.* The data being stored in each mobile unit will be encrypted, and the applications will have access security. This should aid in protecting the firm in cases where a laptop is lost or stolen.
- *Increased availability for hot-line support.* Agents will require technical assistance during non-traditional business hours when they are working at the site of a disaster.

Create the required replication objects

For this case study, the application development team has most of the responsibility for creating the necessary replication objects. They will work with the existing system and network support staff to ensure that a smooth integration of this new mobile computing paradigm occurs. The team that currently supports the replication of OLTP data to the OLAP environment will provide assistance. They will advise, provide training for the existing scripts and tools that help to automate the object create process, and ensure that the development effort complies with all best-practice guidelines.

Code and test the application

Because this application will be distributed to many mobile units, a strong testing effort is necessary. The goal is to minimize release upgrades because upgrading all mobile units is expensive, both in time and in resources. Change management is a big issue in a mobile environment. Upgrades are usually accomplished by downloads to an agent's laptop during a data transfer session. Multiple "fixes" should be bundled so that clients are minimally affected when upgrades do occur. In addition, all upgrades should be scheduled so that agents can plan their work to accommodate them.

Test recovery scenarios with replication in place

Because the host system will perform nightly backups for all mobile units, software should be obtained or developed that performs fast backups and fast loads. The agents and the firm do not want to be unable to work for any lengthy period. This software and its associated procedures should be thoroughly tested before the application rolls out to the mobile users.

Certify the application for WAN use with replication in place

Because many users are part of the mobile community, the communication sessions should be very efficient. Only the condensed reference data changes should be forwarded, and fast data transfer techniques should be used for the laptop backups. WAN analysis tools should be employed to verify the efficiency of these communication sessions.

Tune for performance

Monitoring software should be used to identify areas where tuning or network capacity need to be increased. In addition, if the number of concurrent communication sessions becomes an issue, either the existing host should be upgraded to handle more concurrent users or a second host should be installed to distribute the sessions and provide the necessary scalability.

Create thorough documentation

In addition to providing the documentation normally supplied at completion of an application, the following should also be supplied:

- *Operating procedures with recovery scenarios for the synchronization of reference data with the host system.*
- *Operating procedures with recovery scenarios for the transfer of claims data to the host environment.*
- *Operating procedures for nightly database backups on the host and recovery procedures, should the need arise.*
- *Users' handbook and troubleshooting guides for all claims agents.* These manuals should explain in business terms the use of the claims entry system and the data synchronization procedures.

Migrate to the production environment

Now that all of these tasks have been completed, this mobile computing environment can be phased into the production environment. It should fit well into the physical infrastructure, and it should serve an as example for future mobile computing endeavors.

Case Study 4—Using Replication for a Fault-Tolerant Warm-Standby

This case study illustrates the use of replication to provide application failover. When a hardware or software error occurs to the primary data server or at the primary server location, the application is switched over to use a standby data server. The business user experiences just a short delay before the application can continue. This type of fault tolerance can be provided in either a "hot-standby" or a "warm-standby" mode.

DIFFERENCES BETWEEN HOT- AND WARM-STANDBY ALTERNATIVES

Fault-tolerant systems provide redundant components and/or redundant data to ensure against loss of service. When data redundancy is used to increase fault tolerance, the standby replica can be kept synchronized in either real-time or near-real-time. If a real-time alternative is chosen, the standby data server is called a *hot-standby,* whereas if the near-real-time alternative is selected, the standby is called a *warm-standby.* For a hot-standby replica, both the primary resource manager and the target standby replica are always totally consistent. This total data consistency can be achieved by either a hardware or a software mechanism. If a hardware alternative is selected, then the hardware provides for dual writing across redundant devices. This alternative is attractive, but it does have disadvantages. For example, the redundant devices usually have to be in close proximity to each other. Therefore, this alternative protects against database failure but does not handle location failures, such as a failure caused by a flood. An additional disadvantage of a hardware alternative is that any errors that cause disk data corruption at a primary will be duplicated into the standby replica. If a software alternative is used to provide hot-standby functionality, then synchronous replication is employed to keep the target standby replica's data synchronized with that of the primary. Remember that synchronous replication uses a two-phase commit protocol to coordinate the distributed unit of work across multiple databases. See Appendix A for a complete discussion of a two-phase commit protocol. The same disadvantages of using distributed units of work, as addressed earlier, come into play again. Distributed units of work are not application transparent—that is, the application code has to be modified to incorporate this fault-tolerant functionality. In addition, some application performance degradation can occur due to locking across multiple resource managers and the associated additional communications.

By contrast, a warm-standby replica is kept synchronized with the primary source by means of asynchronous replication. This means that there is always some degree of latency before the originating event at the primary is reflected within the target standby replica. The advantages to an asynchronous approach for fault tolerance include the following:

- *It can be implemented in an application-transparent manner.* In other words, no application code needs to be modified to incorporate this functionality.
- *It does not need to support concurrent locking across multiple resource managers.*
- *It does not require that the primary and the target standby replica be in close proximity.* This allows the warm-standby system to handle both database and location failures.

In essence, the warm-standby replica provides a data source that is in relatively close consistency with the primary source. It can be used to replace the primary data source in the event of failures at the primary. The failure could be due to a corrupted database, a corrupted disk device, or a damaged CPU, or it could be due to a location failure caused by a flood, fire, or sabotage. To be effective, the switch over to the standby should occur with minimal preparation, by means of established procedures, and in a predictable amount of time.

It is worth noting that, depending on what architectural approach is used to implement the asynchronous replication, some minor degradation in performance of the originating event could occur. This depends entirely on the mechanism used to capture the originating event. If the path length of the originating transaction is increased, for example, due to extra application calls, then the transaction's performance will be affected. This should be considered when selecting an asynchronous replication approach.

Generally, two accepted approaches can be used to implement a warm-standby replica. The first is to roll the database log of the primary into the standby replica, and the second is to use asynchronous replication. Rolling the database log encompasses the periodic dumping of the database transaction log of the primary database and the subsequent applying of that log data to the standby database. Rolling the log usually implies a greater degree of latency at the standby replica than does continuous asynchronous replication. In general, the larger the data latency, the higher the potential for "lost" transactions when the primary database fails. When rolling the log is used, there is also the potential of duplicating the effect of software errors that could have corrupted a database or device. A further negative to rolling the log is that during the apply log process at the standby replica, the database is in a recovery mode and is usually unavailable to application users.

If asynchronous replication is used to support the warm standby database, usually a database-to-database type of asynchronous replication is used. With this type of event propagation, there is little likelihood that any database corruption could be forwarded to the target replica. In addition, generally the degree of latency is smaller than with rolling the log approach. Therefore, less data has the potential to become "lost." The negative of using asynchronous replication over rolling the log is that the asynchronous replication solution is slightly more complex to implement and maintain.

ISSUES ASSOCIATED WITH USING A WARM-STANDBY ALTERNATIVE FOR FAULT TOLERANCE

Multiple issues should be addressed when considering the implementation of a warm-standby alternative for fault tolerance. A warm-standby definitely does *not* provide the full functionality for fault tolerance that a hot standby does. Because the warm-standby replica's state always lags that of the primary, the following issues should be considered: the lag of the standby replica, due to the asynchronous replication infrastructure, and the transaction volume generated at the primary replica; the transactions in the store-and-forward queue that have not yet been delivered to the standby replica ("lost" transactions); and the approach used to resolve these "lost" transactions when the primary replica is restored. Lost transactions are not really lost; they are only perceived as lost because they are not visible to the users of the standby replica when it becomes active as the primary. In reality, they are recently committed transactions from the primary replica that have not yet been asynchronously propagated to the standby replica.

Infrastructure issues

The infrastructure that supports the warm-standby replica must have the capacity to keep up with the transaction volume generated by the application systems using the primary replica. This concern is application-specific in that different applications generate different amounts of transaction volume. If the infrastructure can keep up with the transaction volume, then there will be very few transactions in the store-and-forward queue when and if a failure occurs at the primary server or location. If there is a large buildup within the store-and-forward queue, then all these transactions could be perceived as lost. To be considered successful, a warm-standby replica should lag the primary replica by only a few transactions.

Dealing with "lost" transactions

Transactions that are perceived as "lost" must be resolved when the primary location is restored. If the store-and-forward queue is up to date with applying transactions, only a very few of these transactions should be "lost." Some vendor-supplied asynchronous replication software provides functionality to force the apply of the these recently committed transactions that are still in the store-and-forward queue before the standby replica is allowed to become the active primary.

Why is a resolution effort necessary? The example that follows uses the investment banking trade entry system discussed in Chapter 10. Suppose that when a database failure occurs, two recently committed transactions are still in the store-and-forward queue. One of these is a trade entry transaction, and the other is a cancellation for the sending of a settlements statement. The trader for the entered trade notices that the trade just entered is not being displayed. Therefore the trader re-enters it, and it becomes visible from the warm-standby replica. In the second example, no one notices the cancellation of the settlement statement. Therefore, the settlement statement is sent. Both of these situations must be resolved when the originating primary is restored as active.

If the primary restore process only pushes all the changes made on the standby replica back to the originating primary, these two situations will cause errors. For the trade entry, there will already be an existing trade row at the primary replica because that transaction had been committed at the primary before it was put on the store-and-forward queue. For the cancellation request, the request to cancel and the settlement statement that was generated and possibly sent are in conflict. Therefore, data modifications will be required to correct these situations.

There are multiple configuration approaches that can be used to resolve the lost transaction problem. These approaches include the following:

- *Allow the warm-standby replica to be used in read-only mode.* This allows querying against the standby database, but no update activity is permitted. If the outage is for a short duration, this is a viable alternative because it avoids the complexities of trying to resolve conflicting data situations. However, if this approach is used, it must have the full support of the business users of the applications involved.

- *Have the originating primary site be restored from the standby by means of a full backup and load.* Before the primary replica is restored all transactions that were in the store-and-forward queue should be resolved.
- *Implement full conflict detection and resolution for the primary and standby replicas.* The mechanism implemented must be able to ensure full detection and resolution of all conflicts during the restore of the primary database to active status and vice versa. When this approach is used, the standby replica feeds all of its captured changes back to the primary to restore it to active status.

 TIP

In general, using an automated decision process to switch over to the standby replica is not recommended. In other words, an application that cannot access the primary data source should not automatically start using the standby replica. A good deal of effort is needed to synchronize a primary source after a switchover to a standby replica has occurred. Therefore, the outage should be assessed and deemed appropriately severe before a switchover is performed. The unavailability of the primary could just be a transient situation, such as a brief network problem. In this situation, the administrative costs associated with switching and then synchronizing the primary could be avoided.

OVERVIEW OF THE STEPS NECESSARY TO IMPLEMENT A WARM-STANDBY REPLICA

The steps needed to implement asynchronous replication for a warm-standby replica include the following:

- *Selection and implementation of the asynchronous replication mechanism of choice.*
- *Initialization of the warm-standby database.*
- *Thoroughly defined procedures that are used to fail over to the standby database.* As mentioned above, an assessment of the

problem should occur prior to switching to the warm-standby replica. If the replication software of choice allows a procedure to force the apply of the transactions still in the store-and-forward queue, it should be part of these procedures.

• *Switch back to the primary database.* It is during the fallback to the original primary that lost transactions should be resolved.

 WARNING

When asynchronous replication is used to support a warm-standby database for fault tolerance, the standby replica's state always lags that of the primary version by some time. Therefore, the probability is very high that when the primary version of the database fails, some transactions will be "lost." The switchover process should strive to limit the number of lost transactions, and the reconciliation process, which occurs when the primary database is restored, should synchronize both databases.

OVERVIEW OF BUSINESS PROBLEM

A travel and vacation company that offers all-inclusive holiday packages to global resorts needs to upgrade its existing fault-tolerance mechanisms to a more robust approach. The firm owns and manages all the resorts to which it offers holiday packages, as well as some of the travel agencies that offer these packages. To ensure that the resorts are filled with vacationers, the firm also accepts reservations from a number of independently owned travel agencies. These independent agencies receive commissions from the firm to encourage selling its holiday packages. As a strategic marketing move, the firm plans to offer bookings and reservations by means of its home page on the World Wide Web. With the addition of this new functionality, the firm expects that it will have to upgrade the hardware and software that currently support the existing reservation systems. In addition, it plans to enhance the existing fault-tolerant mechanisms. By enhancing existing fault-tolerant mechanisms, the decision makers within the firm believe that the following objectives will also be met:

- *Increased sales.* The existing hardware and software systems have been experiencing frequent outages, which have the undesirable effect of making the reservation systems unavailable. The firm has monitored the effect of these unplanned outages and has noticed that sales from the independent agents always drop after one of these failures. The firm believes that the independent agents become discouraged and frustrated with the poor quality of its systems and therefore book their clients on vacation packages offered by competing firms. By providing a more robust, fault-tolerant system, the firm believes that sales from independent agents will increase.
- *Decreased time spent on bringing up a backup system once a failure has been detected.* The firm currently uses a rolling the log approach with a 15-minute interval. With this approach, bookings and reservations have been lost. In addition, it has generally taken close to an hour to make the standby system active.
- *Increased marketing and trend analysis by using the new standby database for decision support.* The firm believes that by upgrading its existing hardware and software systems and by incorporating a robust standby database that can also be used for decision support, it will have a marketing edge over its competition.
- *Increased global sales by means of an interactive presence on the Internet.* This new form of electronic commerce has become popular among the demographic slice of buyers that the firm considers its ideal market—young, upwardly mobile professionals.

Assumptions and requirements regarding the environment for this case study include the following:

- *All data needed to complete a reservation is maintained by systems on the host in New York City.* This reference data will be available to both the new reservations systems and the interactive Web application.
- *The firm currently rents space for computer operations near its headquarters in New York City.* Their disaster recovery approach has been to store backup tapes in rented space in Staten

Island, New York. The new approach will incorporate a near-real-time warm-standby. The location for this fault tolerance system is yet to be determined.

- *The firm will train and hire developers for the Web portion of the new reservations system.*
- *In addition to corporate headquarters in New York City, the firm has three owned and managed travel agencies.* The travel agents in the New York office and the other three agencies execute approximately 50 percent of all resort bookings for the firm. Each agency has small LANs that provide personnel productivity tools for all agents. These productivity tools include word processing, spreadsheet, and presentation software. Each agency has network connectivity to headquarters in New York City for data entry and query purposes. In addition, each agency has a small, local database use for local administration and management; however, all reservation applications use databases in New York for data persistence. All daily reservations become part of that night's batch processing.
- *Currently the service-level requirements for applications that perform reservations entry are quite loose.* Agents generally work with customers either in person or by phone and tentatively book resort packages. Later that same day they will make the actual reservation entry. Batch processing formalizes and confirms all tentative reservations. One of the goals of the new system is to formalize reservation entry and confirmations while working with the customer.
- *All back-office reservations processing occurs nightly at the headquarters in New York City.* Results of all batch processing will be replicated to the standby database for decision-support querying.
- *The firm supports a reporting database that is refreshed at the end of the nightly batch processing cycle.* All agents and analysts have access to this database. It is anticipated that most of the analytical processing will be executed against the standby database. Removing query users from the OLTP databases should enhance the performance of the reservation entry systems. Reservations entered via the Internet will execute against the OLTP databases while Web browser activity—"surfing" marketing information about the resorts—will execute against the standby server.

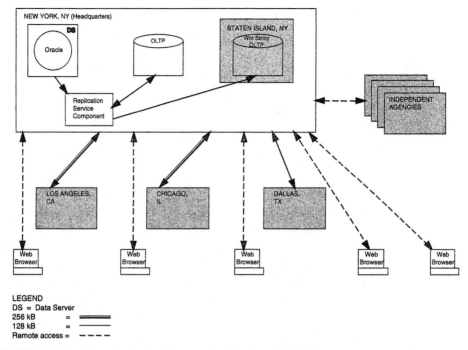

FIGURE 13.1 Case Study 4—Using replication for a fault-tolerant warm-standby.

- *Remote access to the OLTP databases, the decision support systems, and Web browsers will definitely increase the number of connections that the hardware and software currently support.*
- *Data distribution and replication services for the reservation systems and Web initiative must be scalable and flexible to support future anticipated electronic commerce.*

The goal of the firm is to increase reservation efficiency by enhancing the existing application systems, provide a stronger fault-tolerant environment, and increase sales by entering into the new Web model for commerce. Figure 13.1 illustrates this new topology for the firm.

APPLYING DATA DISTRIBUTION METHODOLOGY

As with the previous case studies, the distribution methodology presented in Chapter 5 is used as the workplan for the following section. All data distribution decision points will be thoroughly identified and explained.

Prepare an application distribution profile

The suggested deliverable for this task is an application distribution profile, which describes the distributed nature of the application and should aid in solidifying network requirements. Table 13.1 presents a completed profile for this case study. As with the

TABLE 13.1 Application Distribution Profile

Application Name: Case Study 4—Using Replication for a Fault-Tolerant Warm Standby

Location types	Locations	User types with anticipated numbers (by location)	Business transactions with anticipated execution rates (by location and user types)
Headquarters	New York	Travel agent manager (1) Travel agents (40) Market analysts (4)	Agent performance reporting (daily/distributed to all offices) Resort capacity planning (350/daily) Bookings entry (480/daily)
Owned and managed travel agencies	Los Angeles	Office manager (1) Travel agents (25) Market analyst (1)	Resort capacity planning (200/daily) Bookings entry (210/daily)
	Chicago	Office manager (1) Travel agents (15) Market analyst (1)	Resort capacity planning (120/daily) Bookings entry (130/daily)
	Dallas	Office manager (1) Travel agents (10) Market analyst (1)	Resort capacity planning (120/daily) Bookings entry (90/daily)
Independently owned and managed travel agencies	40 agencies dispersed across the 48 contiguous states	Travel agents (250)	Resort capacity planning (360/daily) Bookings entry (900/daily)
Web Home Page	Global access		Anticipated initial bookings of 200 daily

case study depicting a mobile environment, the logical location types and user types are few, but the number of members of these types will be large. Because the firm is entering into a new marketing arena by introducing Web access, it will be difficult to predict just what the Internet usage might be. The firm plans to tally the number of times its current Web site is visited. Using this as a predictor of potential reservation usage, it will increase the number of available connections accordingly.

Prepare a physical infrastructure profile

The suggested deliverable for this task is a physical infrastructure profile, which should document the physical resources available at each potential deployment location and identify any potential distribution constraints. Table 13.2 presents a completed profile for this case study. Because reservations data currently resides only in New York, the distribution decision for this case study involves where to place the warm-standby data server.

Create referentially tied data recovery groups

The objectives of this task are to identity data recovery groups and to identify potential opportunities for implementing data partitioning by physical location. This warm-standby implementation does not require the typical data analysis needed by other applications because, by definition, a warm-standby replica is a complete copy of its primary source. Because the firm also wants to use the warm-standby database for decision support, it must understand the trade-offs associated with this decision. The major advantage for this decision is that it moves query users off the OLTP database, thereby enhancing OLTP performance. The major disadvantage associated with using the same database for warm-standby and decision support is that the data model used for the warm-standby database should be identical to the OLTP database. This eliminates a good share of the opportunities to tune the warm-standby database for better query performance. When the OLTP applications are switched over to the standby database they expect the same physical data structures. In most

TABLE 13.2   Physical Infrastructure Profile

Application Name: Case Study 4—Using Replication for a Fault-Tolerant Warm Standby

Location/ Location type	Network connectivity (WAN and LAN)	Hardware resources (e.g., servers)	Software resources (e.g., OS, DBMS)	Security level code	Availability level code	Administrative support and constraints	Additional constraints and concerns
New York /Headquarters	256 kB—Los Angeles 256 kB—Chicago 128 kB—Dallas • Multiple connections for remote access from independent agencies and Web users	• 1 Sun SPARC 2000 • Budget has been allocated for a second Sun SPARC 2000 • 50 workstations • 2 Pentium Pro servers	• Sun Solaris • Oracle RDBMS • Oracle Symmetric Replication • NT Server to be used as Web servers	High	7 × 24	Full support	Full technical support provided to all local branches
Los Angeles /Owned and managed travel agency	256 kB—New York Ethernet	30 workstations	Oracle RDBMS	Medium	10 hours/day 8 AM–6 PM local time	Minimum local support during office hours	
Chicago /Owned and managed travel agency	256 kB—New York Ethernet	20 workstations	Oracle RDBMS	Medium	10 hours/day 8 AM–6 PM local time	Minimum local support during office hours	
Dallas /Owned and managed travel agency	128 kB—New York Ethernet	14 workstations	Oracle RDBMS	Medium	10 hours/day 8 AM–6 PM local time	Minimum local support during office hours	

TABLE 13.2 (cont.)

Location/ Location type	Network connectivity (WAN and LAN)	Hardware resources (e.g., servers)	Software resources (e.g., OS, DBMS)	Security level code	Availability level code	Administrative support and constraints	Additional constraints and concerns
80 Independently owned and managed travel agencies	Connectivity to host machine in New York	Mixture of various platforms	Unknown	Unknown	Unknown	Unknown	
Web server access for bookings and reservations	Individual users with Web browsers and modems		85% have Intel-based PC with Netscape, Microsoft Explorer, or subscribe to a service like America Online or CompuServe	Light	7 × 24	Minimum support from various vendor hot-lines	

situations an OLTP data design is not optimized for query usage. Few summary or aggregate columns are included, and queries will require multiple joins to retrieve the requested information. These facts were pointed out to the decision makers of the firm, and after reasonable deliberation, they decided to proceed with the warm-standby solution despite its less-than-optimal query performance. They felt that the marketing analysts are not running massively complex queries, and they were willing to sacrifice query performance in favor of a near-real-time standby that will ensure the availability of the reservation systems. When and if the size of the analyst group increases, the firm will address implementing a separate OLAP database designed and tuned specifically for decision support. Initial analysis demonstrates that the typical query will return results in less than two minutes.

Prepare a process-to-data use profile

The objectives of this task are to identify data usage across application processes and to highlight "heavy-hitter" processes. Because this application represents the implementation of a more robust, fault-tolerant system, this task is not applicable for that aspect of this case study. An analysis of query usage across the database would be beneficial because it could be used to determine if the creation of additional indexes on the warm-standby database would increase query performance for the decision support users. Care must be used to ensure that these additional indexes do not cause the failure of any transactions in the apply portion of the replication effort. This would create an inconsistent warm-standby database.

Integrate global data usage with the process-to-data use profile

The objectives of this task are to integrate global data usage with the application's process-to-data use profile and to negotiate service-level agreements. For this case study there is no data integration across applications. The input is the complete OLTP databases that support the reservation application systems, and the output is the warm-standby replica. No further data analysis is required for the completion of this aspect of the task.

Two areas that should be addressed, however, are the degree of data latency of the warm-standby replica and the overall replication throughput. Both of these concepts are tightly tied. The degree of latency at the standby replica reflects the throughput of the complete replication infrastructure. The replication infrastructure is composed of the hardware, the replication software, and the network capacity of the physical environment supporting replication. If the infrastructure cannot keep up with the replication traffic generated by the primary source, then the warm standby will eventually have an ever-increasing degree of data latency. In other words, the standby replica will get further and further behind in terms of data consistency. The larger the apply queue becomes, the more transactions will be considered "lost" when a switchover to the warm standby is required. This thwarts the objective of implementing a warm-standby replica for fault tolerance. Careful analysis should be conducted to validate that the replication infrastructure can support the transaction volumes at peak periods. Invariably, failures occur during times of peak usage.

During this task, the developers should start considering how to resolve those transactions perceived as "lost" during the switchover processes. Does the tool of choice have a mechanism to apply by force the transactions still in the store-and-forward-queue? If this is an option, the number of conflicts during the synchronization of the original primary will be greatly reduced. In addition, users of the warm-standby database will be able to view their recently committed transactions. If a conflict detection and resolution scheme is deemed necessary to help resolve these situations, now is the time to start defining its requirements.

Create data placement scheme

The objective of this task is to integrate all of the knowledge assembled thus far and to formulate a first-pass data placement scheme. For this case study, this task involves choosing the location for the warm-standby replica.

Multiple options are available to the firm for placement of the warm-standby replica. These include placing it at any of the other firm-owned agencies or placing it at a location near the current OLTP databases that reside in New York City. If any of the owned agencies are used, issues associated with getting quick access to it from the other locations will surface. Currently the network topology is a hub with all connections radiating out from New York. If one of the owned agencies is used, network enhancements would be required. A further complication is the lack of 24-hour by 7-day support at the other agencies. This would require hiring and training staff and integrating administrative support procedures across the two locations. After a cost analysis was performed, it was decided to place the standby replica somewhere in the New York City vicinity, thus alleviating the support issues; the existing support staff in New York would support this new environment. It will, however, involve implementing a robust network connection between the primary source and the warm-standby replica. When a failure occurs and the OLTP users are switched over to the warm standby, the switch should be completely transparent to these users.

Validate placement scheme against existing constraints, capacities, and technologies

The objective of this task is to ensure that the existing physical infrastructure can support the proposed data distribution scheme. As with the other case studies, it entails a methodical review of each deployment location with respect to any and all constraints, possible capacity limitations, and any lack of support for specific technological requirements. For this case study, there are really only two deployment locations: the primary OLTP environment and the warm-standby replica.

This is where the initial analysis regarding replication throughput is validated. Transaction volumes at peak times should be tested with the replication tool of choice and the firm's existing infrastructure to ensure that the anticipated replication traffic can be supported. If it cannot, then possible tuning alternatives should be explored. If after the tuning opportunities are researched and tested, the desired throughput still cannot be maintained, then enhancements to the physical infrastructure are required, possibly including hardware upgrades and network enhancements.

The firm upgraded the existing hardware and budgeted for the purchase of an additional machine in anticipation of this fault-tolerant upgrade. It was confirmed that with a network enhancement between the two New York locations the infrastructure would support the anticipated replication traffic.

Validate placement scheme against service-level requirements

The objective of this task is to ensure that the proposed distribution scheme and the existing physical infrastructure can meet the performance requirements specified in the service-level agreements. For this case study, two areas must be addressed: the time required to switch over to the warm-standby replica and then subsequently fall back to the original primary and the validation of expected response times for query users.

After initial analysis, it is believed the defined procedures for switching over to the warm-standby will meet the requirements of the reservation systems users. After the procedures have been coded, further testing and tuning will be performed. For the synchronization of the primary for the fallback, some issues are still open. The firm has decided initially to use a dump of the standby database to restore the original primary. It would eventually like to use the asynchronous replication of the transactions from the standby to the primary, but at the present time it is not confident that it can implement a thorough conflict detection and resolution mechanism. Therefore it has decided to postpone the implementation of this type of fallback until a later phase of the project.

It is accepted that query user response time will be less than optimal for this first implementation. The DBAs will perform some database tuning. Once this fault-tolerant effort has been completed, the firm is open to the possibility of implementing a separate OLAP database for decision-support users.

Implement distribution scheme

The proposed warm-standby distribution scheme can now be implemented. The firm will lease space in the New York City vicinity for use as the warm-standby location. After a number of sites were explored, the firm decided on available space in Staten Island. The new space is near the site currently used to store the disaster recovery backup tapes.

The firm will also progress with initiatives to upgrade the network connections between the two New York City locations. In addition, they will increase the number of available user connections to both locations.

IMPLEMENTING APPLICATION WORKPLAN

The application workplan presented in Chapter 9 is used as the workplan for the following section. As with the previous case studies, all decision points will be thoroughly identified and explained.

Obtain appropriate training

The firm has very little expertise in data replication; therefore, training appropriate individuals is necessary. Individuals involved as part of this training effort include one systems administrator and one database administrator. In addition, a part-time consultant was hired to help the firm get the replication infrastructure defined and implemented. After completing the vendor training, these individuals, with the assistance of the experienced consultant, will be given the task of defining appropriate standards and best practices for the use of data replication within the firm. The tasks, as outlined in Chapter 8, will be included as part of the development of the best-practice guide. Once the infrastructure and best-practice guide have been defined, the consultant will be used only on an as-needed basis.

Because the firm has stated its desire to use the Web as a reservation entry mechanism, it will hire an individual with experience in this area. Two application developers and one network specialist will be assigned to work with the new employee so that a complete knowledge transfer can occur. It is important that a number of individuals will be able to support and administer this new functionality.

Review the distributed nature of the application design

The objective of this task is to validate the data distribution decisions made earlier. Because this case study is for the development of an asynchronous replication solution for fault tolerance, the selection of the standby replica location in Staten Island is the only distribution task that must be addressed. Once the site has been chosen the appropriate network enhancements can proceed.

Validate the selection of the application model

The objectives of this effort are to ensure that the final design for this warm-standby replica not only reflects a tactical solution but also integrates well into the existing physical infrastructure of the firm. This review effort should involve not only application team members but also participants from other technical support areas within the firm.

For this case study, the model selected is for the use of asynchronous replication to implement a warm-standby fault-tolerant system. Illustrations that exemplify this model are depicted in Chapter 2. Once the firm masters the use of replication to support this model, it can reuse and modify its approach to provide fault tolerance across other systems.

Define specifications for all data mapping and transformational service requirements

Because, by definition, the warm-standby replica will be identical to the primary data source, no data mapping or transformational services are required. It is important, however, to have a procedure to ensure that the data structures across the primary and the warm-standby replica remain identical.

Vendor-supplied replication software varies in its support of propagating DDL (data definition language) statements executed on the primary to the warm-standby replica. In other words, new or altered tables, indexes, stored procedures, permissions (grant statements), and the like may not automatically be forwarded to the target replica. If the vendor-supplied software does not support this functionality, then it is the responsibility of the database administrator supporting the databases to ensure that these changes are applied to both the primary and the standby replica.

Define configuration parameters for resource managers

Because identical reservation processes will be executed on both the primary data source and the standby replica, the same database configuration parameters should be used at both locations. In the past, the firm has identified the sort order and character sets that it deemed appropriate for use across all of its data servers. For this case study, there are no further issues to address with respect to configuring resource managers.

Assist with configuring the replication infrastructure and software

Because this case study addresses fault tolerance, a number of infrastructure and component placement alternatives should be discussed. A major consideration is the placement of the replication software components. One of the goals of a warm-standby solution is to minimize the number of "lost" transactions when the switch to the standby replica occurs. Placing the replication components and the store-and-forward queue on a machine that is *not* the one being used for the primary database is the best approach. If different machines are used and the machine that supports the primary database crashes, then the replication distribution and apply processes located on another machine can continue to apply transactions in the store-and-forward queue. This is especially critical if the application traffic at the primary data source is bursty or very uneven. If a failure occurs during a time of heavy traffic and a latency lag is experienced, then there is a good chance that many of the transactions in the store-and-forward queue can still be applied.

For this case study, the replication volumes from the primary data source were estimated. Then the replication software was installed and configured to handle the predicted capacity. Areas of particular concern are the size of the store-and-forward queue and any product-specific save parameters that could aid in recovery procedures should a replication component fail. A further concern is predicting a reasonable value for the number of concurrent users. This number should be monitored so that host capacity limits are not reached.

Address any application-specific issues related to the model being implemented

For the use of replication for fault tolerance, the issue that must be addressed is how the user applications are switched over to the warm-standby database and how they are switched back to the primary once the primary is resynchronized. Multiple alternatives can be used. The critical factor is that the option selected must integrate well with the asynchronous replication mechanism being used. Some possible alternatives include the following:

- *The vendor replication software of choice incorporates this functionality.* In this situation, the implementers need only define the required parameters.
- *Applications can use an environment variable or a file that indicates the name of the current primary database.*
- *Applications can incorporate the testing of which is the primary by looking up a value in a known table.*
- *The naming services that a data server uses to resolve locations can be switched to point to the warm standby.*

Once again, the same warning issued above applies. Do not let applications automatically make a decision to switch to the standby. A DBA or designated systems person should take some action to permit the use of the standby database.

Create the required replication objects

For this case study, the database support staff will have the majority of the responsibility for creating the necessary replication objects. The application developers for the Web portion of the application and the decision-support systems administrator will also have input. Because this is the first use of data replication within the firm, any scripts and tools created to help automate the object create process should be designed and coded with reuse in mind. This will simplify the create process for other developers in the future.

Code and test the application

Because the replication portion of this fault-tolerant system requires no application code, there is no specific application code to test; however, the replication infrastructure should be tested to validate that the warm standby replica is receiving all the changes applied to the primary. In addition, peak latency times should be monitored to see how far behind the warm standby becomes at the highest level of throughput.

A further area of required testing is the switchover mechanism that will be employed to point applications to the designated primary. If application code is used to query a table for the designated primary, this code must be thoroughly tested.

Test recovery scenarios with replication in place

Even though a warm-standby database is implemented, regularly scheduled backups of both databases should also be taken. These backups are useful when any of the following types of failures occur:

- A widespread failure causes both the primary and the warm-standby replica to become unavailable or corrupted.
- After the applications have been switched over to use the warm standby, that system will represent a single point of failure until the primary database is restored.
- An application modification could introduce an error that gets

replicated to the warm standby in such a fashion that both databases become corrupted.

In any of the above situations, the backup can be used to restore the databases to a consistent state pre-failure. Therefore testing these recovery scenarios is important.

In addition, recovery from any replication component failure should also be tested. This recommendation applies to any replication usage. Recovery procedures should be defined, tested, and documented before any application using replication is migrated into the production environment.

Certify the application for WAN use with replication in place

Even though the asynchronous replication for the warm standby occurs across a local campus, testing the network usage would be beneficial for the firm. Network analysis tools should be employed to verify the efficiency of the asynchronous replication. These tools should also be employed for testing the remote query usage from remote agencies and for the Web access when that portion of the application is implemented.

Tune for performance

Monitoring software should be used to identify where tuning, network capacity, or available connections need to be increased. As the number of concurrent communication sessions becomes an issue, either the existing host should be upgraded to handle more concurrent users or a second host should be installed to distribute the sessions and provide the necessary scalability.

Create thorough documentation

The following documentation should be supplied as part of the migration of the warm-standby database into the production environment.

- Operating procedures that identify the switch over mechanisms being used by applications to point them to the designated primary.
- Operating procedures for the resynchronization of the primary.
- Operating procedures for regularly scheduled database backups for both the primary and the warm-standby databases.

Migrate to the production environment

Now that all of these tasks have been completed, this fault-tolerant system can be migrated into the production environment. It should fit well into the physical infrastructure, and it should serve an as example for future use of asynchronous replication for fault-tolerant endeavors.

Two-Phase Commit Protocol

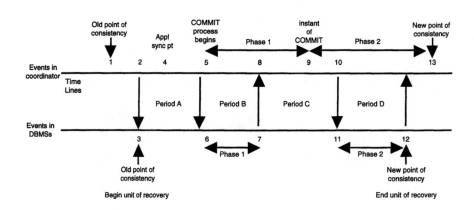

Detailed explanation of a two phase commit protocol:

At 1   The data in the commit coordinator is at a point of consistency.

At 2   The coordinator via an application program issues a statement to perform an update.

At 3   The unit of work begins. This is the start of a unit of recovery.

At 4   The coordinator via an application program or process reaches a point of synchronization.

At 5   The coordinator starts the commit processing. Phase 1 of the commit process begins.

Detailed explanation of a two-phase commit protocol:

At 7   The DBMSs successfully complete Phase 1 processing and notify the coordinator.

At 8   The coordinator receives the notification from the DBMSs.

At 9   The coordinator successfully completes its Phase 1 processing. The coordinator records the instant of commit, i.e., the irrevocable decision to make the changes. The coordinator begins Phase 2 processing.

At 10   The coordinator notifies the DBMSs to begin their Phase 2.

At 11   The DBMSs begin their Phase 2 processing.

At 12   The DBMSs successfully complete their Phase 2 processing and then notify the coordinator that they have finished.

At 13   The coordinator finishes its Phase 2 processing. The data involved in this unit of work is now consistent.

If a failure occurs while the coordinator is connected to the DBMSs, the DBMSs must determine during restart whether to commit or roll back any units of recovery. For certain units of recovery the DBMS has enough information to make the decision. For others it must get information from the coordinator when it reestablishes its connection.

Period a or b   The failure occurred before the DBMS completes its Phase 1. During restart the DBMS backs out the updates.

Period c   The failure occurred after the DBMS PHASE 1 but before starting the DBMS's Phase 2. Only the coordinator knows whether the failure happened before or after the "instant of commit." If it happened before, the DBMS must back out its updates; if it happened after, the DBMS must commit the updates. At restart, the DBMS waits for information from the coordinator before processing this unit of recovery.

Period d   The DBMS failed after it started its own Phase 2 processing. At restart, the DBMS commits the updates.

"if-abort"   The DBMS failed after a unit of recovery began to be rolled back but before the rollback process was completed. During restart, the DBMS continues to back out the updates. (This is not shown on the illustration.)

Note: This protocol is based on data from IBM Corp.

ACID Properties of Transactions

Transactions provide a simple model for success or failure. A transaction either totally commits—all its actions happen—or it totally aborts—none of its actions happen. This can best be defined by the so-called ACID properties of transactions. ACID is an acronym for Atomic, Consistent, Isolated, and Durable.

- *A transaction is atomic.* This means that either all its actions happen or none of them happen.
- *A transaction is consistent.* This means that the transaction as a whole represents a correct transformation of the resource managers involved. For example, it takes the databases from one consistent state to another consistent state.
- *A transaction is isolated.* This means that each transaction executes as though there are no other concurrent transactions.
- *A transaction is durable.* This means that the effects of a committed transaction survive failures.

Both database management systems and TP systems provide ACID properties for transactions. To accomplish this, they provide such functionality as locking mechanisms, logs, and two-phase commit protocols. All the programmer needs to do is provide an identifiable transaction demarcation symbols; usually this entails bracketing the transaction with the BEGIN and COMMIT keywords.

Note that locking mechanisms enable isolation in the face of concurrency. Various degrees of locking can be attained. These degrees of locking vary in range from 0 to 3, as described by the following:

- *Level 0 (Chaos).* This level does not acquire any read locks and releases write locks immediately. This allows other applications to read and/or write dirty data pages. With this locking level, updates can be lost.
- *Level 1 (Browse access).* This level does not allow overwrites of dirty pages of data. Therefore, it eliminates the problem of lost updates. Writes are committed at the end of the transactions; however, dirty data pages can be read by other transactions.
- *Level 2 (Cursor stability).* This level allow no lost updates or dirty reads. In other words, even browsers must wait for the updated data page to be released. This level acquires short-lived read locks that are released immediately. Once released, other transactions can acquire these read pages for update.
- *Level 3 (Repeatable read).* This level allows no lost updates or dirty reads. All read and update data is locked for the duration of the transaction.

Glossary

Because this book contains many terms that may be unfamiliar to the reader, the following glossary has been included. Some very technical definitions have been simplified to help with the overall understanding to the topics. I trust that no one will be offended by the latitude that I have taken.

4 GL fourth-generation language. Languages that were developed to simplify the coding process. Although easier to use than older languages (3GL), these languages are still aimed primarily at technology professionals.

ACID properties acronym for Atomic, Consistent, Isolated, and Durable. The requirements for a true software transaction as defined by the Transaction Processing Performance Council. See Appendix B for a detailed discussion of the ACID properties of transactions.

Application partitioning the breaking up of the functionality of an application into tiers or layers.

Application transparency the details of the mechanism(s) used to solve a problem that are masked from the applications using the solution.

API an acronym for Application Programming Interface. It is a well-defined and published interface to specific tasks performed by a process. It allows programs from multiple vendors to be integrated.

Architecture   a disciplined approach to the art and science of building frameworks or structures.

Asynchronous data replication   provides what is called "loose consistency" between data stores. The latency before data consistency is achieved is always greater than zero. This means that the replication process occurs asynchronously to the originating transaction. There is always some degree of lag between when the originating software transaction is committed and when the effects of the transaction are available at any replicas.

Attribute   a field in a relational database.

Authentication   process of having every user, host, or application server prove it is who it says it is.

Authorization (access control)   process that ensures that authenticated users have the necessary permissions to use designated resources.

Business transaction   business event. It can be composed of multiple software transactions.

Client   a single-user computer that is connected by means of a network to one or more shared computers, called servers. Data storage and processes are distributed among the client and servers in multiple ways (i.e., two-, three-, or *n*-tier architectures).

Composite key   a key in a database table that is made up of several columns.

CORBA   an acronym for the Common Object Request Broker Architecture, as specified by the Object Management Group.

DA   an acronym for Data Administrator.

Data extract   the process of copying data from one system to load it into another system.

Data latency   amount of time a target replica can be in an inconsistent state with its designated primary sources before data consistency is achieved.

Data owner   the person or group that defines the business and administrative rules governing that data element.

Data replication   encompasses the analysis, design, implementation, administration, and monitoring of a service that guarantees data consistency across multiple resource managers in a distributed environment. See also *synchronous data replication* and *asynchronous data replication.*

Data warehouse   a copy of transactional data that is specifically structured for query and analysis.

DBA   an acronym for database administrator.

DBMS   an acronym for database management system. It is used to store, process, and manage data in a systematic fashion. Different DBMSs use a variety of underlying storage methods. These include relational, network, hierarchical, or multidimensional.

DCE an acronym for the Distributed Computing Environment. It is a set of integrated services that work across multiple systems and yet remains independent of any single system. DCE software includes tools and services that function as a layer of software that masks the differences among different kinds of computers.

DCE/DFS an acronym for DCE's Distributed File Services. These services provide a single view of all files, both UNIX and non-UNIX, across all systems to all users.

DCE/DTS an acronym for DCE's Distributed Time Services. These services run on every host computer and keep the associated host clocks closely synchronized.

Denormalize to allow data redundancy within or across data structures (e.g., relational tables).

DML an acronym for Data Manipulation Language. It includes data modification statements such as INSERT, UPDATE, and DELETE.

DSS an acronym for decision-support system. These systems are used for analysis of large quantities of data.

Entity Relationship Diagram a model of a firm's data in which all redundancy has been removed.

Foreign key a field in a database table whose values are drawn from the values of a primary key in a different table.

Gigabyte (GB) 1,024 megabytes. Generally accepted to represent 1,000 megabytes or 1 billion bytes.

Grain of the fact table the meaning of the lowest level of recorded data within the fact table of a star join schema. A star join schema is used in a data warehousing application to enhance performance by reducing the number of relational joins required to build the answer set of a query.

Groupware an application that allows a workgroup to share information. Updates by any of the users are made available to the others. This is accomplished by means of automated replication or concurrent sharing.

GUI acronym for Graphical User Interface. An example would be an application that makes use of windowing technology within its presentation layer.

Identical replicas replicas that have the same platform, same informational content, and same data types. If replicas are not identical, then they should be semantically equivalent.

Kilobyte (KB) 1,024 bytes. Generally accepted to represent 1,000 bytes.

LAN acronym for local area network. It comprises a high-speed connection between locally stored desktop PCs and server machines. The server machines could include file servers, application servers, print servers, or other services.

Legacy system an existing application system used for entering data about the operations of the business.

MDDB acronym for multidimensional database. An MDDB stores data in structures that offer an alternative way of organizing summary data. Through the use of optimizing, cross-indexed hierarchical structures, data is organized into dimensions and measures, by time.

Megabyte (MB) 1,024 kilobytes. Generally accepted to represent 1,000 kilobytes or 1 million bytes.

Meta-data data about data. It represents any data that is maintained to support the operation or use of a firm's data users and/or processes. For example, it is used to define data structures and calculation rules.

Middleware a generic term used to describe a layer of system software that isolates programmers and end users from differences in services and resources used by applications.

MPP an acronym for massively parallel processing. A computer hardware architecture designed to obtain high performance through the use of large numbers of individually simple, low-powered processors. Each processor has its own memory.

Multidimensional a data structure that has three or more independent dimensions.

Nonrepudiation process of ensuring that any authenticated and authorized user cannot deny that it used a designated resource.

Normalize the process of removing redundancy within data structures.

OLAP an acronym for online analytic processing. It is a loosely defined set of principles that provides a framework for decision support.

OLE an acronym for object linking and embedding. A Microsoft Windows technology for presenting applications as objects within other applications and hence for extending the apparent functionality of the client application.

OLTP an acronym for online transaction processing. It describes all of the activities and systems associated with entering data reliably into a resource manager.

OO   an acronym for object-oriented. A method of developing applications that allows the reuse of program components in other contexts.

OSF/DCE   an acronym for the Open Software Foundation's Distributing Computing Environment. It defines a strategic framework for a distributed computing environment. See also *DCE*.

Platform   the combination of an operating system and a database management system.

Primary key   a field in a database table whose values uniquely identify the records within that table.

Quiesce   the process of clearing all transactions that are in still in the distribution phase of replication without actually shutting down or halting the system. When a replication system is quiesced, no new updates flow through the system, and all replication queues are flushed (i.e., applied to targets).

RAID   an acronym for redundant arrays of inexpensive disks. It is a technology for improving the performance and tolerance of hard drives. To have the benefit of RAID, you need to purchase special RAID hardware.

RDBMS   an acronym for relational database management system. See also *DBMS*.

Referential integrity   a mandatory condition in a database where all of the foreign keys are subsets of the existing primary keys.

Replica   a copy of an object.

Replication   see *data replication*.

Semantically equivalent replicas   replicas that have the same informational content but reside on different platform and possibly have different data types.

Server   a computer servicing a number of users.

Service   logical groupings of automated tasks that support a well-defined piece of functionality. A service can perform either a business or technical purpose.

SMP   an acronym for symmetrical multiprocessing. A computer hardware architecture that distributes the computing load over a small number of identical processors that share memory.

Software transaction   an indivisible unit of work. An end-to-end action whose effect is to change the persistent state of the firm from one consistent state to another. A transactional processing system either performs an entire software transaction or it does not perform any part of the transaction. Software transactions exhibit the ACID properties.

Sparse only a small proportion of potential data actually occupying a data structure.

SQL an acronym for Structured Query Language. It is the standard data structuring and access language used by relational databases.

Star join schema a relational database schema used to represent multidimensional data. It is composed of a central fact table and its associated dimensional tables. The central fact table has a composite key comprised of all of the single primary keys of the dimension tables. The fact table is joined to a number of the single-level dimension tables.

Synchronous data replication provides what is called "tight consistency" between data stores. The latency before data consistency is achieved is zero. Data at all replicas is always the same no matter from which replica the update originated. This can be accomplished only through a two-phase commit protocol.

Templates principles, policies, patterns, or frameworks that allow architects to reuse proven rules, strategies, techniques, and tools in the construction of new systems.

Terabyte (TB) 1,024 gigabytes. Generally accepted to represent 1,000 gigabytes or 1 trillion bytes.

Three-tier software architecture an architecture that usually has a first tier composed of presentation and some application logic. This tier communicates with the second tier, application business logic, via message passing. The second tier communicates with the data management tier via data passing.

TP an acronym for transaction processing. It includes the operational systems used to collect and manage the base data of a business entity.

Two-tier software architecture cooperative processing where two logical software tiers interoperate by exchanging data or messages. Within this framework, the first tier is composed of presentation and business logic, which jointly reside within one process space. The second tier is the data management layer, which is the resource manager or DBMS component.

WAN acronym for wide area network. A network usually composed of two or more geographically dispersed LANs connected by lower-speed links.

Warehouse see *data warehouse*.

Index